THE COMPLETE BOOK ON
OVERCALLS
AT CONTRACT BRIDGE

A MIKE LAWRENCE
BRIDGE CLASSIC

Master Point Press
331 Douglas Ave.
Toronto, Ontario, Canada
M5M 1H2   (416)781-0351

Email: info@masterpointpress.com

Websites: www.masterpointpress.com
               www.masteringbridge.com
               www.bridgeblogging.com
               www.ebooksbridge.com

Library and Archives Canada Cataloguing in Publication

Lawrence, Mike
       The complete book on overcalls in contract bridge / Mike
Lawrence – 2nd ed.

ISBN 978-1-897106-45-7

       1. Contract bridge--Bidding. I. Title.

GV1282.4.L38 2009   795.41'52   C2009-904839-6

Editor   Ray Lee
Copy editor/interior format   Sally Sparrow
Cover and interior design   Olena S. Sullivan/New Mediatrix

2 3 4 5 6 7   14 13 12 11 10

PRINTED IN CANADA

For Karen, who made sure I said what I meant and said it correctly. "Thanks."

CONTENTS

CHAPTER EIGHT: RAISING PARTNER'S OVERCALL WHEN RHO PASSES 121

CHAPTER NINE: RAISING PARTNER'S OVERCALL WHEN RHO BIDS 132

CHAPTER TEN: PARTNER OVERCALLS AT THE TWO-LEVEL 150

CHAPTER ELEVEN: 1NT AND 2NT RESPONSES TO AN OVERCALL 159

CHAPTER TWELVE: THE RESPONSIVE DOUBLE 162

FOREWORD TO THE FIRST EDITION

Introducing a bridge book by Mike Lawrence is like introducing a horn solo by the Angel Gabriel. Understandably, therefore, I'm a bit embarrassed at writing these words; and I do so only to please the author and the publisher, good friends and modest men. So let me begin by saying that it is an honor and a privilege to be bringing this book to your attention.

Of course you know that Mike Lawrence was a charter member of the Aces, that he has won two world championships, about a dozen North American championships, and more than ten thousand master points.

Obviously he is a performer. But can he pass on something that will improve *your* performance?

You would not ask this question if you had read his first book, *How to Read Your Opponents' Cards*, or his second, *Judgment at Bridge*. Both were practical, down-to-earth, helpful and instructive. This is in the same tradition. We're just beginning 1980, and already I am convinced that this will be Bridge Book of the Year in the annual listing of one widely-read bridge columnist.

How good a bridge player must you be to get your money's worth out of this book? You should be breathing, you should know enough about the English language to understand a bridge book, and you should be in the habit of playing bridge at least once or twice per month. This book will help a rubber bridge player. It will help you more if you play in club duplicate games. It will help most of all if you chase master points in important tournaments.

Why will this book help you?

Nobody else has written anything at all about overcalling on a four-card suit, about the difference between safe and dangerous overcalls on weak suits, about the jump response to an overcall and when it should be strong and when weak. You won't find much else in the literature about responsive doubles or about how the bidding develops after an overcall.

Much of the material in this book will be useful even if you're just an individualistic rubber bridge player who wants to get better results in a pivot game. Even more of the book will be useful if you spend endless hours discussing bidding with your favorite partner, as all "serious" players do. And the best serious players always use Lawrence's method of illustrative hands, varying the bid after changing just a card or two.

One word of warning: this book is deceptively easy and enjoyable to read. Don't think you've mastered it after just one reading. Read it a second time. Then make your favorite partner buy a copy; and lock him up until he also has read it.

A strange thing will happen. Your overcalls and your partnership will improve, but that's not strange. You'll even play the cards better. The reason for this strange development is that any influence that gets you into the habit of thinking when you're at the bridge table will improve your performance in all departments of the game.

But enough. I mustn't keep you from the book. If you read several bridge books per year, you're already on your way to the cash register. If you read only one bridge book per year, this should be it.

–Alfred Sheinwold
1979

INTRODUCTION

Playing matchpoints with your favorite partner, you pick up some hand like the following, an ordinary eleven-count.

♠ J 10 7
♡ K J 9 8
◇ Q 8 6 3
♣ A 2

Vulnerable versus not, your partner opens with 1♣ and RHO passes. You respond 1♡ and partner raises to 2♡. Deciding your hand is not quite worth a game, but certainly worth a try, you bid 2NT. Over this, partner signs off in 3♡, showing a minimum but confirming four-card support. Having nothing extra, you pass on the theory that it is not necessary to push to questionable games at matchpoints.

An easy hand to bid? Yes. At every stage you were able to make a useful and convenient bid. Both you and your partner had ample time to describe your hands and your final decision was well judged. Nicely bid.

Now, let's start over. Partner bids 1♣, as before, and RHO bids 1♠.
What now?

Let's assume for the moment that you don't play negative doubles. What are your options?

Well, you can't double for penalty; your spades aren't good enough.

Nor can you bid notrump without a spade stopper.

This leaves you with either 2♡ or 2◇. But they both have imperfections. Partner will tend to play you for a five-card suit, or at least a better four-card suit. But assuming you are happy with either of these choices, how happy are you going to be when partner raises to three? Do you know what to do next? Very difficult.

How about a weaker hand such as the following?

♠ Q 10 3
♡ K 8 7 6 5
◇ Q 9 2
♣ 4 3

With neither side vulnerable, partner deals and bids 1◇. When RHO passes you respond 1♡. This hand is no bargain, and if partner shows no ambitions you will be happy to make a partscore. But if partner has a good hand game is possible. 1♡ is a fine start toward whatever contract you will eventually hope to declare. Again, an easy hand.

1◇ – 2♣ – ?

But what if RHO, instead of passing, overcalls 2♣?

You are stuck.

If you pass, you have misgivings about the heart suit or perhaps the marginal diamond support. A 2♡ bid seriously overstates the hand, and 2◇ would overstate the diamond support and would probably lose the heart suit. Awful.

Is there a solution?

If you use the negative double, you can attempt to solve the two hands in this fashion:

1♣ – 1♠ – ?

♠ J 10 7
♡ K J 9 8
◇ Q 8 6 3
♣ A 2

An ideal hand for the negative double. You have four cards in the unbid suits and sufficient values to protect against mishap.

With this hand, not much can go wrong because of your extra high cards. But partner may have doubts about introducing hearts on ♡7642, and there may be some difficulty in working out whether you have a spade stopper for notrump. And even if you do have a spade stopper, you have to decide how high to go. It is not that easy. But the negative double did help, and it's certainly better than nothing.

How does it work on the second hand where RHO overcalls 2♣?

1◇ – 2♣ – ?

♠ Q 10 3
♡ K 8 7 6 5
◇ Q 9 2
♣ 4 3

It doesn't work very well, does it? You won't like it if partner bids 2♠. And you will like it even less if he bids them at the three- or four-level.

You hope partner will bid hearts or rebid diamonds. But you know as well as I do he's going to bid spades far too often to make a negative double work with this hand. The answer? There is no perfect answer. The 2♣ overcall has put you in a difficult bind.

Am I trying to talk you out of the negative double? No, not at all.

What I am trying to do is show you how hard a simple hand becomes when your opponents get into your auction.

If you look at both hands you will note that in each case the overcall took away the one-level response you would have had available. This effectively cut the amount of information you would like to have exchanged by half or more. Very simple and very effective.

Now, if you find that you have trouble with these rather ordinary hands for the simple reason that an opponent has overcalled, is there any reason to believe that your opponents will not have the same problems if they open and you overcall?

I assure you they will have problems.

Why Should You Overcall?

There are actually quite a few reasons for overcalling.

1. You may buy the contract for a successful game or partscore.
2. You may get partner off to a good lead.
3. You may push the opponents too high; perhaps, on occasion, at considerable expense to them.
4. You may find a successful sacrifice.
5. You may cause the opponents to misjudge their hands and either miss a game or slam or get to the wrong game or slam. Or for that matter, the wrong suit, period.

Most of these reasons are well known. They do not need elaborating. The reason I spent so much time on the two example hands was because I wanted to emphasize as strongly as possible this one aspect of overcalling. It makes life difficult for the side that opened.

I intend to cover the range of hands on which I believe you should overcall. This will be done by way of examples for the reason that general rules just don't make it in an area such as defensive bidding. Not to say that I don't believe in them. I just don't think they do the job.

Later, I intend to get into a structure of responding to partner's overcall.

Occasionally I will make a distinction between matchpoints and IMPs.

Something About This Book

As you probably know, *Overcalls* was published in the eighties, and it was a first. No one had written about overcalls other than to give them a token mention. Discussing responding to overcalls was not heard of. *Overcalls* broke new ground and now, after quite a few years, this version will do the same. Much of what was included in the original was correct but there were some errors in judgment and the tools were more limited than they are today. In this version of *Overcalls* I have changed the answers to some of the example hands, have added new hands, and have introduced something that is completely new. In much of this book I will focus on basic methods. The new methods will have a section of their own. At the end of the book there will be a large quiz that will look at traditional methods and which will touch on modern methods, something I will address in its own section. There will also be additional quizzes along the way.

PART ONE

OVERCALLS

CHAPTER ONE
ONE-LEVEL OVERCALLS

Neither vulnerable. RHO opens 1♣.

♠ A Q 10 7 6	♠ 4	♠ A K Q 9 7
♡ 4 2	♡ K Q 10 7 6 5	♡ Q 5 4
◇ K 3 2	◇ A 6 5 4	◇ 4
♣ A 10 6	♣ 3 2	♣ 10 7 6 5

♠ Q J 10 8 7 5	♠ K 4	♠ K 5
♡ 4	♡ 3	♡ A Q J 10 8 7
◇ A Q 5	◇ A J 10 8 7	◇ A J 3
♣ Q 10 7	♣ K 9 8 7 6	♣ 4 2

These hands should all be automatic overcalls regardless of the form of bridge you play. In all cases you have both a good suit and values approximating an opening bid. If you felt like passing any of these hands, I would have to say you were being far too conservative. Also, if you passed any of these you will find some of my later ideas hard to accept.

At the other extreme, none of these hands is worth a takeout double with the intention of showing a suit later. That action would be too aggressive.

In the following hand, neither side is vulnerable and RHO opens 1♣.

♠ K Q 10 9 7
♡ 5 4 2
◇ K 8 3
♣ J 2

At matchpoints, where overtricks are of such concern, there is much to be said for overcalling at the one-level on any hand including a good suit. Here, 1♠ has almost everything going for it except that game is unlikely.

You want a spade lead. Your overcall will take away significant bidding room from the opponents. It's better for you in general to bid right away rather than to wait and permit the opponents an unimpeded discussion. True, you may be able to balance later, but why wait? This hand is also sufficiently strong to bid 1♠ at IMPs, although that is beginning to stretch things.

IMPs vs. Matchpoints

When considering whether or not to overcall, you should realize the distinction between matchpoints and IMPs. Matchpoints is a wild struggle where every hand is a separate battle. Winning a hand by an extra trick may be as good a result as getting +800. The worst you can do is get a zero. If on one round you steal a trick in 2♣ and make an overtrick for +110 and get a top on the first board, and then on the next board you go down 800 and get a zero, you have achieved an average round.

At IMPs, you may gain one IMP for your extra trick in 2♣, but you may lose 14 for your –800, and your net is minus thirteen IMPs. A disaster. This means that at IMPs you must be far more conscious of safety than at matchpoints. As you will see, I recommend an aggressive stance at IMPs as well as at matchpoints, but tempered with a reasonable amount of caution.

Incidentally, there is one aspect of matchpoints which will become more and more evident as we go along. I will refer to it constantly.

Good matchpoints is almost never good bridge.

You have to learn to play badly. There's a number of things you can do which are theoretically wrong, but at matchpoints they work a high percentage of the time. And this is what matchpoints is all about. If you want to win, and to win a lot, you have to learn what works and what doesn't. And you have to be able to take the hard knocks with the rest of your results. If you can't stomach going for your life every now and then, you will probably get a lot of 167's and 172½'s but you won't get many wins. You have to determine your goals.

1♣ – ?	Here, 1♡ is fairly straightforward. Your suit affords protection against a double and prospects for a small plus score are adequate. Overcall at IMPs as well.
♠ K 2	
♡ A Q 10 9 8	
◇ 10 7 6	
♣ 9 8 3	

1♣ – ?	1◇. Again, it should be automatic. Good hand. Good suit. Game is not even unlikely. An important point of this hand is that your 1◇ overcall does not do much to inconvenience your opponents.
♠ A 3 2	
♡ 7 4	
◇ K Q J 8 7	
♣ K 5 4	

OBSTRUCTION

You should be aware of two situations when considering an overcall. These auctions, 1♣-1♠ or 1◊-2♣, are far and away the most difficult for your opponents to handle. You have effectively removed the one-level from their available responses, making it hard for them to cope. Anytime responder has a few points, but not enough for a two-level response, he is going to be awkwardly placed. Some of the time he may be able to make a negative double but as you've seen, that may not work if responder's hand is unsuited.

Conversely, 1◊ over 1♣ and 1♠ over 1♡ do little to obstruct the opponents. This means that on hands where you are not sure about overcalling, you might lean toward bidding if your bid will prove awkward for the opponents.

In the following hands, they open 1♣ on your right. Assume that no one is vulnerable.

1♣ – ?

♠ Q 10 8 7 4
♡ 8
◊ K 7 6
♣ A Q 4 2

Bid 1♠. Even though the suit isn't quite up to what you would like it to be, the rest of the hand more than makes up for it. Likewise at IMPs. Clear-cut.

1♣ – ?

♠ K 9 8 7 5
♡ K 7 4
◊ J 4 2
♣ Q 10

Bidding with this hand is a stretch. I might think of bidding 1♠ on the theory that it makes things hard on the opponents, but even at matchpoints pass is probably best. At IMPs this is a clear-cut pass. Your maximum is likely to be a partscore and you could easily go for a substantial number. If you can get four tricks out of this, down three would still be –500 if 1♠ gets doubled.

1♣ – ?

♠ K Q 10 8 7
♡ K J 9
◊ 5 4 2
♣ 7 4

This hand has the same high cards and the same distribution as the previous hand. But now the high cards are all working in that they reinforce each other. And your suit is now rather good. Before, it was not. At matchpoints this becomes a reasonable overcall and even at IMPs it is an acceptable minimum. Even though you may go for a number, you are well placed to contend for a partscore. And you do want a spade lead. Again, the quality of your suit is a major consideration when making an overcall on a minimum hand.

1♣ – ?

♠ J 8 7 4 2
♡ 8
♢ A K 3
♣ A J 4 2

1♠. This hand falls into a family of hands where you have good values but no particularly good bid. It is true that some good hands afford no convenient way to enter the auction. But, when you have a good hand which includes a five-card suit, even a bad five-card suit, it may be possible and even desirable to overcall. Even at IMPs, an overcall is clear-cut. Look at your potential. If partner has as little as any four spades, you can probably make a partscore and even game is possible. Here is the kind of layout you hope to find. You might make game with these two hands.

♠ J 8 7 4 2	♠ A 10 5 3
♡ 8	♡ Q 9 7 6 4
♢ A K 3	♢ 10 2
♣ A J 4 2	♣ Q 5

Even if partner has as little as ♠103 ♡J97642 ♢652 ♣Q5 you will probably be able to make 1♠ or 2♠.

1♣ – ?

♠ 9 6 5 4 2
♡ A 3
♢ A Q 8 7
♣ K 2

Again, bid 1♠. Your offensive potential makes this worth an overcall at matchpoints or IMPs. Anytime you feel that a moderate fit will provide some future, you should bid. Note that when you overcall with a bad suit, you are doing so at the one-level only. And when you overcall with a bad suit the rest of your hand is good. You will need an opening bid or exceptional distribution to take the risk. Also, your high cards should be aces and kings.

1♣ – ?

♠ 8 7 6 4 2
♡ K J
♢ K Q 7
♣ K J 5

This hand is dangerous for an overcall. Your suit is bad and opposite a weak dummy you could find yourself never being able to lead toward your hand to score all those kings and jacks. If at matchpoints you wanted to overcall 1♠, well, okay. This is the kind of bad bid you may make at matchpoints. It has a chance to work. Don't do this at IMPs, however.

1♣ – ?

♠ 8
♡ 6 5 4 3 2
♢ A Q 3 2
♣ A K 4

1♡. Could your suit be worse? This may seem a bit contrary to what you've been accustomed to, but if you've been able to accept some of the earlier examples you should be right at home with this one. In terms of offense, you have an excellent hand. If partner can suggest a game you should be happy to accept, your trump suit notwithstanding.

This is an important hand. It contradicts most widely-accepted notions of competition and yet so much is at stake here that passing can lead to all sorts of bad results. I intend to spend quite some time on this example.

First, there is the obvious objection that partner may get off to a bad lead. This is true. He may lead a heart from the doubleton king or queen and this may not be best for your side. But for this to occur requires a number of things to happen. One of these is that partner has to be on lead, and that is not necessarily going to happen. One of the results of your overcall is that your side often ends up playing the hand. In those cases where partner is on lead you will frequently find that partner's lead of the doubleton king or queen does not cost a trick. The opening bidder on your right may well have the ace, so your partner's king was dead in any case. Perhaps there was no best lead for your side. Admittedly, in the actual hand you would prefer that partner lead a club or a diamond, if that should be his natural choice. But if the opponents end up in notrump your partner might well lead a spade, which would do your side no good at all.

Let's say that LHO does bid 1NT and gets raised to 2NT or 3NT. Let's say partner leads his king from the doubleton ♡K7 and everyone gets a good laugh as dummy on your right puts down ♡QJ10 and declarer takes the ace. This looks bad, but it may well be that this is the only lead to defeat them. You have all sorts of entries and may be able to establish your hearts for the setting tricks. Now, if partner had led a spade from ♠Q10752, his lead would also give declarer an extra trick, but in that case there would be no chance for the defense to recover.

The next obvious objection is that you may get doubled. This can happen and once in a while it will happen. I won't try to tell you 1♡ is entirely safe, because it's not. But then, nothing is safe. Some people open a short club on ♣862, and I can't believe that is safer than overcalling 1♡ on ♡65432. It's difficult to argue this point. A big penalty is hard to ignore. But I will say this. I would overcall 1♡ at IMPs even if vulnerable. The net benefits to bidding 1♡ are so substantial that the occasional penalty is worth the price.

There is also the possibility that even though you could have gone for a number, the opponents fail to catch you. Or, perhaps one of your opponents decides not to sit for the double. Or, perhaps you escape to diamonds, or for that matter, clubs, spades, or notrump. You will be quite surprised at how seldom you get penalized heavily for overcalling on a hand such as this. Admittedly, I am asking you to accept this on blind faith. But if you have the proper outside values necessary to overcall when the suit is so bad, you will find yourself doing quite well.

What happens when partner doesn't like hearts and bids something else? What happens when partner doubles the opponents, expecting you to have good hearts? Let's see.

W	N	E	S
		1♣	1♡
1NT	2♠		

♠ 8
♡ 65432
◇ AQ32
♣ AK4

You bid 1♡ and the bidding continues as shown. Do you like your hand? You should. Your hand is outstanding, aside from lack of spade support. Partner is probably short in hearts, or he would have raised your overcall. This means your bad heart suit is not a liability at all. It means your high cards are all working and partner will actually be delighted with your dummy. However, if your hand were ♠8 ♡KQJ42 ◇K76 ♣K542 then it would not be nearly as useful to partner in a spade contract. If partner had a singleton heart he would have to get in, then set up the hearts, get in again, and somehow get to dummy to use the heart tricks. The actual hand has ready-made tricks.

If partner should decide to double the opponents, your hand will not be a disappointment at all. You have excellent defensive strength — ◇AQ and ♣AK. If partner doubles something and it makes, partner should either have a better hand for the double or else the defense wasn't so hot. You need have no apologies for the overcall. You had your values.

And finally, if partner raises hearts you should be pleased. One of the purposes of overcalling is to find a fit and arrive at a good contract. A raise from partner is good news indeed. I repeat that this hand is clearly worth a bid, at any vulnerability and at any form of the game, including IMPs. It's entirely possible that you might do some further bidding with this hand. But, more on that later.

1♣ – ?

♠ 82
♡ AJ3
◇ 87642
♣ AK10

Pass or 1◇. Experience has shown there isn't much future in overcalling with a bad minor suit, as opposed to a bad major suit. It does little to get in the way of the opponents. You do have a good hand so you could overcall, but with anything less you ought to pass. Perhaps later you can reenter the auction if it's convenient.

There is one more area, or style, of overcalling which, when properly used, can accurately be termed as devastating. There is very little literature on it, so for the most part, people are unfamiliar with it. Which is certainly to my advantage. Quite frankly, I would just as soon that my opponents were not into this particular strategy. Perhaps this is why no one has bothered to discuss it in print. Anyway, here goes...

CHAPTER TWO
OVERCALLING ON FOUR-CARD SUITS

Every now and then, you are going to find yourself with some sort of goodish hand and your RHO will open the bidding. Feeling like you should take some action, but finding nothing convenient, you pass and later discover you had a game or partial available on a hand where neither you nor partner had been able to enter the auction. Certainly there are hands with which you would open the bidding but with which you can't compete after an opening bid. Some of these hands, however, can be handled through the tactic of overcalling on a four-card suit. There are many cases where this is correct.

If you are thinking of doing this, there are four rules you must follow. I will give you the rules now and will refer to them throughout this chapter. I will repeat them later for emphasis.

RULES

1. You overcall with four-card suits only at the *one-level*.
2. You need an *opening bid* or close to it when you overcall with a four-card suit.
3. You need a *good suit* when you overcall with a four-card suit.
4. Your hand does not offer a better alternative, such as a takeout double.

The concept of overcalling on a four-card suit was first seen in print when *Overcalls* came out in 1980. It is still a widely ignored bidding trick and if you use it properly you will still be way ahead of the majority of players, who have a stubborn streak or who have not read about it.

Following are a number of examples. With neither vulnerable, RHO opens 1◇.

1◇ – ?

♠ K Q 10 9
♡ 4 2
◇ A Q 6 5
♣ K 5 4

Bid 1♠. One of the few generalities I can give is that overcalling on a four-card suit requires a very good suit. Partner is going to raise you whenever possible and three small should be quite adequate support if his hand is otherwise suited. Responder should not have to worry about the quality of your overcalls.

1◇ – ?

♠ 8 2
♡ A Q 10 7
◇ 10 7 6 5 4
♣ A Q

1♡. If the possession of five cards in the suit opened bothers you, forget it. Your length in diamonds plus opener's length assures you that there are not a lot of diamonds for your partner and LHO. This means your partner is likely to have heart support. The length in diamonds therefore is not a minus, but rather an asset. Perhaps the two hands are something like this:

♠ 8 2	♠ A 9 7 6 4
♡ A Q 10 7	♡ J 8 3
◇ 10 7 6 5 4	◇ 3
♣ A Q	♣ 7 6 5 2

With a diamond lead and a heart return, you should make seven to nine tricks. Not bad considering that dummy is not all that good. If dummy had a fourth heart ten tricks would be possible, and if you found dummy with five of them, game would depend on winning either the club or heart finesse. With the opening bid on your right, game should be nearly a cinch.

If the two hands below offer a good play for game, it would be nice to find a way to bid it.

♠ 8 2	♠ A 9 4
♡ A Q 10 7	♡ J 9 5 4 2
◇ 10 7 6 5 4	◇ 3
♣ A Q	♣ J 9 4 2

Or, if you can't get to game, at least get to hearts. Making +170 is better than being –110 or –90, or some such partscore. If you don't bid 1♡ right away you will never be able to reach 4♡ or, for that matter, hearts, period.

1◇ – ?

♠ K Q J 9
♡ A 2
◇ J 3
♣ J 8 7 4 3

1♠. This hand may appear similar to the prior hand, but in fact it is quite different. There is a rather subtle difference. The points are the same. The distribution is the same. The hand contains a good four-card suit and a crummy five-card suit. Neither hand contains a singleton. The difference? It is in the auction. In the previous hand the opening bid was in your weak five-card suit. This had the effect of implying that your partner could have substantial distributional support for your four-card suit. Even if you found partner with no high cards at all, you were assured of some kind of fit.

In this hand, however, the opening bid was in one of your doubletons. Therefore, even though it's correct to bid 1♠ you do so in the hope, rather than the expectation, that partner can provide some sort of fit. If worse comes to worst, you will probably take three spade tricks and the ♡A. But my estimation of this hand is that you will seldom get fewer than five tricks, even opposite nothing. There are many hands with five-card suits on which nearly everyone would overcall which could easily end up taking fewer tricks.

1◇ – ?

♠ A Q 8 6 2
♡ A Q 3
◇ 4 2
♣ 9 7 3

This hand, if doubled in a 1♠ overcall, could conceivably take only two tricks. While two tricks is admittedly unlikely, the possibility of taking three or four is very real. And yet, nearly everyone would hasten to bid 1♠ on this hand, and hasten equally quickly to pass the hand just being discussed with ♠KQJ9.

My own feeling is such that I would be quite pleased to hold ♠KQJ9 ♡A2 ◇J3 ♣J8743 and be able to overcall 1♠ at matchpoints, rubber bridge, or IMPs. There is another aspect of this hand which is important to recognize. If you elect to overcall 1♠ you have to be prepared to lose the club suit. There is no way you can ever hope to get the club suit mentioned without partner assuming (rightly) that you have as many or more spades than clubs.

Hands like these are inflexible. Either you don't bid at all, or you bid (as in the example) 1♠ and then usually subside. The only way you can bid again is when partner shows a good hand, forcing you to make another decision.

ANOTHER LOOK AT WHY FOUR-CARD OVERCALLS ARE SO EFFECTIVE

You may wonder why overcalling on four-card suits is so effective. In addition to the usual reasons, a four-card-suit overcall needs a good suit by definition, so it is certainly a suit you want partner to lead. The fact that you have such a good suit suggests partner won't have much in that suit, and it might not occur to him to lead it without a suggestion from you. Furthermore, the quality of your suit is such that the opponents may be shy about contracting for some number of notrump. They may credit you for a longer suit and decide on a partscore when 3NT is cold.

Having only a four-bagger also works well when the opponents end in a suit contract. Each opponent, holding three or even four small, may have been hoping his partner held shortness in the suit. When this happens, you will occasionally find the opponents playing in a suit contract when they should have been in 3NT. If they end in the wrong game, it can be a terrific result for you.

By now, if you've not been convinced that overcalling on four-card suits is a good thing for your side if done properly, do this. During the next session or two you play, note the ease or difficulty you experience when your opponents overcall. If you are convinced that you do not like it when they bid, then consider this. It is a fact that most people do not compete with four-baggers. If a partnership which did not tend to do this decided it was right, then they would be in a position to compete on from one to three or four hands more per session than they had been in the past. My experience suggests that in general, my results are excellent when one of these overcalls has been used. Out of ten occurrences I would expect two or three tops, four very good results, an average or two, and perhaps one bad result. This is true at both matchpoints and IMPs.

If you give these a try, you will be well placed. At least until everyone else learns as well. I do understand that if you are not accustomed to something like this, it is difficult to make the transition. I hope you don't make it against me.

Some more examples in the same vein. This time you are not vulnerable vs. vulnerable and your RHO opens 1♡.

1♡ – ?

♠ KQ108
♡ 32
◇ AJ43
♣ K65

Don't get carried away. This is a takeout double, not a 1♠ overcall.

1♡ – ?

♠ A2
♡ 108654
◇ A2
♣ KQJ8

Pass. Overcalling at the two-level requires a five-card suit. Good suit and all, 2♣ is not acceptable.

1♡ – ?

♠ K1097
♡ AQ542
◇ 42
♣ A3

This is the kind of hand on which a theoretically unsound bid of 1♠ could work well. It's the sort of 'bad' bid you can get away with at matchpoints, but definitely not IMPs. Bear in mind that you are trading heavily on the fact that you expect to find a fit because of your heart length.

Even though you don't take much room away from the opponents with your 1♠ overcall, look what might happen. Compare these three auctions that show what happens when East opens 1♡ and South does or does not bid.

1.

West	North	East	South
		1♡	pass
1NT	pass	2♣	?

2.

West	North	East	South
		1♡	pass
1NT	pass	pass	?

3.

West	North	East	South
		1♡	1♠
pass	2♠	?	

In auction one, the opponents have been able to find their best fit (probably) and whether or not your side balances, they can judge what to do over your belated competition. Likewise, in auction two. If you bid 2♠ now it is somewhat dangerous, although probably correct. In auction three, however, you have kept the opponents from their smooth exchange, and at the same time you got to 2♠ because your partner likes spades, which on auctions one and two was not so clear.

1♡ – ?

♠ AKQ9
♡ 872
◇ QJ3
♣ 1097

After a 1♡ opening it is marginal to bid 1♠ at matchpoints, but only at matchpoints. You would have preferred the opening bid to be 1♣ or 1◇ instead of 1♡ because you would have deprived the opponents of important bidding room.

1♡ – ?

♠ QJ42
♡ 87653
◇ K10
♣ K2

Pass. Your suit is not good enough to bid, your hand is not good enough to bid, and that adds up to two strikes. One strike is usually enough. Having said that, I admit that if I had the ♠KJ98 I might try 1♠ if I felt I needed a good result.

1♡ – ?

♠ Q987
♡ 87642
◇ KJ3
♣ A

When you gain experience with four-card overcalls you will see how effective they can be. Knowing this, you may be tempted to overcall more often than you should. Resist that temptation. You can pass hands like this one, reserving your four-card overcalls for hands that qualify.

1♡ – ?

♠ QJ97
♡ 86542
◇ A
♣ AQ10

This is an acceptably marginal 1♠ bid. Your suit is pretty good and you have a full opening bid. Not vulnerable I would overcall at matchpoints and at IMPs. The following layout is what you are hoping for.

♠ QJ97	♠ K8642
♡ 86542	♡ J
◇ A	◇ 1086
♣ AQ10	♣ J932

If spades divide 2-2 and RHO has the ♣K you may be able to take ten tricks, a result that you would never achieve if you do not overcall 1♠. Even if your side does not find a lot of games, you will be competing for partscores and will be a general pain in the opponents' auctions. Results like this are likely.

♠ QJ97	♠ 10863
♡ 86542	♡ Q3
◇ A	◇ KQ63
♣ AQ10	♣ 964

With this dummy you can make 2♠ or 3♠. At the same time, they can make up to 3◇ in spite of your impressive trump holding.

1♡ – ?

♠ KJ87
♡ 42
◇ AK
♣ Q6432

Pass is probably best. With no reason to expect a fit, it is too dangerous to attempt any action. If you must bid something I suppose 1♠ is best, but I don't care for it. Be sure you understand why this hand is a pass when it is actually better than some of the previous examples.

1♥ – ?

♠ K Q 10 5
♥ J 8 6 4
◇ A J 3
♣ 7 6

1♠ is reasonable at matchpoints. Holding four hearts is not as great an inducement for you to bid as holding five hearts would be, but they do suggest a fit is possible. Don't try this one at IMPs.

1♥ – ?

♠ K Q J 3
♥ 8 7 6
◇ A J 4
♣ K J 5

This is a better double than it is a 1♠ bid. If partner has four spades, he will bid them. If not, the odds favor his holding a five-card minor. One thing is clear. This is a good hand and you should bid something if there is a good bid available.

Here are those four rules again, offered for reinforcement. I have found that when I discuss four-card overcalls, most players tend to forget at least one of these rules.

Remember this

1. You overcall with four-card suits only at the one-level.
2. You need an opening bid or close to it when you overcall with a four-card suit.
3. You need a good suit when you overcall with a four-card suit.
4. Your hand does not offer a better alternative, such as a takeout double.

CHAPTER THREE
VULNERABILITY

So far, this discussion has basically ignored vulnerability. So far it hasn't been important. What I've been trying to do here is to present a style of overcalling and to give you an idea of what works. If you have been able to accept my ideas to this point, then you should have no trouble judging when to bid or not bid according to vulnerability changes.

Regardless of anything else, it is more expensive to go down vulnerable than not vulnerable. Therefore, you need a better hand for your vulnerable overcalls than for your non-vulnerable overcalls. A look at a few examples should suffice.

VULNERABLE OVERCALLS AT THE ONE-LEVEL

With everyone vulnerable, the auction proceeds as indicated:

1♡ – ?

♠ A J 10 8 7
♡ 4 2
◇ K J 3
♣ Q 9 7

This is a reasonable vulnerable 1♠ call. You can make this bid at matchpoints or at IMPs. Note the importance of the spot cards. If your spades were ♠AJ632, passing would be reasonable if vulnerable.

1◇ – ?

♠ Q 10 8 7 5
♡ K 2
◇ 4 2
♣ A K 10 6

1♠. An average vulnerable overcall. I would do this at IMPs too. I would feel better if I had the ♠J or even the ♠9 too.

1♣ – ?

♠ 8 7 6 5 4
♡ A K 3
◇ 4
♣ A Q 6 5

1♠. You may get opinions to the contrary but this is not a bad hand for 1♠, even vulnerable. The first two hands had better suits, but they offered little chance for game unless partner had a mallet. With this hand, the chances of game are substantial if partner has the right minimum. It follows that this hand is a must-overcall hand at IMPs as well. The chance for game makes it well worth the risk.

1♢ – ?

♠ K J 9 8 7
♡ 4
♢ A 10 7 6 5
♣ J 3

1♠. Good potential for game opposite a fit. More likely, you will be able to jack the auction up to 2♠ or 3♠, forcing the opponents to make the last guess. As vulnerable overcalls go, this one is minimum. You are counting on your good shape to protect you.

1♢ – ?

♠ 8 2
♡ A J 10 8
♢ A Q 9 5 3
♣ 5 2

Clear-cut 1♡ bid at matchpoints. Also, for that matter, at IMPs. There's no way you will get hurt in 1♡ and if partner raises, this hand will be more than adequate. It is okay to bid, vulnerable, because you have a good hand and a good suit and you do not mind if partner wishes to bid on. You have values that will be useful for him if he bids a new suit or if he bids notrump.

1♡ – ?

♠ K 10 9 7
♡ A J 8 6 3
♢ 3
♣ K Q 2

1♠ is reasonable, but the suit is just about as bad as you would ever have vulnerable. The reasons you would overcall here are the fit implication (five hearts) and your good hand, comprised of aces and kings, rather than a lot of queens and jacks. I admit I would bid 1♠ at IMPs but with mild trepidation. Remember that your partner is entitled to raise you with ♠843 if his hand is otherwise suitable.

1♢ – ?

♠ Q 9 8 7
♡ 4
♢ A 10 9 8 7
♣ A J 3

Pass. Now and then a 1♠ bid might work, but it would be exciting. When you overcall on four-card suits vulnerable, they should be good suits. Following is a list of the kind of suits you need.

A K Q 7
A K J 8
A Q 10 7
A J 10 8
K Q J 8
K Q 10 7
K J 10 9

While you might sneak in a weaker suit on occasion, the rest of your hand should be super.

CHAPTER FOUR
TWO-LEVEL OVERCALLS

After the somewhat complex considerations of overcalling at the one-level, the discussion of two-level overcalls is going to be a breeze. Comparing one-level and two-level overcalls is like comparing night and day.

Why is this so?

Well, first is the simple fact that overcalling at the two-level means contracting for eight tricks rather than seven. This means you need extra values to give you a shot at taking that extra trick. So right away, all of those weakish hands which qualified for one-level overcalls are eliminated.

Overcalling at the two-level requires a good suit, so all those hands with K8642 or J10632 or 87632 are eliminated.

Overcalling at the two-level guarantees your suit will be five cards or longer. So all those nice four-card suits are eliminated.

So, what's left?

What's left is good hands with good suits. There just isn't the room for tactical actions that there is at the one-level. This does not mean there is no flexibility at all. Not true. Given the basic premise that a two-level overcall shows a good hand and a good suit, there are a few things that can be done.

TWO-LEVEL OVERCALLS, NOT VULNERABLE

Opener bids as indicated.

1♠ – ?

♠ 10 6
♡ A Q J 9 6
◇ A 10 4 2
♣ Q 3

This is a very reasonable 2♡ call at matchpoints. It's typical of the risk you are willing to take. Game is not too likely but you do have good chances for a partscore. In IMPs, a 2♡ call would be much more dangerous. While it's true you have good chances for a plus score, your most reasonable expectancy is 110 or 140, or perhaps a small plus by defeating the opponents. However, there is potential for a bad result too. This could be the layout.

♠ 10 6	♠ K J 5 4
♡ A Q J 9 6	♡ 8 3
◇ A 10 4 2	◇ J 8 3
♣ Q 3	♣ K 6 4 2

2♡ doubled could go for 300 quite easily. And it could be worse. Dummy has two trumps. Sometimes it has only one.

I would rate your chance of making a game at about 20% of your chance of going for a number. Repeating, in matchpoints you are concerned with, "How often can I get a plus score?" whereas at IMPs you are concerned with, "How big is my potential plus score? How big is the risk?" But before you decide never to bid at the two-level again, I note that your partner might have a third heart, in which case your 2♡ bid will not be a disaster.

Remember this

If they open and you overcall at the one-level and get doubled, you need seven tricks for your contract. If you overcall at the two-level and get doubled, you need eight tricks for your contract. Seems elementary. One of the consequences is that if you are doubled at the one-level, not vulnerable, and go down one for –100, you are in contention for a few matchpoints if they can make a partscore. If you are doubled at the two-level, not vulnerable, and go down two for –300, you will get a horrible score unless they have a game.

Further, many opponents are reluctant to double you at the one-level but are willing to double you at the two-level. It is just flat out more dangerous to overcall at the two-level than the one-level.

1♡ – ?

♠ 8
♡ A 10 7 3
♢ K Q 9 8 2
♣ K 5 4

Bid 2♢. Once again, there is the consideration that you hold length in the opener's suit. Whereas three cards is a very poor holding (particularly Qxx or worse), four- and five-card holdings are good and excellent respectively, and should encourage you to bid whenever possible. This point is strong enough that I would feel more comfortable bidding with this hand than on the prior hand, which may have appeared stronger. Stronger, perhaps, but safer, no. This hand, while not likely to produce a game, just barely qualifies for a call at IMPs as well.

One other point of this hand is that your overcall has stolen the one-level from the opponents. There remains an unbid major suit and your bid will make it difficult for the opponents to untangle their suits and values. While this is true to some extent of all overcalls, you should be aware of the degree of effectiveness of any given action. As I mentioned earlier, bids that get in the way of responder's bids are more effective than bids which do not take away responder's bids. The key is whether your bid takes away responder's bid of one of a major.

1♢ – 2♣ Gets in the way of both majors
1♣ – 1♠ Gets in the way of hearts and diamonds
1♢ – 1♠ Gets in the way of hearts

These calls make it hard for responder to show a major if he has one. Compare them with 1♠ – 2♣. This call takes only the 1NT response away. Had responder wanted to bid hearts or diamonds at the two-level, he can still do so with no loss of bidding room. Worse is 1♠ – 1◊, which gets in the way of nothing. 1♠ – 2♡ gets in the way of 2♣ and 2◊, but this is not a big deal.

The nature of bridge scoring is such that bidding is geared toward finding either a major suit fit or notrump. If responder has enough to respond 2♣ or 2◊ had you not overcalled, then he probably has enough strength that your 2♡ overcall will not have accomplished much in terms of making life difficult for the opponents. On the other hand, there are many, many hands where responder can bid 1♡ or 1♠ if you do not overcall but which just come nowhere near being worth bidding 2♡ or 2♠ when you interfere.

1♠ – ?

♠ 3
♡ A 3
◊ 10 5 4 2
♣ K Q J 7 6 3

A fairly straightforward 2♣ call. Note that when your overcall does not get in the way of a major suit, you do not have 'obstruction' going for you.

1♠ – ?

♠ 10 6 5 2
♡ A J 10 9 6 3
◊ A 3
♣ 5

This is the sort of hand on which many people pass, yet which is nearly a mandatory bid at all forms of bridge. Game could be cold opposite a singleton spade and four hearts to the king. Unlikely? Perhaps. But opposite a doubleton spade and three hearts to the queen, you have a play for 3♡. And no one can say that that is asking too much. If partner raises to 3♡, it would be reasonable to carry on.

How does this hand fulfill the requirements for a good hand and good suit? Well, the suit is obviously good enough and the hand qualifies as good because of the excellent distribution.

What is the risk of overcalling here? Opposite a bad hand you might go for a number, but that would be extreme and pessimistic. Your good heart spots should keep you safe against almost any mishap, such as a foul trump break.

Will partner be disappointed with your defensive potential if he doubles something? He shouldn't be. This hand rates to take two tricks, which on defense is quite adequate for an overcall.

1♠ – ?

♠ 872
♡ AJ10863
◇ A2
♣ 43

This hand is similar to the previous hand but it has one less spade and one more club. This has the effect of taking away one potential winner (the fourth spade you hoped to trump in dummy) and replacing it with a club loser. Now overcalling is marginal at best. A 2♡ bid *could* create some action, and for that reason *could* work at matchpoints, but it is fraught with danger.

1♠ – ?

♠ 432
♡ A42
◇ KQ987
♣ K5

Pass, double, or 2◇? This hand is balanced and it has three cards in opener's suit, always a bad sign. I would pass with this hand at any vulnerability.

1♡ – ?

♠ 8
♡ A1073
◇ KQ982
♣ K54

This is a hand from earlier in this chapter. I suggested bidding 2◇ after a 1♡ opening bid. I am showing it again to emphasize the value of good distribution. Do not get attached to points. There are other things to consider.

TWO-LEVEL OVERCALLS, VULNERABLE

Vulnerable two-level overcalls require a bit more in high cards, distribution, or a longer suit. In the example hands, everyone is vulnerable.

1♡ – ?

♠ 8
♡ A1073
◇ KQ982
♣ K54

Pass: While this was a routine 2◇ bid not vulnerable, it becomes a marginal 2◇ bid now. If either of those kings were an ace, I would swing in the other direction. If at matchpoints you want to bid, then go ahead. It can certainly work. But not at IMPs.

1♠ – ?

♠ 10762
♡ AQJ963
◇ K4
♣ 2

Bid 2♡. The excellent six-card suit makes this worth a bid. Take away a spade and add a club and the hand is not worth a bid.

1♠ – ?

♠ QJ3
♡ KJ872
◇ A43
♣ QJ

This hand is a disaster. It's not worth a bid anywhere or anytime. Strictly a trap for point-counters. Vulnerable, bidding 2♡ is just awful. Words fail me.

1♠ – ?

♠ 32
♡ QJ7642
◇ AK97
♣ 5

At matchpoints, vulnerable, 2♡ is clear enough. At IMPs, it is borderline. You are a favorite to get six tricks, but fewer would be a strong possibility. Again, at matchpoints you bid when you think you can improve your result by any amount, no matter how small. Add the ♡10 and it would become a minimum vulnerable IMP overcall.

1♡ – ?

♠ K2
♡ J63
◇ KQ8654
♣ AJ

This is typical of a matchpoint overcall which should be overlooked at IMPs. It is not safe and game potential is minimal. Even though you have a six-card suit, your hand won't be worth much if partner has a singleton diamond and not much on the side. The reason for passing at IMPs is that your hand has too few tricks for a vulnerable bid. If your LHO has ◇A1072, you might end up with eight losers for down three. Balanced hands are always nervous, but vulnerable they are more nervous than ever.

1♡ – ?

♠ K2
♡ 73
◇ AQ10872
♣ AK7

Bid 2◇ all the time. You may have been wondering what the upper limit may be for an overcall. Where does an overcall leave off and where does a takeout double followed by bidding a new suit begin? I'll cover that later. In the meantime, this hand does not qualify for anything but an overcall.

1♠ – ?

♠ 8
♡ 1098642
◇ AQ10
♣ AKJ

Here is an extension of those bad five-card suits that were sometimes worth a one-level overcall. You have added one card to the trump suit and the rest of the hand is outstanding. Bid 2♡ at matchpoints or IMPs at any vulnerability. It's clearly right to bid something and no other bid comes to mind.

1◇ – ?

♠ 4 3
♡ A Q 7 5
◇ 8 3
♣ A K J 9 7

Bid 2♣. Do not bid 1♡ and do not double. It is likely that you will be able to show your hearts later. If LHO bids 2◇ and that is passed to you, you can bid 2♡. Or your partner may bid something and you can bid hearts then if the auction allows. What you do not want to do is misdescribe the lengths of your two suits. Getting to the right trump suit is important because the wrong choice can make a huge difference in the tricks you take. Note that since you are vulnerable, you need a hand like this one to plan on bidding both of your suits.

1♠ – ?

♠ A 3
♡ 10 9 8 7 4
◇ A K Q 10 7
♣ 8

When I wrote the original text to *Overcalls* I suggested bidding 2♡ with this hand, intending to follow up with a diamond bid. This was acceptable because the hand is so good. Today, however, there is lots of available science. Best now is to bid 2♠, a variation on the Michaels cuebid. A 2♠ bid here shows five hearts and a five-card minor. Partner does not know which minor it is, but he knows you have five hearts and usually he can guess which minor you have. If he is not sure, he can ask you which minor you have if he is interested. This bid has the advantage of showing both suits at once and it also makes it tougher for the opponents to sort out their values. More on this convention later in the book.

1♡ – ?

♠ 5 2
♡ 8 7 2
◇ A K Q J 10
♣ J 8 7

At matchpoints, this is a good hand for a 2◇ overcall. Your expectancy is probably as low as any hand you may ever have, and you are hoping the opponents can't cope. This is a valid hope, since many people just don't know how to handle an overcall. It's obvious that you could go for 800 opposite a poor dummy, but the risk is worth it. Note that the only time you might purposely make a bid like this is when you have a solid trump suit. Neither opponent will be too eager to double you. If partner raises you may not like it, but if partner raises you on what must be poor trump (you have 150 honors) he will have something useful outside. Perhaps you will be able to escape for down one undoubled.

Please don't try this at IMPs.

CHAPTER FIVE
OVERCALLING WHEN BOTH OPPONENTS HAVE BID

When you are considering an overcall, or any other action for that matter, one of the most important factors you have to look at is how the auction has gone. Specifically, are you acting directly after the opening bidder, or are you acting after a response to the opening bidder? For some reason, a lot of players seem to think they are the same thing and they act accordingly. And they get bad results without knowing why. There are a number of specific cases, each different from the others. Here they are.

1. RHO bids a new suit at the one-level and you overcall at the one-level.
2. RHO bids a new suit at the one-level and you overcall at the two-level.
3. RHO bids 1NT and you overcall at the two-level.
4. RHO raises and you overcall at the two- or three-level.
5. RHO bids a new suit at the two-level and you overcall at the two- or three-level.

In some of these cases it is almost incumbent on you to act, and you should do so except when it is clear to pass. In some of these cases it is dangerous to act, and for the most part you will pass unless your hand is something special.

As it is easier to understand principles with examples, we'll look at the various cases. This is an important section in that you will see why a hand may be a clear-cut overcall on some auctions and a clear-cut pass on others. There are a few things to consider that apply when your opponents have had a chance to open and respond. You should be aware of them.

Firstly, your RHO, or responder, has made a bid. His call, whatever it was, has conveyed a significant amount of information. A 1NT response to 1♣ or 1◇ tends to show a balanced hand with 6-10 points or some similar range. A 1NT response to 1♡ or 1♠ has two meanings today. Traditionally, it showed about 6-10 points, no support for the major, and no suit higher ranking than the opener's. Since 2/1 bidding became popular, a 1NT response to a major is now a forcing bid. Usually responder has the same hand as always but may have an assortment of hands in the 11- or 12-point range. These are few, but you do have to be aware what it shows when it comes up at the table.

A raise shows about 6-10 points and a fit. If the opening bid was 1♣ or 1◇, then responder probably won't have a four-card major. His hand is limited. A new suit at the one-level shows 6+ points with length in the suit bid. Note that RHO has not limited his hand. He can have 20 or more points and still respond at the one-level.

A new suit at the two-level shows 10+ points and is also unlimited. RHO can have a huge hand. If your opponents are playing a 2/1 method, a response at the two-level promises even more than normal. Responder will have 12 or more points, not just 10 or more.

Once RHO has made a bid, you could say that their auction has established a rapport and it is going to be more difficult for you to interfere effectively. Remember. If you overcall after an opening bid on your right, the opponents must somehow communicate both their suits and their strengths. But when there has been a response, much of that information will have been exchanged. They are probably going to be involved in raising each other or bidding notrump, or conceivably in doubling your overcall. They may still be involved in searching out a new fit, but after the first response this is no longer as likely as before.

This does not mean your overcall has no effect on the opponents' bidding. If the auction has gone 1♣–pass–1◇, a 1♠ bid here may make it difficult for the opponents to locate their heart fit. But if the auction has been 1◇–pass–1♡, a 1♠ bid by you will have no preemptive or obstructive value. You should remember this rule in deciding whether to overcall.

RULE

When overcalling, part of the value of your bid is how difficult it is for the opponents to overcome it. If your bid does not take up some useful space, then your hand must be correspondingly better in terms of suit and hand quality.

ONE-LEVEL OVERCALLS AFTER A 1/1

The first case to cover here is when RHO has responded and you are considering a one-level overcall. There are only three auctions where this can occur. These are:

LHO	PARTNER	RHO	YOU
1♣	pass	1◇	?
1♣	pass	1♡	?
1◇	pass	1♡	?

If RHO has bid 1♠ or higher, you won't be able to bid a suit at the one-level. Here are some things to consider.

1. **Partner has passed, suggesting he may be weak.** This is not a guarantee, of course, but the possibility is greater than if he had not had a chance to bid.

2. With the opening bid on your left, your high cards will be in greater jeopardy. Opener rates to have most of the outstanding strength so your finesses will be generally unsuccessful. This particular objection holds true whenever LHO has opened the bidding. It's the sort of thinking which should become second nature to you when deciding whether to take action on this or any other occasion.

3. There is the danger that you will get doubled. Opener can count on his partner for a modicum of strength and if he feels there is a misfit, he might well decide to take a shot at your overcall. For that matter, RHO may want to double you. RHO's one-level response, while promising only 6 or so points, is unlimited, and he can have quite a good hand. Note that when the auction goes 1♣–pass–1♡, RHO does not deny a spade suit. He may easily have both a good hand and length in the suit or suits higher than the one he has just bid.

4. Lastly, if you judge that opener on your left is going to be declarer, you want to be careful about suggesting a lead to partner.

This all boils down to a fairly straightforward rule.

RULE

When there has been an opening bid and response and you are considering a one-level overcall, bid if you have any kind of *constructive* reason for doing so. Have either a good hand or a good suit. There is too much danger to bid on some of the trash on which you would have overcalled had there been an opening bid on your right.

With neither side vulnerable, the auction goes as indicated on the left.

W	N	E	S
1♣	pass	1◊	?

♠ K Q 10 8 5
♡ 7 3
◊ A J 9 7
♣ 8 6

A normal 1♠ call. Clear-cut at IMPs, too. Note that you have a good spade suit and a fairly good hand.

W	N	E	S
1♣	pass	1♢	?

♠ J 8 7 6 5
♡ 8
♢ K Q 9 6
♣ A 10 8

Again, 1♠. Note that even though the suit is bad, you have some expectation of a mild fit with hopes for more. The safety factor suggests a call at IMPs as well. One curiosity here. Your 1♠ bid makes it difficult for them to find their heart fit, but on the other hand, you know that hearts are not breaking well for them.

W	N	E	S
1♣	pass	1♡	?

♠ J 8 7 5 4
♡ K 5 4
♢ A 2
♣ K 9 7

Pass. This is the kind of hand you give up. While you might try 1♠ after an opening bid of 1♣, you should not bother here. Under no circumstances should you ever contemplate an overcall at IMPs.

W	N	E	S
1♢	pass	1♡	?

♠ A Q J 8
♡ A 10 8 4 2
♢ 3
♣ 8 7 3

1♠. Regardless of the auction, a good four-card suit is adequate if the rest of the hand warrants a bid. You will find that most hands which warrant an overcall on four-card suits tend to meet the requirements for safety, and therefore qualify for an overcall at IMPs as well. Note that if you pass and opener rebids 1NT, you will have to make a decision at the two-level. If you choose to pass it out in 1NT your partner will usually lead a club, which you don't like, and might even lead a diamond, which you would hate. Wouldn't you prefer to see him lead a spade? One of the rules for bidding a four-card suit at the one-level is that you have an opening bid. This hand is not strictly worth an opening bid but it does have excellent cards. Judgment applies here.

W	N	E	S
1♢	pass	1♡	?

♠ A Q 10 7
♡ Q 6 3
♢ 4
♣ A 8 6 5 4

Double. 1♠ would give up on the club suit.

W	N	E	S
1◇	pass	1♡	?

♠ A K J 8
♡ 8 7 2
◇ A 5 4 2
♣ J 2

You can bid 1♠, but you must be aware that this is far more dangerous than if you were bidding 1♠ over an opening 1◇ bid. Once the opponents have had an exchange, they will be well placed to double you when you are in trouble. For this reason you would tend to give up the IMP overcall. As usual, you need either safety or some expectation of game to justify bidding at IMPs.

W	N	E	S
1♣	pass	1♡	?

♠ A K 8 2
♡ 8
◇ 9 7 6
♣ A K 4 3 2

Here, 1♠ is certainly worthwhile, but is hardly safe. You have length in a suit bid by an opponent, but it was bid on your left. This suggests that your RHO may be able to overruff dummy in the event that you try to ruff clubs. Also, in this case there is the danger that the defense will start with hearts, forcing you to ruff. Note that had there been an opening 1♣ bid on your right, you would have bid 1♠ with way more expectations. The defense would be expected to lead clubs and your trumps would not be subject to immediate danger. But after 1♣–pass–1♡, the picture is completely different. It is very important to understand the differences involved.

The reason you might bid 1♠ at IMPs as well is that you have a very good hand which rates to take some tricks. Your safety is not predicated on a hoped-for fit, but rather on the useful high cards you yourself hold in hand.

W	N	E	S
1♣	pass	1♡	?

♠ K Q J 8
♡ 10 6 5
◇ 3 2
♣ A Q 9 6

1♠. When you overcall on four-card suits you have to consider how the defense will go. If you expect the defense will be able to negotiate a forcing game where they make you ruff, then you should not rush to call on four-card suits. Here, your doubleton is in diamonds, an unbid suit, so there is no reason to expect the defense to lead them. Once again, this is an IMP overcall as well.

Vulnerable, you are going to need a better hand, of course, but the considerations are still the same. If you have a four-card suit or a bad five-card suit, you should still get in there if you feel the hand otherwise meets the requirements. If this hand had the ♣K instead of the ♣Q, bidding 1♠ would be routine when vulnerable.

TWO-LEVEL OVERCALLS AFTER A 1/1

These are going to be somewhat similar to overcalls directly over the opening bidder. You will remember that by definition, two-level overcalls show good hands and good suits. The fact that both opponents have bid should encourage you toward caution. This is one of the more dangerous moments for you to act and you should be on reasonably firm ground. The dangers to you are similar to those I described when making a one-level overcall after RHO has responded, but they are more pronounced. I am going to summarize them briefly.

1. Partner has passed. He could easily have a weak hand. Remember that RHO, while showing only 6 points for his 1/1 bid, has not denied a good hand. There is no upper limit on his values. Compare this with a 1NT response showing 6-10 (or 8-10 for some players).
2. The opening bidder is over you. Your high cards may be poorly placed.
3. It is far more likely that you will get doubled in a two-level overcall than in a one-level overcall. It's amazing how many tops are acquired by doubling an indiscreet overcall and collecting a number. I am not trying to scare anyone into passing. This is a book on bidding, after all, and bidding is the name of this game. I'm just trying to get you to stop making bad or silly bids.

Other common considerations:

1. Does your bid deprive the opponents of any useful bidding space?

LHO	Partner	RHO	You
1♣	pass	1♡	2♢

Your 2♢ bid means LHO cannot rebid 1♠, 1NT, or 2♣. While losing 1NT and 2♣ may not be much of a loss, losing the 1♠ bid may turn out to be serious. The important point is whether or not there is an unbid major and whether or not your overcall makes it hard for the opponents to locate it.

LHO	Partner	RHO	You
1♡	pass	1♠	2♢

There is no unbid major here so your bid loses much of its obstructive value.

LHO	Partner	RHO	You
1♣	pass	1♠	2◇

Here there is an unbid major, but opener, if he was going to bid it, would have had to do so at the two-level. Your 2◇ bid does not actually take away as much room as first appears. This means that after RHO has responded, some of your overcalls can be obstructive, and you should be aware of these. Here is a simple hand to show you how it feels from the opener's point of view.

♠ A K 7 3   ♡ Q 3   ◇ 4 2   ♣ K Q 8 7 6

LHO	Partner	RHO	You
			1♣
pass	1♡	2◇	?

They gotcha. Your nice 1♠ rebid is not available and you haven't the values for 2♠. You must pass. Whatever happens now doesn't really matter. What does matter is that your side will have to work harder to get back to par.

2. How has the auction gone? Once again, the auction is all-important. If I emphasize the point once, I'll emphasize it a hundred times. It is very possible that on a given hand it might be right to overcall after an opening 1♠ bid on your right but wrong to overcall after 1♣–pass–1♠.

Let's look at cases.

Neither vul.

W	N	E	S
1♣	pass	1♡	?

♠ 4 2
♡ A J 7
◇ A Q J 9 7 6
♣ J 3

This is a reasonable 2◇ call at either IMPs or matchpoints. You have a good suit and a good hand as well. Your heart holding is over the bidder. With any luck at all you could have two heart tricks. This sequence is also good for you in that it makes it difficult for your opponents to find a spade fit. Note that East's bid is two-edged. It tells you that your RHO is not broke, which lessens the chance that your partner has values. But at the same time it tells you something about their values, which may be useful information.

Which hand here is worth more?

LHO	Partner	RHO	You
1◇	pass	1♠	?

Hand One
♠ 4 2
♡ A Q 10 8 7
◇ K J 7 6 5
♣ 3

Hand Two
♠ K J 7 6 5
♡ A Q 10 8 7
◇ 4 2
♣ 3

In my opinion, the second hand is worth from two and a half to three tricks more than the first. The ♠KJ765 is a huge plus. The honors are well located and with any luck LHO will lead one. The ◇KJ765, however, is poorly placed and there is no chance at all that LHO will lead the suit for you.

LHO	Partner	RHO	You
1♡	pass	1♠	?

Hand One
♠ A 8 4
♡ K J 3
◇ K Q J 8 7
♣ 5 4

Hand Two
♠ K J 3
♡ A 8 4
◇ K Q J 8 7
♣ 5 4

These two hands are also easy to compare. In hand one, the ♡KJ3 is a very dangerous holding while on hand two, the ♠KJ3 could easily provide two tricks. I would bid 2◇ on the second hand at any vulnerability at matchpoints and even, perhaps, at IMPs. The first hand might be a non-vulnerable 2◇ call at matchpoints, but surely not at IMPs. While it's not too hard to evaluate a hand on any particular auction, it is very necessary that you do it. Taking all available facts into consideration will help your evaluation and consequently your bidding.

Both vul.

W	N	E	S
1♣	pass	1♠	?

♠ Q 8 4
♡ A K J 7 4
◇ Q 5
♣ K 8 6

At matchpoints 2♡ might work, but I'd be nervous to try it, even not vulnerable. Passing is best. Your black suit holdings are not worth much at all. On a bad day you could go for 1400. On a good day you could make 140. In spite of 15 points, your game potential is as good as nil.

Both vul.

W	N	E	S
1♣	pass	1♡	?

♠ K 8 7 6
♡ K 2
♢ A Q J 10 7
♣ 4 2

Double. You don't want to lose the spade suit.

Both vul.

W	N	E	S
1♣	pass	1♠	?

♠ K 10 6 5
♡ A J 10 8 6 5
♢ Q 5
♣ 7

A clear-cut 2♡ bid at matchpoints, and reasonable at IMPs. You'd rather the ♢Q were the ♠J, but nothing is perfect. The spade length (four) is an asset.

Both vul.

W	N	E	S
1♣	pass	1♠	?

♠ 7
♡ A J 10 9 7 5
♢ Q 5
♣ K 10 6 5

2♡ at matchpoints, but consider passing at IMPs. Even though your hearts are better, your clubs are going to be a liability. The opening leader will probably lead a spade, and that doesn't rate to be of any help to you.

Both vul.

W	N	E	S
1♣	pass	1♠	?

♠ K 4 2
♡ A Q 10 7 4
♢ K 2
♣ K J 3

Dangerous hand. Your ♠K is the only well-placed card you have. The distribution is vile and the rest of your high cards are of unclear value. When you consider that partner doesn't rate to have much more than 3 or 4 points, you can see the lack of future for this hand. Overcalls are made of tricks, not points. 2♡ here might be okay not vulnerable at matchpoints, but if you can bring yourself to pass, you will be taking a step in the right direction.

Both vul.

W	N	E	S
1♡	pass	1♠	?

♠ 8 6 2
♡ Q J 3
◇ A K Q 8 7
♣ K 3

This is typical of most well-judged passes. While 2◇ might work at matchpoints, it would be frightfully excessive at IMPs. The best you can hope to achieve is a small plus, while risking a large minus. Look at all the defects this hand has.

1. You have the worst possible spade holding. Three small in the suit bid on your right.
2. You have secondary honors in the suit bid on your left.
3. The opponents have bid both majors. 2◇ by you has little to gain tactically.

Here is a typical layout which you might find if you bid 2◇:

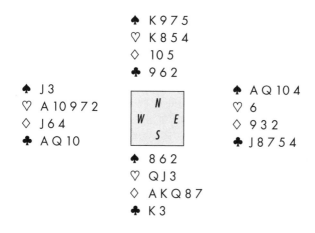

```
              ♠ K 9 7 5
              ♡ K 8 5 4
              ◇ 10 5
              ♣ 9 6 2
♠ J 3                          ♠ A Q 10 4
♡ A 10 9 7 2      N            ♡ 6
◇ J 6 4       W       E        ◇ 9 3 2
♣ A Q 10          S            ♣ J 8 7 5 4
              ♠ 8 6 2
              ♡ Q J 3
              ◇ A K Q 8 7
              ♣ K 3
```

While you are lucky, sort of, to find dummy with two kings and diamonds dividing three-three, you are going to go down four tricks against best defense. They will take three spades, the ♡A and two heart ruffs, two clubs, and then lead a fourth spade, allowing West to score his trump jack. That's –400. If East makes a sporting double, it's –1100. A stiff price considering their maximum is 120 in notrump or 130 in clubs.

Neither vul.

W	N	E	S
1♣	pass	1♡	?

♠ A 2
♡ 9
◇ A K Q J 7 5
♣ J 7 6 4

2◇ is right in all forms of the game. Don't consider doubling with an eye to bidding diamonds later. Partner would be entitled to compete in spades and might get you too high for the wrong reasons. Note that 2◇ makes it hard for the opponents to find spades. It would be an error to bid 3◇ unless you play that as strong. Most play that 3◇ would show a weak hand, which you do not have.

N-S vul.

W	N	E	S
1♣	pass	1♠	?

♠ 8 2
♡ K Q J 10 8 7 5
♢ A 4
♣ 3 2

Bid 2♡. The good suit should encourage you to bid. The vulnerability and bad distribution should discourage you from bidding too much. If partner can't contribute anything to the auction, you should go quietly. This hand rates to produce a sure partscore for you but game is most unlikely. On hands where game is out of the question, or seriously against the odds, you need a good suit.

Both vul.

W	N	E	S
1♣	pass	1♠	?

♠ A Q 10 3
♡ 10 9 7 5 4
♢ 4
♣ A K 7

I would bid 2♡. The reasons you can try this on such a suit are as follows.

1. Game is possible if you have any kind of fit. If partner has four hearts, you might easily come to ten tricks. Note that on the previous hand four-card heart support can't even guarantee a partscore.

2. You have a good hand. You have sure tricks, not unsupported kings and queens.

3. Your spade length suggests a mild heart fit is probable and a good fit is likely.

4. Your spade honors are well placed. Even better is that LHO may well lead one. This will not hurt your chances. When you overcall with such suits it is exceptional, and you need outstanding side values.

Both vul.

W	N	E	S
1♣	pass	1♠	?

♠ 4
♡ 10 9 7 6 5
♢ A Q 10 7
♣ A K 5

Double. I hate to make takeout doubles when holding a five-card major but bidding hearts here is just too dangerous. The defense is likely to lead spades and you will be subject to the tap sooner than you wish. When you can predict that the opponents can establish a forcing game (making you ruff) you must have good trump suits. In the previous hand the bidding was the same but your short suit was diamonds, a suit they do not rate to lead.

♠ A Q 10 3   ♡ 10 9 7 5 4   ♢ 4   ♣ A K 7

Here is the previous hand. After LHO bids 1♣ and RHO bids 1♠, you can bid 2♡ without fear that they will lead a diamond, potentially tapping you. The auction suggests you will get a spade or club lead. The forcing game is not a serious threat and can be discounted.

Here is a summary of a two-level overcall after a 1/1 response:

1. It is more dangerous than overcalling directly after an opening bid.
2. You need a good suit or a good hand that suggests you can take tricks.
3. You should not count random unsupported kings and queens at full value except when they are in the suit bid by RHO.
4. Length in RHO's suit (four-cards or more) is a plus.
5. Length in opener's suit (four-cards or more) is only mildly advantageous.
6. Any three cards in RHO's suit is a minus.
7. Any three cards in opener's suit is a minus.
8. Your overcall is less likely to be obstructive. Know the exceptions!

TWO-LEVEL OVERCALLS AFTER ONE-OF-A-SUIT–PASS–1NT

For a change, we are into an area of competitive bidding where you should be encouraged to bid as opposed to the safety-first approach of the previous two sections. When the bidding goes:

1♣ pass 1NT	1♡ pass 1NT
1◇ pass 1NT	1♠ pass 1NT

there are some very important facts you should immediately recognize. Let's assume 1NT is a natural bid. Then we know (probably):

1. RHO has 6-10 HCP. Sometimes their range is even tighter.
2. RHO does not have a suit higher ranking than opener's.
3. RHO rates not to have support for his partner. This is usually true of a 1NT response to a major. It is not necessarily true of a 1NT response to a minor. Some opponents use a forcing notrump response to a major suit opening but it usually turns out to be a normal bid. Do not worry about this.

What this means to you is that on some auctions you will be able to take certain liberties. Here's why.

1. When RHO responds 1NT he shows 6-10 HCP, averaging perhaps 7, maybe 8. When RHO responds in a new suit, he shows an unlimited hand. After a 1NT response, therefore, you are entitled to a moderate amount of optimism regarding your partner's strength. It will probably average out to a queen or so more than when RHO's bid was one of a new suit.
2. This is the real bonus. License to steal. When RHO bids 1NT he is denying a suit higher than the suit opened, and this in turn means it is that much safer for you to compete in one of these *higher ranking* suits. I would say

that when RHO bids 1NT, it is incumbent on you to consider bidding. One warning here. Do not lose sight of the fact that when RHO bids 1NT he may very well be loaded in many or all of the lower-ranking suits. This is an extremely important distinction, as you will see in the example hands. Let's get into specifics.

W	N	E	S
1♣	pass	1NT	?

♠ K Q 8 7 6 5
♡ J 8 7
♢ 3
♣ A 5 4

Bid 2♠. Quite clear-cut at any game. Right away you should begin to feel that on some auctions it is safe for you to act, and this is one of them. You have a higher ranking suit well worth mentioning and a decent hand besides. Your chances of finding a fit are very good. RHO's 1NT bid is usually based on four clubs, as he didn't seem to have a suit worth mentioning. This suggests that your partner has only one or two clubs. This in turn increases the chances of partner holding a few spades. You can just about expect three spades, you can hope for four spades, and if you should find only two in partner's hand that would be a bit unlucky. One or none is possible but not common.

Once in awhile you will run into someone who for some reason chooses to open 1♣ with only two. And now and then his partner decides to bid 1NT with one or two four-card majors. When this happens you may get nailed, but even against these people, it's unlikely. If they bid this way their defense won't be any better. Don't worry about the occasional fix you suffer. These people will be repaying you with interest for their other mistakes.

One last aside here. Some people play that 1♣–pass–1NT shows a good hand in the 8-11 point range. If this is the case, you should tighten up just a little bit.

Neither vul.

W	N	E	S
1♣	pass	1NT	?

♠ A Q 3
♡ K 10 9 7 5 4
♢ 8 7
♣ 10 5

Bid 2♡ at matchpoints. When you are faced with a 'safe' auction, try to get in there whenever possible. Even at IMPs, 2♡ would not be terrible.

Neither vul.

W	N	E	S
1♣	pass	1NT	?

♠ Q J 10 8 3
♡ 8 7
◇ A K 6 5
♣ 4 2

Not vulnerable at matchpoints, there is a lot to be said for 2♠. You have a good suit and decent shape which includes useful side values. Minimum hands that have all their values concentrated to best advantage are usually better than hands with greater point count but with honors scattered all over the place. If vulnerable, you might try this if you were a passed hand. Partner would not expect more.

Some people insist on substantial values for overcalls on the theory that partner will always protect (balance) when the auction dies. This is nice when it works, but I can't expect partner to reopen if 1NT is passed to him.

LHO	Partner	RHO	You
1♣	pass	1NT	pass
pass	?		

Is partner supposed to bid with this hand?

♠ 9 7 2   ♡ K J 4 2   ◇ Q 3   ♣ K 9 7 5

This is too rich for me. His hand is good enough that our side can make 2♠ or 3♠ with no trouble. If 1NT is passed out they may or may not make it. I like the odds for bidding and not defending. Remember, though, that much of the reason you are acting on some of these marginal hands is that the auction is one defined as 'safe.' One other reason for bidding 2♠ is that the auction might very well continue in this fashion:

LHO	Partner	RHO	You
1♣	pass	1NT	pass
2♣	pass	?	

If RHO passes 2♣, then you can reopen with 2♠, which is fine. But if RHO raises to 3♣ it will be all over for you. And believe me, it can go that way. If you choose to bid 2♠ at your first opportunity, LHO may not be able to bid 3♣ because of insufficient values and RHO may be hesitant about competing to 3♣ because he fears that opener may have only three clubs.

Neither vul.

W	N	E	S
1♣	pass	1NT	?

♠ 10 3
♡ J 10 7 5 4 2
♢ 3
♣ A K 8 7

This is an example of the extremes you can go to in order to get involved. 2♡ is quite reasonable and is far safer than it might first appear. Note that partner almost surely has a stiff or doubleton club. He probably has a weakish 4-4-4-1 or perhaps 4-3-4-2. Note that the objection to overcalling on a weak suit doesn't apply here because partner is unlikely to be on lead. For that to happen LHO would have to end up in clubs, which suits you fine, or he would have to rebid 2♠ or 3♢, which is most unlikely. Even if this happens, partner's lead doesn't have to be costly.

Neither vul.

W	N	E	S
1♣	pass	1NT	?

♠ 4 2
♡ A K Q 10 3
♢ 8 3
♣ 10 6 5 4

Because of the safeness of the auction and the length in clubs, implying a fit, I would bid 2♡. Note that the opponents do have a club fit, which hints of a heart fit for us. The real danger in bidding is not that you will go down in 2♡. It is that your partner will raise you to 3♡, which will be in danger of going down.

Neither vul.

W	N	E	S
1♢	pass	1NT	?

♠ 4 2
♡ A K Q 10 3
♢ 10 6 5 4
♣ 3 2

It's more dangerous to bid 2♡ here than on the previous hand. While RHO may have some diamonds, which would mean your partner is short in diamonds, your RHO may have a bunch of clubs and no diamond support. This would mean your partner's diamonds are not necessarily as short as you would like.

    Remember: 1♣–pass–1NT guarantees a fit.
                        1♢–pass–1NT suggests a fit.

Neither vul.

W	N	E	S
1♢	pass	1NT	?

♠ A Q 10 7 6
♡ 4 2
♢ A 4 3
♣ K 6 5

It's reasonable to bid 2♠. RHO doesn't have hearts or spades so it becomes a safe auction for an overcall. LHO may have spades but you are 'safe' from both opponents having them. Compare with the next hand:

Neither vul.

W	N	E	S
1◇	pass	1NT	?

♠ K 6 5
♡ 4 2
◇ A 4 3
♣ A Q 10 7 6

Pass. Very dangerous. When RHO responds 1NT, he is denying length in partner's suit and in higher ranking suits. This perforce means he has length in the lower ranking suit or suits. After 1◇–pass–1NT, you can be sure that RHO has clubs. On this sequence, a 2♣ bid by you must show a very good suit. If you don't have it, you're going to go down and likely doubled in the bargain. This auction is curious as it is one of the few that tells you in advance how your prospective trump suit (clubs) will divide. If you had one more club and one less card elsewhere, bidding 2♣ would be much safer.

Both vul.

W	N	E	S
1♡	pass	1NT¹	?

1. Forcing

♠ Q 3
♡ A 4 2
◇ Q J 9 7 6
♣ A J 7

Be careful. Bidding 2◇ is rather risky. After 1♡–pass–1NT it is 'safe' to bid spades, which is a suit higher ranking than opener's. It is not 'safe' to bid diamonds. You can hope to find partner with a few points, but you cannot really hope for a fit. There is the real danger that partner won't have any support for diamonds, and even if he does they may well break poorly. RHO rates to have clubs and diamonds (he doesn't have hearts or spades). Note that if 1NT is not forcing, rare today, you can pass it and may be on lead. This is fine with you since you have a good lead and you have entries that will help you set up and use your suit. You can not double 1NT, if you were thinking of it, because that would be a takeout double showing the three unbid suits.

Neither vul.

W	N	E	S
1♣	pass	1NT	?

♠ Q 10 8 7 6
♡ A 2
◇ A 6 5
♣ Q 8 5

Get in there with 2♠ at matchpoints, but not at IMPs. You are taking a calculated matchpoint risk that your partner has a few spades. Some would call it a matchpoint prayer. If you find a fit it may carry you through. ♠J52 ♡Q10643 ◇K74 ♣102 is enough to get away with this smelly overcall. Do not try this one when vulnerable.

Neither vul.

W	N	E	S
1◇	pass	1NT	?

♠ K J 8 7 6
♡ A Q 10 6 4
◇ 3 2
♣ 7

You should want to bid something and the question is, what? Your choices seem to be 2♠, 2♡, 2◇, and double. Two things you shouldn't do are bid 2♡ or double. If a 2◇ cuebid would show the majors (highly recommended), it is the best bid. If you do not have a Michaels cuebid in your system you should bid 2♠, reserving the possibility of bidding hearts next.

Neither vul.

W	N	E	S
1◇	pass	1NT	?

♠ 3
♡ Q J 10 8 7 6
◇ A 10 6 5
♣ 10 3

When you have a hand with a good suit and other factors are in your favor, you should bid. The auction is 'safe' and you can hope reasonably for a fit of some sort. It might be minimal, in which case you will get no higher, but it could be spectacular, in which case you might even make a game. In practice, I would expect +140 as against –120 or –110. Some of the time you get a small plus when the opponents go down 50 or 100. All of these are better than passing. A minor aside here is that if you pass, your partner might reopen with 2♣. Now if you wish to play in hearts you will have to do so at the three-level.

Neither vul.

W	N	E	S
1♡	pass	1NT[1]	?

1. Forcing

♠ A 2
♡ 4 3
◇ K 7 6
♣ K Q J 8 7 5

Bid 2♣. This is clear enough, but you should not feel too optimistic about this hand. You are not likely to find much of a fit, and even with this hand you might be doubled and go for a couple of tricks. In your favor is that you will get a club lead if opener plays the hand. And on occasion you will be able to compete higher if partner's hand is suitable. Note that overcalling in a suit lower ranking than opener's requires that you have a decent hand and a good suit.

Conversely, of course, when you are contemplating overcalling in a suit higher ranking than opener's you can take all sorts of liberties.

One more important point to make here. After a 1NT response your overcalls will never have significant obstructive value. There is no sequence where your overcall makes it impossible for opener to show an unbid major when he would have wanted to do so.

1♠-pass-1NT-2♣	Opener can always show hearts or diamonds if he wants to do so.
1♡-pass-1NT-2◇	Opener can't rebid 2♣, but this is a small loss in general. If opener wants to show spades or rebid his hearts, he can do so.
1◇-pass-1NT-2♠	Opener can't show any suit at the two-level, but he has already been able to show his diamonds. Since their side does not have a heart fit, opener won't be interested in looking for that suit. Note that however small the obstructive value of 2♠ may be, it is still much more annoying to the opener than 2♡, 2◇, or 2♣, each bid being less obnoxious than the previous one.

Neither vul.

W	N	E	S
1♡	pass	1NT	?

♠ K J 4 2
♡ 3
◇ A Q 2
♣ Q 6 5 4 2

Double for takeout. Under no circumstances bid 2♣.

Overcalls When RHO Has Responded With a 2/1

This one is easy. Don't.

Of all the situations where it is dangerous to bid, this one is the worst. It's scary. Fortunately, it is easy to see why this is so. Four simple reasons:

1. LHO has an opening bid, and may have more.
2. RHO has 10+ HCP, and may have more than that if using 2/1 bidding.
3. Their side has 24 HCP, and may have more.
4. Your side has 16 HCP on a good day, and usually has less.

This means if you hear the bidding go 1♠–pass–2◇ and elect to get involved, you will be trying for eight or nine tricks on hands where you can't possibly have more than 40% of the high cards. If you overcall and fail to find a fit, or if dummy is particularly broke, you have had it.

Does this mean you should never bid after a 2/1 response? No, but it does mean your tactics must lean strongly toward safety. You must have values in your own hand, both in the form of good suits and a good hand. Under no circumstances should you hope to find useful high cards in partner's hand. You won't find them. At least, you won't find them often enough to make it worthwhile. You may, however, hope to find a fit when your hand suggests it might exist. Hoping for a fit and hoping for some high cards are not at all the same thing.

Neither vul.

W	N	E	S
1♠	pass	2◇	?

♠ K 3 2
♡ Q 10 7 6 5
◇ K J 7
♣ A 2

Pass these hands. You have a broken suit. You have a balanced hand. Your ♠K is suspect. You don't want a heart lead. You will never be able to outbid the opponents. There is nothing good about bidding 2♡. Assume the best that can happen. Give partner 3 points, the most he can have. Let's imagine he has the ♡K. The best of all worlds. If partner happens to have four hearts, then nothing much will happen. You won't get doubled. The opponents will get to wherever they were going and they will get an average. Perhaps declarer will play the hand well as a result of your overcall and will get a top. If partner has one, two, or three hearts to the king (we're still hoping), then you may get doubled or the opponents can still do whatever else they like. There's just nothing good that can happen for you as a result of your overcall.

Here's a common result stemming from a 2♡ overcall:

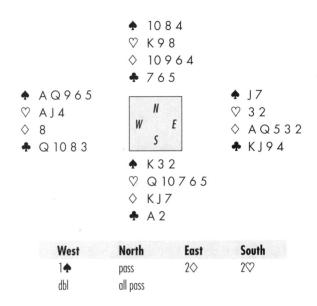

♠ 10 8 4
♡ K 9 8
◇ 10 9 6 4
♣ 7 6 5

♠ A Q 9 6 5   ♠ J 7
♡ A J 4   ♡ 3 2
◇ 8   ◇ A Q 5 3 2
♣ Q 10 8 3   ♣ K J 9 4

♠ K 3 2
♡ Q 10 7 6 5
◇ K J 7
♣ A 2

West	North	East	South
1♠	pass	2◇	2♡
dbl	all pass		

A well-judged double by West netted 500 out of nothing. Some would say that East does not have enough for 2◇. He could have more. And your partner could have less and might also have fewer hearts. You might go for more than 500, with –800 or –1100 being possible.

N-S vul.

W	N	E	S
1♡	pass	2♣	?

♠ K J 10 7 6 5
♡ A 8 2
◇ K J 7
♣ 3

Pass again! This hand came up in practice and was judged to be worth 2♠. It wasn't. Dummy had a scattered 4-count which turned out to be worth zero. Minus 1100. Note that the vulnerability given here was vulnerable vs. not vulnerable. Bidding was rather idiotic. So much so, in fact, that you shouldn't bid even with neither vulnerable. The only time you could consider acting with this hand is not vulnerable vs. vulnerable, and your objective would be less to find a good contract than it would be to find a save. Note that you have no reason to expect a fit and even not vulnerable vs. vulnerable, –300 could be bad if they have no game.

Both vul.

W	N	E	S
1♠	pass	2◇	?

♠ K J 8
♡ A K Q 8 7
◇ 5 4 2
♣ K 9

Believe it or not, you should pass. Even better if you can pass for the right reasons.

The facts here are:

1. Partner is broke.
2. Your spades are likely worthless.
3. Your diamond holding is atrocious.

With the expected diamond lead and spade return this hand could easily fall apart. You haven't the slightest reason to expect that partner has heart support. If you bid 2♡ you could go for 200 to 800. This will happen almost anytime one of your opponents has four hearts. Some important points here:

1. Even though the opponents are thinking of bidding to game, you have enough defense that they may not have one. If they do not have a game a penalty of 200 or more will be a bad result.

2. Both opponents are likely to double you. RHO has a good hand and will be happy to double whenever his hand is suitable. Furthermore, opener, if unsure of what to do, can pass, expecting his partner to bid again. If RHO has something like ♠3 ♡J96 ◇AKJ76 ♣QJ82, he would certainly take a shot at 2♡ after the auction 1♠-pass-2◇-2♡-pass-pass-?.

Neither vul.

W	N	E	S
1♠	pass	2♣	?

♠ 3
♡ K Q J 4 2
◇ 3 2
♣ A Q 8 6 5

Here it is right to act. You have a decent suit and you have every right to hope for a fit. If partner has three hearts and no high cards at all, 2♡ could succeed. The implied fit is all-important here. If partner likes hearts, you have a good save or even a make.

Neither vul.

W	N	E	S
1♠	pass	2◇	?

♠ 3
♡ K Q J 4 2
◇ 3 2
♣ A Q 8 6 5

Whatever you do, don't bid 2♡. Either double (best) or bid 2NT, unusual.

N-S vul.			
W	N	E	S
1♠	pass	2♡	?

♠ 4 2
♡ K 2
◇ A Q J 8 6 5
♣ K Q 3

Pass! Pass! Pass! You are too high and you are outgunned. Dummy has nothing. On a good day, you get seven tricks. Whenever it is wrong to bid, you get doubled and you go down. It is never right to bid. *Pass.* The only conceivable rationale you can have for bidding is that you suspect LHO is psyching. But there is no reason to assume that, and if your assumption is wrong, you pay the price. Here is a possible hand from opener's point of view:

♠ A Q 9 8 5   ♡ 9 6   ◇ K 10 4   ♣ A 10 5

After 1♠–pass–2♡–3◇ opener should double, especially in view of the fact that the 3◇ bidder is vulnerable.

Both vul.			
W	N	E	S
1♠	pass	2♣	?

♠ 9
♡ A 8 7
◇ K Q J 10 7 3
♣ 10 5 4

In spite of only 10 HCP, you should bid 2◇. This hand is going to take tricks no matter what partner has. If you are unlucky, you may go down 500. On some of the 'better' hands shown earlier you would have to be lucky to go for *only* 500.

Both vul.			
W	N	E	S
1♠	pass	2♣	?

♠ 8 6 5
♡ A K Q J 8 7
◇ 7 3
♣ 4 2

It's right to bid 2♡, but you shouldn't be thrilled. If you bid 2♡ and feel sort of blah about it, that's about right.

Neither vul.			
W	N	E	S
1♡	pass	2◇	?

♠ J 10 8 7 6 5
♡ 3
◇ A Q 9 6 3
♣ 5

I would bid 2♠, hoping to find a fit. If partner has dull support, nothing much will happen. But if he has good support and can raise, you could have a good save or even a game. It's safe to bid here because you know where your tricks are coming from.

Neither vul.

W	N	E	S
1♡	pass	2♣	?

♠ J 10 8 7 6 5
♡ 3
◇ A Q 9 6 3
♣ 5

If you want to experiment you could try 2♠. You have no reason to expect a fit, but if partner does have a few spades you can do well.

The dangers here as opposed to the previous hand are worth noting.

1. The chances for a fit are substantially less.

2. You are likely to get a diamond lead on the first hand but not on the second.

3. If the opponents play the hand your partner will probably lead a spade, and this may work out poorly. Note that this objection doesn't hold true for the first auction, 1♡–pass–2◇–2♠. If you pass instead of bidding 2♠ partner, if on lead, would usually select an unbid suit, that is, clubs or spades, and you don't particularly care for either. On the other hand, after 1♡–pass–2♣, 2♠ tends to ensure a spade lead and you actually would prefer a diamond lead. Had you remained quiet, partner might well have selected one.

Oh well, pay your dues, take your chances.

The rule to follow after a 2/1 is simple. You bid when it is safe to do so and you have a good reason for bidding. *Points by themselves* do not constitute safety. They do not take tricks. They are not a reason to bid.

RULE

After a 2/1 your overcalls show tricks, not points.

It is safe to bid when you have tricks. These are usually in the form of good suits or hands with distribution where the auction has told you to expect a fit. Partner should not expect too much of you when you do overcall after a 2/1. Your side has few high cards so anything you make must be on the basis of a fit with good distribution. There is no way your side can make 3NT.

LHO	Partner	RHO	You
1♠	pass	2♣	2♡

They have two thirds of the high cards. They may bid and make 3NT. Your side will never bid and make 3NT. Your partner should recognize that you bid 2♡ with a shapely hand, not a good hand.

Think about it. In practice, the only bids the partner of the overcaller can make are to raise or to double. A raise should show a good hand with useful cards. It should not be made on garbage points including questionable high cards.

Both vul.

W	N	E	S
		1♠	pass
2♣	2♡	pass ?	

♠ Q 10 7 6
♡ 10 6 4 2
◇ Q 10
♣ K 10 7

You should pass. With most of your values in the opponents' suit, you don't have much to offer partner.

Both vul.

W	N	E	S
		1♠	pass
2♣	2♡	pass ?	

♠ 10 8 7 6 5
♡ Q 10 6 5
◇ K 4 2
♣ 3

But with this hand you should bid 3♡, or even 4♡. Probably 4♡ is best. Your values are all working overtime with no wastage. More on this later.

OVERCALLS AFTER A RAISE

LHO	Partner	RHO	You
1♣	pass	2♣	?
1◇	pass	2◇	?
1♡	pass	2♡	?
1♠	pass	2♠	?

This section is also easy. When they bid and raise, you should be anxious to find a bid. If there was ever a sequence where you should compete, this is it. Everything is in your favor. Here's what you have going for you. It's compelling and overwhelming.

1. RHO has a limited hand.
2. Some of RHO's values will be distributional, implying the possibility of even fewer HCP.
3. After 1♣–pass–2♣ or 1◇–pass–2◇, RHO won't hold a major suit. After 1♣–pass–2♣, RHO probably won't have a diamond suit. After 1♡–pass–2♡, RHO probably won't have a spade suit. (A responder holding

♠Q1062 ♡K83 ◊42 ♣K1087 should raise 1♡ to 2♡, in spite of holding ♠Q1062. There are enough bad bidders out there who bid 1♠, though, that in practice a heart raise does tend to deny spades.)

4. Opener will not be inclined to double an overcall by you. More likely than not he will bid again, even when he should pass. Even when opener should be doubling you he may bid instead. Human nature is such that when a fit is found, most people try to outbid the opponents in lieu of other actions.

5. Because of opener's propensity for bidding again after an overcall, you will often be pushing the opponents too high. This is especially important on hands where your partner could not reopen had you passed.

A NEW THOUGHT: PRE-BALANCING

When your opponents bid and raise a suit, there is the possibility that it may be passed out there. If you have a weakish hand with a fair suit, you can bid right away in an effort to make sure the bidding is not passed out. This bid is called a 'pre-balance' bid, the idea being that you are making a balancing bid yourself. This is not a classic balancing situation but it is a sane one. This trick requires that your partner does not take your overcalls seriously, something that may cause you to miss some games. Still, bidding aggressively after a raise is a good idea. I will discuss this theme in the following hands.

Neither vul.

W	N	E	S
1♣	pass	2♣	?

♠ KJ875
♡ 3
◊ K872
♣ A53

2♠. Clear-cut. Above average in values. Note that RHO does not have four spades or hearts.

Neither vul.

W	N	E	S
1♣	pass	2♣	?

♠ 3
♡ KJ875
◊ Q872
♣ A53

2♡. Slightly fewer values than the preceding hand. One additional reason for bidding here is that you don't want to hear partner reopen with 2♠.

Neither vul.

W	N	E	S
1♣	pass	2♣	?

♠ 8 7 2
♡ 4 3
◇ K Q 10 9 7
♣ A 8 7

2◇ at matchpoints. Pass at IMPs. At matchpoints, when the opponents have opened and raised, you need little excuse to bid at the two-level. When your suit is good you really don't need much more. At IMPs you do have to keep an eye out for safety, so some matchpoint bids must be overlooked. Another reason for bidding 2◇ is that if you pass, your partner may reopen with 2♡, something you do not care for.

Neither vul.

W	N	E	S
1♣	pass	2♣	?

♠ Q 10 9 6 4 2
♡ A J 3
◇ —
♣ 8 7 6 5

2♠. That length in clubs makes this safe enough for IMPs as well. Your partner is sure to have two clubs maximum and may have one. One measure of whether you should bid 2♠ is this. Are you happy if your partner raises? I would love it myself since I have an extra spade, super shape, and the values I have are excellent.

Neither vul.

W	N	E	S
1♣	pass	2♣	?

♠ A Q 8 6 5
♡ 4 2
◇ K 10 8 7 6
♣ 3

Bid 2♠. When RHO raises opener an interesting situation arises.

1. If you have length in their suit, you can overcall safely because partner rates to have a fit for your suit.

2. If you have shortness in their suit, you should try to overcall because partner may not have the distribution to reopen. After 1♣-pass-2♣-pass-pass-?, partner will not reopen with ♠J73 ♡A953 ◇Q9 ♣K964 or other balanced minimum hands including length in the opponents' suit. Therefore, you should try to take the pressure off of partner whenever you can. In other words, when they raise, you should always bid unless you see a reason not to bid.

Neither vul.

W	N	E	S
1♣	pass	2♣	?

♠ 4 3
♡ A J 10 8 7
◇ K J 4 2
♣ 3 2

2♡ at matchpoints and IMPs. When you have any excuse to bid at the two-level, do so. Note that the emphasis here has been on bidding at the two-level. This is because any suit available to you at the two-level is defined as safe, because RHO would likely have bid it.

Overcalls at the three-level after RHO raises opener are not nearly as safe. While it is true that RHO has a limited hand, he can hold substantial values in any or all lower ranking suits. This is similar to RHO's responding 1NT to the opening bid. 1NT denied a higher ranking suit and it denied a fit, so consequently implied length in the suits lower than opener's.

N-S vul.

W	N	E	S
1♣	pass	2♣	?

♠ 3
♡ A K 8 7 6
◇ A 4 3 2
♣ 8 7 3

2♡ always. Even vulnerable. As overcalls go, this is a good one. If your partner raises, continue to game.

N-S vul.

W	N	E	S
1♣	pass	2♣	?

♠ 8
♡ K J 8 6 2
◇ 8 2
♣ A 8 6 3 2

2♡ always. When you have a guaranteed fit you should get in there. Here, partner will likely reopen if 2♣ is passed to him, but there are the dangers that:

1. Partner will reopen with 2♠.
2. Opener will bid some number of notrump and partner will lead a spade or a diamond. Of importance is that you do not worry about your five clubs. These are a good reason to bid, not a good reason to pass.

Both vul.

W	N	E	S
1♣	pass	2♣	?

♠ K Q J 9 3
♡ ?
◇ ?
♣ ?

This is just to emphasize that when you have a good suit that can be bid at the two-level, you should strive to do so. If the other eight cards are random small ones you may pass, but if you can think of any excuse to bid you probably should. On auctions like this one, people lean much too far in the direction of caution. Unless you are a confirmed maniac you should step out in this area and start bidding it up.

Neither vul.

W	N	E	S
1♣	pass	2♣	?

♠ ?
♡ ?
◇ ?
♣ ?

Who cares what your hand is? After this sequence you can bid any of the remaining suits at the two-level. They are all safe to bid. RHO is limited, etc, etc, etc. Of all the auctions in the world, here it is most incumbent upon you to bid. If you can't overcall, perhaps you can make a takeout double. More on this later. Whatever else, don't pass unless you have to.

Neither vul.

W	N	E	S
1◇	pass	2◇	?

♠ 3 2
♡ K J 8 7 6
◇ 9 2
♣ A K 8 6

After 1◇–pass–2◇, you should feel almost the same enthusiasm for bidding that you did after 1♣–pass–2♣. The only difference, of course, is that one suit has become relatively more difficult for you to bid. But this suit is a minor (clubs), and both majors are available. If you can bid one of them, you should. 2♡ is correct here.

Neither vul.

W	N	E	S
1◇	pass	2◇	?

♠ 3 2
♡ A K J 8 7
◇ 3
♣ J 9 7 6 3

Here also, 2♡ is right. With such disparity between your clubs and hearts it would be wrong to try 2NT, unusual. (See next hand.)

Neither vul.

W	N	E	S
1◇	pass	2◇	?

♠ 3 2
♡ Q 9 7 6 3
◇ 3
♣ A Q J 8 7

If you play that 2NT is unusual, to show the lower two unbid suits, that would be correct. If not playing this, it would be right to bid 2♡. It is important to understand that it is far safer to bid 2♡ than 3♣.

1. You are at the two-level.
2. RHO does not have hearts.
3. Clubs would require action at the three-level.
4. RHO could easily have clubs.

Neither vul.

W	N	E	S
1◇	pass	2◇	?

♠ K 4
♡ K 10 7 5 4
◇ 9 8 3
♣ A 9 7

This isn't much of a hand but what you have is okay. At matchpoints a 2♡ bid is reasonable. But not at IMPs. They bid and raised diamonds so you can envision that partner has one or two of them and hopefully some hearts. This 2♡ bid has a name; pre-balancing, mentioned earlier. Larry Cohen, I believe, called this a pre-balancing bid in anticipation that the bidding might die in 2◇ if he did not bid. There is some merit to this thought. What it means is that you will overcall aggressively when RHO makes a simple raise of opener's suit. Mind you, you do this only at the two-level.

Both vul.

W	N	E	S
1◇	pass	2◇	?

♠ 4 2
♡ K 8 7
◇ Q 9 7
♣ A Q J 8 3

Pass. Three-level actions require additional values and they are substantially more dangerous. Anytime you are considering a three-level overcall it is, perforce, in a suit lower ranking than their suit. It is likely that your RHO has length in your suit. For example, RHO could have this hand for his raise to 2◇: ♠K9 ♡93 ◇J1042 ♣K9742.

Evaluate these hands, neither vulnerable:

LHO	Partner	RHO	You
1◇	pass	2◇	?

Hand One
♠ K J 8 7 2
♡ A 6 3
◇ 4 2
♣ K 9 7

Hand Two
♠ K 9 7
♡ A 6 3
◇ 4 2
♣ K J 8 7 2

How do you feel about bidding 2♠ on the first hand? How do you feel about bidding 3♣ on the second? My estimate is that hand one will produce one and a half or more tricks in spades than hand two will produce in clubs. When you consider that you have to bid clubs at the three-level, the relative dangers become more apparent.

Both vul.

W	N	E	S
1◇	pass	2◇	?

♠ 8 3
♡ K J 6
◇ 3 2
♣ A Q J 8 7 5

You could bid 3♣ at matchpoints, and perhaps at IMPs. The important point is that you have an outstanding suit.

N-S vul.

W	N	E	S
1◇	pass	2◇	?

♠ A J 8 7 5
♡ K J 9 8 7
◇ 8 2
♣ 3

2♠. Not only do you bid, but if opener tries 3◇, you will bid 3♡ if given the chance. There are two traps on this hand.
1.   Passing. You will lose all sorts of partscores and a few games besides. It would be most pessimistic to pass.
2.   Doubling. If partner responds 3♣, you are in trouble. You would be very lucky to escape alive if you started with double.
One other possibility is a cuebid, showing the majors. Perhaps a 3◇ bid should show a good five-five with the majors and bidding 2♠ and then 3♡ should show a lesser hand. One thing that is clear is that if you bid a major it should be spades, reserving the option of bidding hearts later.

Neither vul.

W	N	E	S
1◇	pass	2◇	?

♠ K 8 7 6 5
♡ A 5 4 3 2
◇ 3
♣ Q 2

This is a minimum hand, but still worth a bid. Try 2♠. A very important point here is that your doubleton is in clubs, not diamonds. The worst holding you can have in a suit bid and raised is a doubleton. And of these holdings the worst of the lot are Qx, Jx, and QJ. These will be wasted points of no value to you. The fact that you have them means that the opponents do not have them. This means that they have something else to compensate, which in turn means your partner's useful points are likely to be diminished by the margin of these wasted cards you hold. Fortunately your doubleton queen is in clubs, where you can wish for it to be useful.

This hand is tasty, but it is very weak. Because it is weak you cannot afford to bid 3◇, the Michaels cuebid.

AN EXAMPLE OF BAD CARDS

LHO	Partner	RHO	You
1◇	pass	2◇	?

Neither vulnerable, which of these two hands would you prefer to have, and why?

Hand One
♠ A Q 10 6 5
♡ 8 6 3
◇ 4 2
♣ A 8 6

Hand Two
♠ A Q 10 6 5
♡ 8 6 3
◇ Q 2
♣ A 8 6

Both of these hands are worth a 2♠ bid at matchpoints. You would prefer, though, to have the first hand rather than the second. Here's why.

Let's say that the opponents have 22 HCP. In the first hand your partner therefore has 8, and in the second hand he has 6. As far as you are concerned both of these hands are the same, since the ◇Q is worthless. So you would rather have hand one because you rate to find a better dummy.

Another factor on this and many hands is that values in the opponents' suits means your hand is better suited to defense, and on close decisions you might be swayed toward bidding or passing according to what values you hold in their suits.

Both vul.

W	N	E	S
1◇	pass	2◇	?

♠ A Q 8 7
♡ Q 10 6 5 4 2
◇ 3
♣ 9 7

Bid 2♡ and call it quits. Even though you might feel guilty about losing the spade suit, you can at least get one of your suits into the picture. Passing or doubling would be begging disaster. 2♡ does something good and may lead to a worthwhile result. This is typical of hands where you want to tell all sorts of things to your partner but just don't have the tools to do it. When this happens, try to describe the single most important feature if possible. Here you want to show long hearts with spades as well. It can't be done.

Neither vul.

W	N	E	S
1◇	pass	2◇	?

♠ Q 8 6 5 2
♡ K J 3
◇ Q 4
♣ Q 10 7

Pass. Too much garbage. While you should want to bid on this sequence, this hand is just too unreasonable. Your partner has to be able to count on you for something. After discounting the ◇Q you have 8 points, and you can't expect all of them to be useful. In practice, this hand may turn out to be worth only 5 or 6 points.

Neither vul.

W	N	E	S
1◇	pass	2◇	?

♠ Q J 8 7 2
♡ 4 2
◇ A K J
♣ 10 7 6

You have the values for 2♠, and you should bid 2♠, but it's nothing to write home about. If partner has a stiff or doubleton diamond it won't have its normal value, as you don't have any diamond losers anyway.

Neither vul.

W	N	E	S
1◇	pass	2◇	?

♠ Q 2
♡ J 8 7 6 5
◇ K Q 10
♣ K 6 3

Pass. Another case of too much junk and too much wastage in diamonds.

Both vul.

W	N	E	S
1◇	pass	2◇	?

♠ A K 2
♡ 10 6 5 4 2
◇ A 8 7 3
♣ 2

Bid 2♡ and be happy to do it. When RHO has raised, it is no longer necessary to have a good suit to overcall in a higher-ranking suit. When the suit is this bad you do need a decent hand. Here you have tricks in the form of aces and kings and you have a safe auction. Further, you know you have a fit. Bid 2♡, and bid a game if partner raises.

Neither vul.

W	N	E	S
1♡	pass	2♡	?

♠ K 10 7 6 5
♡ Q 4 3 2
◇ A J 3
♣ 3

Bid 2♠. Once again, a safe auction plus a fit, even with a poorish suit. Note that after 1♡–pass–2♡, spades is the only suit available at the two-level. Too bad your queen isn't in spades or diamonds.

N-S vul.

W	N	E	S
1♡	pass	2♡	?

♠ K Q 2
♡ K 7 6
◇ Q 5
♣ A Q 10 6 2

At matchpoints, 3♣ would be dangerous. At IMPs it would be silly. Hands like this have no future. You have no game, so you are competing only for a partscore or a small plus by pushing them too high. If you are wrong, you could be set two or three tricks and, on occasion, doubled. Competing in suits lower ranking than the opponents' is only mildly safe, and you are also one trick higher. If you are wrong to bid 3♣ it can be expensive.

Both vul.

W	N	E	S
1♡	pass	2♡	?

♠ Q 8 7 6 2
♡ Q 10
◇ K 5 4
♣ A 8 7

Pass. Your heart holding is the worst possible. When you have a doubleton in their suit your expectations of a fit are only so-so, and you require a bit extra to take a call. You would feel better about this hand if you did not have the ♡Q. The more wasted values you have in their suit, the less you rate to find in your partner's hand.

Neither vul.

W	N	E	S
1♡	pass	2♡	?

♠ J 10 8 7 5
♡ 3
◇ K 4 2
♣ A K 8 7

2♠. This hand is far too good to pass. Your alternative is to double, but that runs the risk of losing the spade suit. It might become impossible to show a five-card suit.

Neither vul.

W	N	E	S
1♡	pass	2♡	?

♠ J 8 7 6 5
♡ A K 3
◇ A Q 3
♣ 4 3

2♠. Bad suit but a good hand.

Neither vul.

W	N	E	S
1♡	pass	2♡	?

♠ 4 3
♡ A K 3
◇ A Q 2
♣ J 8 7 6 5

Ugh. A good hand, but no worthwhile action is available. At matchpoints you might try 3♣, but only to get the opponents one trick higher. Hope partner doesn't take us seriously. If he does, you should apologize. The reasons you might consider 3♣ on such a bad suit are that RHO's strength is limited and your hearts suggest you will find shortness in partner's hand, and therefore some club support. This is strictly a matchpoint ploy and would be inconceivable at IMPs. It is hard to stomach this bid. The rationale you need to remember is that if you pass 2♡, that will end the bidding and they will be in a perfect (for them) contract.

Neither vul.

W	N	E	S
1♡	pass	2♡	?

♠ A K 3
♡ 4 3
◇ A Q 2
♣ J 8 7 6 5

Double. 3♣ would be awful. Not only is the hand well-suited for a takeout double, but your doubleton heart no longer suggests you will find a club fit. The difference between this hand and the previous one is very important. This hand would be a double at IMPs as well, and at any vulnerability.

Neither vul.

W	N	E	S
1♡	pass	2♡	?

♠ A K 8 7 6
♡ 4 2
◇ Q 8 6
♣ J 9 7

A matchpoint 2♠ call. At IMPs, pass is best.

The most difficult decisions come on those hands that have a doubleton in the opponents' suit. When you have three or more in their suit, you can bid with the assurance of finding some sort of fit. When you have a singleton in their suit, you at least have some distribution. But when you have a hand like the one above, you have no clear-cut directive. Bidding can be right or wrong. How can you tell? You can't, really. But you can be right reasonably often by requiring a little extra in the way of values, either suit-wise or points-wise. This is logical enough because a doubleton in their suit is a distinct minus value and you need something to compensate for it. The important thing here is to recognize this fact. I've been advocating a free-wheeling approach to overcalling when RHO raises and you can compete at the two-level. But in this one case, I suggest you pull in your horns just a little. In any event, your partner may be able to reopen and nothing will be lost.

LHO	Partner	RHO	You
1♠	pass	2♠	?

Whoever owns the spade suit rules, and this auction is typical. Even though it is a safe auction for you to bid on in terms of hoped-for strength in partner's hand, you must bid at the three-level if you compete. If you don't find as much in dummy as you would like, you are more vulnerable to a double than if your bid was at the two-level. Face it, fighting the spade suit is hard. After 1♠-pass-2♠ you are under pressure, and while I still recommend bidding on close hands, you do need something.

Remember that from a distributional point of view, all suits are dangerous. RHO, holding any of these hands, would raise 1♠ to 2♠:

♠ K 8 7	♠ K 8 7	♠ K 8 7
♡ A 10 8 6 2	♡ 4 2	♡ 4 2
◇ 4 2	◇ A 10 8 6 2	◇ J 3 2
♣ J 3 2	♣ J 3 2	♣ A 10 8 6 2

The point of this is that RHO can easily have length in any of the suits lower ranking than that which he is raising.

Neither vul.

W	N	E	S
1♠	pass	2♠	?

♠ 8 7 2
♡ A Q 8 7 6
◇ K J 3
♣ Q 9

Somewhat sketchy. This is a hyper-aggressive 3♡ bid at matchpoints, but under no other circumstances. If you could bid at the two-level your values would be adequate. As it is, it is a scary bid.

Here are three possible layouts.

You	Dummy One	Dummy Two	Dummy Three
♠ 8 7 2	♠ J 4	♠ Q 9	♠ 10 4
♡ A Q 8 7 6	♡ J 5 3	♡ K 5	♡ K 9 5
◇ K J 3	◇ A Q 9 5	◇ 9 8 7 4 2	◇ A 8 5 2
♣ Q 9	♣ J 5 3 2	♣ K 7 4 3	♣ K 8 4 3

Your hand facing Dummy One rates to have two spade losers, a heart loser, and two club losers. You found a 9-point dummy with 7 useful points and three hearts. The opponents may make 2♠, but it may fail.

Your hand facing Dummy Two won't be good. You will lose two or three spades (depending whether the defense lets you ruff one in dummy) and you have a potential heart loser, three potential diamond losers, and one club to lose. Playing in 3♡ is too rich. Clearly, if you could play in 2♡ that would be okay, but the bidding pushes you to the three-level, which is generally too high. Three-level overcalls usually start with a good suit, good shape, or some combination. This hand has a fair suit but it is balanced, which is a warning sign.

Finally, if you find Dummy Three, as good a hand as partner can have, you will make 3♡. But if partner has Dummy Three he would have doubled 2♠ if that came around to him.

Neither vul.

W	N	E	S
1♠	pass	2♠	?

It's clear to bid something, and I would choose 3♡. Double would lose the heart suit, but it could easily work. Don't pass!

♠ 3
♡ A Q 10 6 3
◇ K 5 4
♣ A 6 5 2

Both vul.

W	N	E	S
1♠	pass	2♠	?

3♡. You might go down two. You might make a game. Your good suit and three spades are nice, and your outside values are excellent. Bid 3♡ at IMPs, too.

♠ 8 6 2
♡ Q J 10 9 6 3
◇ A Q 3
♣ 2

Both vul.

W	N	E	S
1♠	pass	2♠	?

Pass. Your spade holding is bad for two reasons:
1.   The ♠Q is probably worthless.
2.   The ♠Q lessens the chance that partner will have useful points for you.
The heart suit is marginal and the rest of the hand doesn't make it worth a bid at the three-level.

♠ Q 2
♡ K J 6 5 4 2
◇ Q 3
♣ K 6 2

N-S vul.

W	N	E	S
1♠	pass	2♠	?

♠ K 3
♡ J 10 7 6 5 4
♢ A K 4 2
♣ 9

Who knows? If you could be sure LHO would lead a spade, you should bid 3♡. Perhaps you should bid 3♡ anyway. At matchpoints I would go ahead. At IMPs, it's exciting. The vulnerability is a bit worrisome, for sure. The ♠K3 is not as good as it might seem. You hope for a spade lead, but a good defender will not lead one from some holding such as ♠AJxxx, even after a raise from partner.

Neither vul.

W	N	E	S
1♠	pass	2♠	?

♠ 8 6 4 2
♡ J 9 8 6 2
♢ A K 3
♣ A

When the auction screams that you have a fit, you can still enter the auction on poorish suits or poorish hands. (Not, please, on both.) Your hand here is quite good enough for 3♡ so the suit quality can be overlooked. Be prepared for good results and bad ones. You may be able to make 4♡ if partner has four hearts, and you may be down if he has only two. Still, 3♡ is a good gamble. You have too much to hope for partner to be able to balance.

CHAPTER SIX
QUIZ ON OVERCALLS

WHAT HAVE YOU LEARNED?

Well, we've now looked at a lot of overcall situations. (There are still a few, but they will wait.) The ideas behind what qualifies for an overcall and what doesn't qualify are complex. Make no mistake about that. It's made more difficult by considerations of vulnerability, auction, strength, distribution, matchpoints, IMPs, etc. This next section will help pull it all together. This is the format: There are three hands. We will look at each of them in light of a number of auctions and see how your considerations change from sequence to sequence.

EQUAL LEVEL CONVERSION

Here is a bidding thought that I need to introduce at some point. Some players, but not all, play that if you make a takeout double and remove a club bid from partner to the next higher unbid suit, you are not showing a big hand; you are showing the two unbid suits. Here is one example hand.

♠ K 10 9 3   ♡ 8 3   ◇ A K J 8 3   ♣ K 8

If you double 1♡ and partner bids 2♣, you can bid 2◇, which does not show a big hand, merely a hand that has spades and diamonds, the other two unbid suits. If you double 1♡ and then bid 2♠ over partner's club bid, this does show a big hand, typically in the 18-20 point range. You and your partner must decide if you wish to use this treatment. It is not automatic and if I had not discussed it in advance, I would expect that doubling and bidding a new suit would show a good hand. Warning. If you use equal level conversion you will have some problems when you happen to have a big hand. If you have 19 points and you double, bidding 2◇ later won't show a big hand. This treatment will be available in a few of the following hands.

This is your hand for each of the following thirteen sequences. Neither side is vulnerable.

♠ A Q J 8   ♡ 4 2   ♢ A 10 8 6 5   ♣ 8 3

W	N	E	S
		1♢	?

1♠. Good four-card suit, implied fit, very obstructive to the opponents. Bidding 1♠ is clear-cut. There are some well-known authors who fuss about overcalls with four-card suits but as long as you adhere to the four rules, you will get consistently good results.

W	N	E	S
		1♡	?

Not clear at all. Your choices are:
1. Pass. Safe. Maybe you can balance later.
2. 1♠. Intending to give up on the diamond suit. If partner can raise, you will be very well placed. Note that you have no presumption of a fit, so it is not particularly safe.
3. 2♢. Also dangerous. Limited future. Even if you have a fit, you are unlikely to be able to outbid the opponents.
4. Double is *not* a consideration unless you play equal level conversion, discussed earlier. If you do play equal level conversion, doubling has the best chance of showing your hand. Be clear that this hand offers no comfortable choice otherwise.

W	N	E	S
		1♠	?

Because of the implied fit, 2♢ would be very reasonable at matchpoints and almost acceptable at IMPs. You are not likely to make more than a partscore, but in that pursuit, you are fairly safe.

W	N	E	S
1♣	pass	1♡	?

Double. Clear-cut.

W	N	E	S
1♣	pass	1NT	?

Awkward. I would try 2♢. It is hard to say what is best. However, this hand is good enough that bidding twice, showing spades later, is possible. No promises with this hand.

W	N	E	S
1♡	pass	1NT	?

Again 2♢, but not with as much conviction as on the previous auction. RHO can easily have diamonds, which means you could be in trouble. If doubled, you will run to 2♠. One danger is that 2♢ won't get doubled and you get left in an inferior contract down a few when something else (spades) would make. At least it's only –50 a trick.

W	N	E	S
1♡	pass	1♠	?

With spades bid on your right, everything is in your favor. Bid 2◇. This doesn't take much bidding room away from the opponents, but with the hope of a fit you may be able to push them past their limit. 2◇ is clear-cut at IMPs, too.

W	N	E	S
1♣	pass	1♠	?

The same. Bid 2◇.

W	N	E	S
1♡	pass	2♣	?

The only reasonable action is double, but with the opponents showing strength you should pass. Any overcall would be suicidal. When they make a 2/1 response you need a really good suit or really good shape to bid.

W	N	E	S
1♣	pass	2♣	?

Bid something. After this auction you bid first, look at your hand later. Try 2◇. You would like to mention spades somehow, but it can't be done. At least not now.

W	N	E	S
1◇	pass	2◇	?

Hard to believe. They're trying to play in your best suit. You hope. But it won't happen. If you pass, LHO will bid some number of notrump or LHO will pass and partner will reopen. If partner reopens, you will get to some decent contract and you will get a par result. If LHO bids notrump, however, your partner will be on lead and will almost always lead one of your doubletons. My suggestion here is to bid 2♠. Overcalling at the two-level on a four-bagger is quite unusual and this hand is a rare exception. You have a very good four-card suit with five cards in the suit raised by RHO, suggesting your partner has a singleton and maybe a void. You are able to bid at the two-level, and finally, you have a good hand as well. I just can't see anything bad happening. Partner has shape so you are safe in 2♠, and will get higher only when partner raises. And if they play the hand, partner will get off to a good lead.

W	N	E	S
1♡	pass	2♡	?

You should want to bid something. Passing just feels terrible. As to what to bid, I don't know. Here are your choices:

1. 3◇. Dangerous. You're at the three-level and you have no expectation of a fit.

2. 2♠. Only a four-card suit but it's a 'safe' suit and you are at the two-level.

3. Double. But if partner bids clubs, as expected, you have to pass with inadequate support or correct to 3◇. This would also imply four spades, but would suggest a much better hand. This hand would work well if you were using equal level conversion. If you do not have this agreement, I would bid 2♠. I choose this because my urge to bid is overwhelming rather than because 2♠ is right. If you choose to pass I would rate that as conservative, but okay. I said passing *felt* terrible. I didn't say it *is* terrible.

W	N	E	S
1♠	pass	2♠	?

3◇. You know you have a fit, and the safety gives you license to bid. The opponents will frequently accept the push and get too high. The only real danger to you is that partner competes too high.

This is your hand for the following eleven sequences. Neither side is vulnerable.

♠72 ♡KQ865 ◇K65 ♣A42

W	N	E	S
		1♣	?

Bid 1♡. Easy. Any game, any vulnerability.

W	N	E	S
		1◇	?

Bid 1♡. Decent suit. Opening hand. You can bid at the one-level.

W	N	E	S
		1♠	?

A dangerous overcall at matchpoints which could easily be wrong. A clear pass at IMPs.

W	N	E	S
1♣	pass	1◇	?

Bid 1♡. Always.

W	N	E	S
1♣	pass	1♠	?

I suppose 2♡ at matchpoints. Ugh. Not at IMPs.

W	N	E	S
1♣	pass	1NT	?

2♡. Only at matchpoints. You should feel a bit better about this than after 1♣-pass-1♠. The 1NT bid limits RHO's hand, which his 1♠ bid does not. Also, RHO may have four hearts after his 1♠ bid. He won't have four when he bids 1NT.

W	N	E	S
1♠	pass	1NT	?

Do whatever you feel like. Whether 1NT is forcing or not, this is an ugly hand. Passing and bidding 2♡ if they get to two of a minor is possible. Basically, that 1NT bid is uninformative and you are facing a guess. Too bad you are so balanced.

W	N	E	S
1◇	pass	2♣	?

Pass. No excuse for anything else. 2/1 auctions are dangerous.

W	N	E	S
1♠	pass	2◇	?

Likewise. You are outgunned. Bidding is a no-win proposition.

W	N	E	S
1♣	pass	2♣	?

Bid 2♡. They bid and raised a suit and you can bid at the two-level. It is as safe as it can be to bid here.

W	N	E	S
1♠	pass	2♠	?

At matchpoints you could risk 3♡. This works often enough that you will end up ahead more often than not. The auction is not as safe as when you can bid at the two-level. RHO has not denied hearts. He can have a lot of them. Plus, you are bidding at the three-level. Your good results will be small ones. Your bad results will be spectacular. This is the sort of thing that suits matchpoints.

This is your hand for the following fourteen sequences. You are not vulnerable vs. vulnerable.

♠ K 6 2   ♡ J 9 7 6 3   ◇ 4   ♣ A K 8 7

W	N	E	S
		1♣	?

1♡. Any vulnerability. IMPs too. The expected-fit factor is overwhelming.

W	N	E	S
		1◇	?

1♡. It's bad practice to make a takeout double with a five-card major. There isn't the same expectancy of a fit so 1♡ is not as safe as after 1♣. Vulnerable at IMPs, 1♡ would be a marginal bid.

W	N	E	S
		1♠	?

Pass. The only time you can bid at the two-level with J9763 (barring an exceptional hand) is after a raise.

W	N	E	S
1♣	pass	1◇	?

1♡. Still more than a minimum overcall.

W	N	E	S
1♣	pass	1♠	?

Pass. Your hearts are not really good enough for a two-level overcall.

W	N	E	S
1◇	pass	1♠	?

Double. Earlier I said you should avoid doubling when holding a five-card major. Here, though, your suit is not good enough to overcall on this sequence. Fortunately, you have the shape and values to make double a reasonable alternative.

W	N	E	S
1♣	pass	1NT	?

2♡, clearly and with no apologies. This is safe within all three definitions. RHO is limited in strength, RHO doesn't have hearts, and RHO has clubs, implying a fit. (If RHO didn't have clubs, he would have a suit to bid.)

W	N	E	S
1◇	pass	1NT	?

2♡ again, although with less enthusiasm. You are missing the strong implication of a fit, as on the previous hand. I would never do this vulnerable, and I might hesitate to do this at IMPs. But it would not be terrible.

W	N	E	S
1♠	pass	1NT	?

Pass. Your ♠K is of unclear value and RHO could easily have the heart suit stacked. Bidding is very unwise.

W	N	E	S
1♠	pass	2♣	?

Pass fast. The best policy after a 2/1. This hand has a weak suit and a dubious ♠K.

W	N	E	S
1◇	pass	2♣	?

Likewise.

W	N	E	S
1♣	pass	2♣	?

Bid 2♡. 100%. No possible reason to pass. Any vulnerability, any game. When they bid and raise, your expectation is that you will find a bid.

W	N	E	S
1◇	pass	2◇	?

Bid 2♡. You should feel that with this hand it is about one and a half tricks more dangerous to bid after 1◇–pass–2◇ than after 1♣–pass–2♣. It is still clear to bid.

W	N	E	S
1♠	pass	2♠	?

Go quietly. You are entitled to be reluctant about passing, but a little discretion is best. In favor of bidding:
1.   You rate to have some sort of fit.
2.   RHO is limited.
In favor of passing:
1.   Your ♠K is a marginal card.
2.   You are at the three-level.
3.   Your suit is bad.
4.   RHO can have hearts.

This is your hand for the following six sequences. You are not vulnerable vs. vulnerable.

♠ A Q 10 7   ♡ 4   ◇ K 8 7 4   ♣ A 10 7 4

W	N	E	S
		1♡	?

Double for takeout. The only reason for showing this hand is to remind you that even in a book on overcalls, one should not always assume an overcall is the first choice.

W	N	E	S
		1♠	?

Pass. What you should not do is double. With no support for hearts, a double is asking for trouble. You might have a successful contract in one of the minors but it is not reachable.

W	N	E	S
1♣	pass	1◇	?

Bid 1♠. The four-card overcall is your only option. Note that you have the ◇K, the suit that RHO bid. If you had the ◇A and the ♣K your hand would not be worth as much.

W	N	E	S
1♣	pass	1NT	?

Pass is best. This is a tempting hand but it does not offer a good bid. Sometimes even a good hand must stay out of the bidding.

W	N	E	S
1◇	pass	1♡	?

Double. You have the two unbid suits and you have opening bid values. This is a fine double.

W	N	E	S
1♡	pass	2♣	?

Pass. When they make a 2/1 bid, a normal takeout double is best rejected. Your partner is broke and if he does not have a four-card fit for you, you will be too high and most likely doubled. They have not found a heart fit yet so your partner could have four or five of them, which means he is less likely to have a good holding in one of your suits. Knowing when to stay out of the bidding is an important part of your bidding judgment.

It's really quite amazing the number of different actions you can contemplate on any given hand. The preceding three hands were rather ordinary but still offered much food for thought. On some auctions it was right to bid. On others it was right to pass. On some a takeout double was best. Some of the decisions were clear-cut. Some were vague or marginal. A curious item is that on one sequence it might be 100% to make a vulnerable two-level overcall whereas on a different sequence with the same hand a non-vulnerable two-level bid would be ridiculous.

Learn to recognize the dangerous auctions and the safe ones. Does your hand and the bidding tell you anything? Can your partner have any points? Do you expect a fit? These are the important things. They will help you with overcalls and they will help you with many other competitive decisions. As you will see in the next chapter.

SOME REFLECTIONS ON THE OVERCALL

So far this entire book has been devoted to the overcall. A lot of space has gone into this topic. And a lot of hands. It was necessary. The decision to overcall is one of the most difficult you'll ever have. This is because it is so committal. So final. If you are wrong there may be no escape.

Look at the other decisions you may have. A takeout double? These almost never get penalized, for the simple reason that a takeout double offers a number of possible contracts. An overcall usually offers only one.

Other decisions, such as raising partner, are safe and easy. When you're thinking of raising you have a fit, which is insurance against disaster. If you are thinking of bidding some number of notrump in response to partner's overcall or takeout double, you are assured of certain values. But the overcaller himself has no such security. His bid is a speculative venture attended by a prayer or two.

Now, I do not want you to stop overcalling. Hardly. I want you to overcall more. But it should be done sensibly. This is why so much time has been devoted to an analysis of each possible auction. When is it safe to bid? When is it dangerous? What kind of fit can I expect? What are my cards worth? How will the hand play? The concepts I have discussed will be new for some. I suspect for quite a few. As far as I know, they have not seen print before. This is surprising because they are so important. They are the basis of what makes good and effective competitive bidding. I hope you will review this section again and again. It's very important that this becomes second nature to you.

Furthermore, an understanding of this section will help you in later situations. In particular, if your partner has overcalled you will find these principles very important in determining whether or not to introduce a new suit. Also other competitive decisions, such as when to raise and when to pass, will be easier to judge. These ideas are flexible and will pertain to more than just overcalls.

For that matter, this material will help your offensive judgment as well on those hands where your side opens the bidding. But that's another book.

PART TWO

RESPONDING TO AN OVERCALL

When your partner opens the bidding, you can generally look at your hand and form some kind of opinion as to your potential. Your auction will be guided by the usual questions such as, "Do we have a game? Do we have a slam? Which suit is best? Should we stay in a partscore?"

Once in awhile the opponents get into the act and the questions now may include those such as, "Should we double them? Should we let them buy it? Should we save?" However, note the sort of questions you must answer when the other side has opened and your side has entered the auction. "How high should we compete? Should we save against their game? What suit do I want partner to lead? Do we have a game?"

It is very important that you understand the differences in the thinking of the side that opens as opposed to the side that overcalls. The side that opens the auction (excluding preempts) expects to get a plus score. The opening bidder assumes the hand belongs to his side. His thinking is along offensive lines with positive expectations. On those occasions when the opponents turn out to own the hand, the opener is disappointed.

The overcaller, however, is in a totally different frame of mind. His expectations are rather negative. Thoughts of slam are almost nonexistent and even thoughts of game are rather the exception. For the most part, the overcaller is happy if he can find a successful partscore or perhaps suffer a small penalty. A good result might be that the opponents somehow missed a game contract or perhaps a slam. An outstanding result might be that the opponents went down in a poor contract when they found the wrong level or the wrong suit.

Given the difference in objectives of an opening bidder as opposed to an overcaller, it seems reasonable that the system of responding to opening bids may differ from the system of responding to an overcall. Different objectives, different methods. Yes? No? Perhaps.

Here are some possible differences.

1. If partner overcalls, should a new suit by you be forcing?
2. If partner overcalls, what should a 1NT response show? Should a jump to 2NT after a one-level overcall be forcing?
3. What is the range for a simple raise? What is the range for a jump raise? For example, 1♣–1♠–pass–3♠. Is 3♠ forcing, invitational, or preemptive?
4. What should a jump shift look like? Should it be forcing? Does it guarantee a game? Does it imply a slam?
5. What would a cuebid mean?
6. Passing with hands that look like they might be worth a bid.

CHAPTER SEVEN

INTRODUCING A NEW SUIT AFTER PARTNER'S OVERCALL

RESPONDING TO A ONE-LEVEL OVERCALL

By my way of thinking, it should be easy to decide whether a new suit should be forcing or non-forcing. If your partner opens the bidding your new suit response is forcing. This is because your side may well have a game or slam. The new-suit-forcing principle caters to finding if you have a game and, subsequently, which one. On occasion, you miss a good partscore when your system didn't give you license to bid a suit because of insufficient values. This may occur, for example, as follows:

Partner	RHO	You	LHO
1♡	pass	1♠	pass
2♡	all pass		

♠ 2		♠ Q 8 7 3
♡ K Q 8 6 4 3		♡ —
◇ K J 3		◇ Q 9 8 7 5 2
♣ A 8 7		♣ K 4 2

You go down three when 3◇ would have made. There was just no way in Standard American, or for that matter most other systems, to get to 3◇.

The reason this kind of bad result occurs is that your system is geared to reaching for game and slam bonuses, at the expense of the occasional partscore.

When an opponent opens and your side overcalls, you are faced with entirely different goals. Game is no longer an expectation and slam is almost entirely out of the question. Instead, you are going to be looking for a good partscore or a good save. Now and then you will be trying to escape from partner's suit when he has picked a poor time to overcall. Usually you will be looking for your best fit, and any games bid and made are nice, but not expected.

It seems to me that if your primary goal is to find a fit, then the best way to do that is to start bidding your suits. If you play that a new suit is forcing, you won't be able to do much exploration because you just won't have enough high cards often enough to justify bidding.

Here is a typical situation.

LHO	Partner	RHO	You
1♣	1♡	pass	?

♠ K 6 4   ♡ 3   ◇ K J 10 9 7 4   ♣ 10 7 6

If you could bid 2◇, non-forcing, you would surely do that. 2◇ rates to be a good spot, and if partner likes diamonds you aren't averse to hearing a raise. Even if partner doesn't like diamonds, you won't mind playing there. What you won't want is to hear partner bid 2♡. If you play 2◇ is a forcing bid, then you can't bid it because you will end up in 2♡ or 3◇, or higher. You want to be in 3◇ only if partner likes diamonds, not because your system forces you to get there.

The following hands should not be difficult unless you are accustomed to high requirements for introducing new suits. One mild warning: You do have to keep an eye out for safety. You can't go around bidding willy-nilly just because it's your turn. On the other hand, if you pass everything in sight you will be robbed on hand after hand. If you blend a bit of caution with some amount of optimism you can more than hold your own.

Neither vul.

W	N	E	S
1♣	1♡	pass	?

♠ K 10 8 7 6
♡ 4 2
◇ A K 8 7
♣ 10 7

1♠. Fairly straightforward. In this case you don't mind if partner bids again, but if he passes it's probably okay. If partner should feel like making a game try (unlikely) you would be happy to accept. Passing 1♡ would be very poor tactics for a number of reasons. If spades are better than hearts, or if you have a game, you will have done the wrong thing and you will have little chance to recover. Let's say that you pass and you get lucky. LHO rebids 2♣, which is passed around to you. You get a second chance.

LHO	Partner	RHO	You
1♣	1♡	pass	pass
2♣	pass	pass	?

What will you do? Do you do anything at all? Do you bid 2♠ and find partner with:

♠ 3   ♡ K J 10 8 7   ◇ Q J 4   ♣ A 9 6 5

1♠, 1NT, 2◇, or 2♣ by the opponents are better than 2♠ by you.

Do you bid 2♡ and find partner with:

♠ Q 5 3   ♡ A K J 10   ♢ 3 2   ♣ K J 8 4

1♠, 2♠, 3♠ or 1NT are better than 2♡. Anyone for 2♣ doubled?

Do you bid 2♢ and find partner with:

♠ J 5 4   ♡ A Q 8 6 3   ♢ Q 2   ♣ K 5 4

Anything is better than 2♢.

Or do you pass and find partner with:

♠ 9 5 4 2   ♡ A K 9 5 3   ♢ 10 2   ♣ A 3

4♠, possibly with an overtrick, is better than beating 2♣ by a trick.

Whatever action you choose may lead to a bad result. Partner will have no reason to overrule you, so if you guess wrong, you lose. If you guess right, you break even. The entire fault of this, of course, was the failure to bid 1♠ over 1♡. This had the effect of shutting partner out of the picture so that he could not contribute to a useful dialogue.

This failure to act immediately is one of the most serious common errors. I imagine that some of the time it is merely bad judgment, but some of the time it is system. Whatever the reason, failure to act at once almost always leads to guessing games. Sometimes, the auction proceeds in such a way that you don't even get a chance to guess.

Neither vul.

W	N	E	S
1♣	1♡	pass	pass
1♠	pass	2♣	?

♠ 10 7 2
♡ 8 3
♢ A Q J 7 5 4
♣ 8 5

On this auction it is just too dangerous to bid. I suppose you could bid 3♢ on the theory that you can't have much because you already passed. But if you go for 300 or more, partner won't be interested in theory. Note how much more constructive it would have been for you to bid 2♢ earlier. If partner doesn't like 2♢ he may or may not do something, but at least you won't be in 3♢. Also, and very important, is the difficulty the opening bidder will have. If you bid 2♢, opener will have to bid 2♠ rather than 1♠. If he doesn't have a good enough hand he may pass, allowing you to make a plus when it was really the opponents' hand.

Or possibly the opening bidder will bid 2♠ or even 3♣ and go down when his dummy is unsuitable.

Or perhaps the opening bidder will rebid on less than sufficient values. When this happens his partner sometimes raises, expecting the opener to have a better hand. Again they go down.

Or perhaps 2◇ gets passed out and it proves to be better than 1♡.

Or sometimes, when the opponents compete, your partner can raise diamonds.

Or sometimes your side can make 3NT, based on running your good diamond suit.

If you pass, none of these good results can occur. You've just got to get in there. Mix it up. The more problems you can create for your opponents, the more often they will go wrong. Whenever they go wrong, you get a good result. As long as you take action whenever possible, you will do well.

Neither vul.

W	N	E	S
1♣	1◇	1♡	?

♠ Q 10 8 7 6
♡ 4 2
◇ 3
♣ A J 8 6 5

Bid 1♠. It is crucial to bid on a hand like this. Most of the time, when you are considering introducing a new suit, it will be at the one- or two-level. This is because you won't often have the strength or the good suit required to try for a three-level contract. At the three-level you just have to have a good hand. You are too high to experiment.

My rule for competition at the one- or two-level is this: When in doubt, bid. Only when it is not right to bid do I pass. Note that this differs from the concept of, "Pass, except when it is right to bid."

Neither vul.

W	N	E	S
1♣	1♡	1♠	?

♠ 10 6 5
♡ Q 2
◇ K Q 10 9 5
♣ 8 6 3

This is a dangerous moment to take a bid, but at matchpoints you could try 2◇. This could easily lead to a poor result because if partner doesn't like diamonds you will have no place to go. Nor do you have any reason to think partner likes diamonds. Other bad features of this hand are the three little cards in both of the suits bid by the opponents.

What you do have going for you is that LHO can't rebid 1NT or 2♣. Also going for you is that when partner does like diamonds, he can raise. In this case, you may be able to push the opponents to the three-level. This is typical of a matchpoint auction where everyone seems to have something to say. At IMPs, the dangers suggest a pass is best. You have too little to gain.

SNAPDRAGON DOUBLES

Modern bidding offers another solution for the previous hand. When RHO bids 1♠, you can double. This is not penalty. The snapdragon double is used when the opponents have bid two suits. It is takeout, showing the unbid suit, diamonds, and a tolerance for partner's suit, hearts. This is not a wonderful convention but since using double for anything else is not a big deal, it has a role when used as snapdragon. If you choose to use snapdragon doubles, you may wish to have the agreement that they only apply when the bidding is at the one-level. With discussion, you may choose to use them at a higher level.

Neither vul.

W	N	E	S
1♣	1♡	2♣	?

♠ 10 6 5
♡ Q 2
◇ K Q 10 9 5
♣ 8 6 3

This is the same hand as the previous. If on the previous auction you felt uncomfortable about bidding 2◊, you should not feel so here. Look at the differences in the two auctions.

1. Your three small clubs are not as clearly a detriment as before because clubs have been raised. Partner probably has a doubleton and perhaps a singleton. This improves your chances of finding a diamond fit in partner's hand.

2. Your RHO did not bid 1♠, as before. If partner has any spade honors, they will be more valuable than in the case where RHO bid spades.

3. RHO's 2♣ bid is limited. He has about 6 HCP with some distribution. In the prior auction, the 1♠ bid was unlimited. RHO could have as much as 10-12 points, which would decrease your partner's expected HCP. This should suggest that you be more cautious when the opponents have not found a fit as opposed to when they have.

Neither vul.

W	N	E	S
1♣	1♡	2♣	?

♠ 8 4
♡ Q 8
◇ K Q 10 7 6
♣ 8 6 4 3

The extra club here (four instead of three) just about guarantees that you have a diamond fit. On this auction it would be very poor tactics to pass at matchpoints or IMPs. Bid 2◊.

♠ 3 2
♡ 8
◇ K J 10 9 3
♣ 9 8 6 4 2

2◊. Scary? Why bid at all? You have five clubs. Isn't it better to pass and hope to beat them? It might be better to try to set 2♣, but if 2♣ should end the auction you will almost certainly find you could have made a good partscore in diamonds. Also, partner is not likely to lead a diamond against 2♣. Partner is more likely to lead his suit, hearts. With your actual hand, you can see that a heart lead could work out very poorly. A diamond lead should be worth at least two additional tricks to your side.

But this is all academic, because 2♣ is unlikely to be passed out. Someone out there is going to bid again. Frequently it will be the opening bidder. The auction is very likely to go:

LHO	Partner	RHO	You
1♣	1♡	2♣	pass
2NT	pass	3NT	

or

LHO	Partner	RHO	You
1♣	1♡	2♣	pass
3NT			

In either of these cases you want a diamond lead. The danger to bidding 2◊ is that partner may get excited. However, in this case partner's enthusiasm will be based on a fit, and with a sensible partner you should be able to survive most of his excesses. More on this later.

You will find rather more opportunities to initiate a new suit in a competitive auction when RHO has raised or passed as opposed to having introduced a new suit himself. When RHO bids a new suit, this leaves only one unbid suit for you. You will not often have that suit plus whatever values you require to bid it.

1♣-1◊-1♡-? You can bid 1♠.
1♣-1♡-2◊-? You must bid 2♠.
1♣-1♡-1♠-? You must bid 2◊.

These auctions do not imply at all that you will find a fit if you elect to bid the fourth, or unbid, suit. This, plus the unlimited nature of RHO's bid, suggests you be rather careful.

Neither vul.

W	N	E	S
1♣	1◇	1♡	?

♠ J 10 8 7 6
♡ 8 7 2
◇ K 3
♣ A Q 3

You can try 1♠. Only in the unlikely event that 1♠ gets passed out and partner has a singleton will you regret this action. Should partner raise, you will not mind. If partner shows game interest you should be pleased to cooperate. This is a clear action at IMPs as well. The poor quality of your suit should not bother you.

Neither vul.

W	N	E	S
1♣	1◇	1♡	?

♠ 9 7 6 4 2
♡ 10 8 4 3
◇ K 2
♣ A 10

Even this hand is not an unreasonable 1♠ call. In practice, this bid seldom comes to any harm. If partner can raise spades you will have a sound basis for competing to the two- or even three-level. Note also that you may be on lead. If you are clearly not going to be on lead, you might give up on the close hands so as to avoid getting partner off to a bad lead. Here your values are sufficient to bid 1♠ and as noted, you may be on lead.

An aside. You may be thinking of using the snapdragon double here. That is a possible bid and it is up to you to decide if you like this convention. As I noted, it has its uses but they are not that big a deal. If you do wish to use it, you may like playing that double shows four spades, not five, on this sequence.

This hand might even take another voluntary bid. Typical matchpoint auctions might be as follows:

LHO	Partner	RHO	You
1♣	1◇	1♡	1♠
pass	pass	2♣	2◇

or

LHO	Partner	RHO	You
1♣	1◇	1♡	1♠
2♣	pass	pass	2◇

These auctions are the sort of thing that effective matchpoints requires. Bid. If all of these bids seem to be overdoing things a bit, consider that either 2◇ or 2♠ should provide a satisfactory resting spot. You would be very unlucky indeed if partner had only one spade and only a four-card diamond suit. I would expect him to have two or three spades or five or six diamonds about 98% of the time.

♠ 97642
♡ 10843
◇ K2
♣ A10

Let's see what partner might have.

♠K 10 3   ♡J 2   ◇A J 10 6 3   ♣Q 9 5

You can make 1♠ or 2♠.

♠A 3   ♡Q J 5   ◇Q J 10 9 7   ♣K 6 4

You can make 2◇.

♠10 5   ♡A 9 7   ◇A Q J 8   ♣9 8 6 2

Even this dummy provides seven or eight tricks at spades. Note that the reason you were able to take two bids on this piece of cheese was that the few cards you had were known to be useful. If your hand were:

♠9 7 6 4 2   ♡10 8 4 3   ◇A 2   ♣K 4

instead, you might still bid 1♠, but perhaps you should give up on later competing with 2◇. The ♣K is of dubious value. When you support partner with a doubleton you need to have something to justify the bid, and on minimum hands you must have guaranteed values. Very rarely, you might introduce 1♠ on a four-card suit. But you should not go out of the way to do this.

Neither vul.

W	N	E	S
1♣	1◇	1♡	?

♠ KQ107
♡ 42
◇ Q9
♣ A6542

Tough, but too good to pass. Bid 1♠, or perhaps 2◇. Or, as already noted, perhaps the snapdragon double is best.

Neither vul.

W	N	E	S
1♣	1◇	1♡	?

♠ KQ107
♡ 542
◇ Q63
♣ K87

2◇. No need to bid a four-card suit when a reasonable alternative is available. Again, the snapdragon double is a possibility.

Neither vul.

W	N	E	S
1♣	1◇	1♡	?

♠ KQ87
♡ Q983
◇ J2
♣ Q97

This hand, 10 points and all, is a pile of junk. Double, showing four spades, is possible. 1NT is possible. Passing is reasonable. Lots of ugly choices.

When RHO passes, you have more room to bid after partner's overcall and you can do so with less pressure or danger. In practice, the situation won't happen too often because RHO will be in there whenever he can.

Neither vul.

W	N	E	S
1♣	1♡	pass	?

♠ K10642
♡ 52
◇ 82
♣ AJ97

1♠. Straightforward. 1♠ is mildly forward-going. With nothing, you should pass.

Neither vul.

W	N	E	S
1♣	1♡	pass	?

♠ QJ8642
♡ 3
◇ A1082
♣ K4

Again, 1♠. You would like to hear partner bid again. A spade raise would be super.

Neither vul.

W	N	E	S
1♣	1♡	pass	?

♠ 8 7 6 5 4
♡ 2
◇ A Q 10 7
♣ K 4 3

1♠. Not running from 1♡. Your suit is bad but your hand is not hopeless.

Neither vul.

W	N	E	S
1♣	1♡	pass	?

♠ 10 8 6 5 4
♡ —
◇ K 6 5 4
♣ J 10 6 3

Pass. A 1♠ bid, while hardly promising a good hand, should show something. If 1♡ gets doubled you may decide to run. But not right away.

Neither vul.

W	N	E	S
1♣	1♡	pass	?

♠ J 9 7 6 4
♡ K 6 3
◇ K 8 2
♣ 10 3

Raise to 2♡. 1♠ would be poor. A new suit response should deny three-card support for partner's major-suit overcall. If partner had overcalled 1◇, bidding 1♠ would be fine, trying to find a major-suit fit. You can raise diamonds later on some auctions.

In most auctions where you are bidding the fourth suit, you will have to do so at the two-level.

LHO	Partner	RHO	You
1♣	1♡	1♠	2◇
1♡	1♠	2♣	2◇
1◇	1♡	2♣	2♠
1◇	1♡	1♠	2♣

etc.

There is one fact you have to recognize immediately. Was RHO's bid at the one-level or the two-level? For example:

LHO	Partner	RHO	You
1♣	1♡	1♠	?

or

1♡	1♠	2♣	?

In both cases diamonds is the unbid suit, and it might appear equally safe to bid them in both of the example auctions. But is it not equally safe, and you should be especially aware of the reasons. You have heard them before but here they are again.

LHO	Partner	RHO	You
1♣	1♡	1♠	?

The 1♠ bid shows a minimum of 6 or 7 points. It does not necessarily show a good hand. He could have as few as 5 HCP.

LHO	Partner	RHO	You
1♡	1♠	2♣	?

This time RHO bid 2♣, a new suit response at the two-level, usually showing 10 or 11 points or more. What this means to you is that your partner's overcall is probably minimum and you should not be bidding in the hope or expectation that partner may have an extra ace or king lurking around somewhere.

The opponents' sequence shows they have a minimum of 23 or more HCP, thus leaving fewer for partner. The auction 1♣-1♡-1♠-? by the opponents shows only 19 or 20 HCP, leaving more room for your partner to have a good overcall.

Let's see how these different sequences affect your decision to bid; that is, introduce the fourth suit. (As you will see, these considerations hold true in other bidding situations as well. More on this later.)

Neither vul.

W	N	E	S
1♣	1♡	1♠	?

♠ 10 6 5
♡ Q 2
◇ K Q 10 9 5
♣ 8 6 3

This hand is from the first part of this chapter. I recommended 2◇. One of the reasons that you can consider bidding with this hand is that the opponents have not yet shown strong hands. See next hand.

Neither vul.

W N E S
1♡ 1♠ 2♣ ?

♠ Q 2
♡ 8 6 5
◇ K Q 10 9 5
♣ 8 6 3

Dangerous to bid 2◇ now. RHO shows a good hand. If the opponents have their values, then your partner is surely minimum. Bidding 2◇ can't possibly gain much because your side is known to have insufficient values for competing. Your lack of distribution merely confirms what you already know. If the opponents want to bid on, they can and will. If they want to double you, they can and will.

Bidding 2◇ is basically offering the opponents a choice of actions. Double you, or proceed otherwise as they see fit. Only in very rare situations will your side be able to conduct further effective bidding. This will be when partner has a super fit. This is not likely.

When your side is known to have very limited high cards you have to be careful about looking for a fit. Note that when you have found a fit, you can bid strongly on minimum high-card values. But otherwise, it is best to go quietly.

One last point in defense of bidding 2◇ for those who just can't stand to pass; the suit here is decent and you may direct partner to the best lead. If you think, though, that you may be on lead, then even this consideration loses its credibility. In practice, when you introduce a new suit at the two-level it will be after a raise or after a pass by RHO.

These are typical auctions:

LHO	Partner	RHO	You
1♣	1♠	2♣	?
1◇	1♡	2◇	?
1♣	1♠	pass	?
1♡	2♣	2♡	?

On sequences where RHO has shown limited strength via a pass or a raise only, you should feel fairly free to get in there with your suit.

Neither vul.

W N E S
1♣ 1♡ 2♣ ?

♠ 3 2
♡ 8
♢ K J 10 9 3
♣ 9 8 6 4 2

As you've seen, this is a 2♢ bid. You have an almost guaranteed fit. This hand is shown again to emphasize the extremes to which you should go to get into the auction. In my mind, this is not even extreme. There will be those who disagree, but their objections will be based on a fear of partner overdoing things, expecting you to have more.

Both vul.

W N E S
1♢ 1♠ 2♢ ?

♠ 9
♡ A J 8 6 5 4
♢ 8 7 6 2
♣ J 3

Even vulnerable, this is worth 2♡. Your four-card diamond holding strongly suggests shortness in partner's hand, and therefore a heart fit of sorts. Here are some possible layouts.

♠ 9	♠ K Q 8 7 6
♡ A J 8 6 5 4	♡ Q 7 3
♢ 8 7 6 2	♢ 4
♣ J 3	♣ A 10 5 4

If partner has the hand on the right, likely given their diamond bids, you have a play for ten tricks. You won't get to 4♡, of course, but you should be able to buy the hand for a successful heart partial.

♠ 9	♠ A K 10 7 2
♡ A J 8 6 5 4	♡ K 10 2
♢ 8 7 6 2	♢ 4
♣ J 3	♣ A 10 5 4

In this layout, partner will raise to 4♡ and you will make it, perhaps with an overtrick or two.

When you can expect a fit the liberties you can take are rather incredible.

Both vul.

W N E S
1♢ 1♠ 2♢ ?

♠ J 2
♡ 10 9 8 7 5 2
♢ A 6 5
♣ Q 3

2♡. Note the expected fit is present here.

N-S vul.

W	N	E	S
1♣	1♠	2♣	?

♠ 4
♡ Q 9 6 5 4
◇ K 9 4
♣ A 8 6 5

Believe it or not, this hand is probably a 2♡ call at any form of the game. All of your high cards are working and you hope partner has just one club, a distinct possibility.

Both vul.

W	N	E	S
1◇	1♡	2♣	?

♠ K J 9 7
♡ 3
◇ 10 6 5
♣ A J 9 8 3

Who knows? It might be right to play in spades or clubs. Certainly the hand is good enough to do something. But what? Eventually I'm going to get into a convention known as the *responsive double*, in a later chapter. For the time being, a hand like this is just a guess. If you are feeling very much as though you want to do something and just aren't sure what, then your thinking is in the right place. More on this later.

Neither vul.

W	N	E	S
1♣	1♡	2♣	?

♠ K 9 7 6 4 2
♡ J 2
◇ A 10 6 2
♣ 9

This is a curious hand. It doesn't look like it, but bidding 2♠ is rather dangerous. Throughout this section, or for that matter throughout the book, I've been emphasizing the aspect of what kind of fit you can hope for in partner's hand. Here, your singleton club tells you nothing about partner's hand. Your partner could have three or four clubs and that does not give you hope for a spade fit. Just one spade is possible. I would guess partner's average holding at about one and a quarter spades. One only is the rule and even a void is possible. Should you pass 2♣? No. Not really, but you shouldn't be too optimistic about your chances of more than a partscore. What is important is that you understand why 2♠ is not as clear-cut as it may seem and why it could easily lead to a minus score.

A few more hands here to re-emphasize some important points:

N-S vul.

W	N	E	S
1♣	1◇	1♠	?

♠ 8 7 5
♡ K Q 10 9 6 3
◇ K 9
♣ 10 4

Bid 2♡, but don't be too sure of its safety. When there is no reason to expect a fit you need a good suit or some amount of compensating high cards. Here your hearts will play adequately even opposite a singleton.

N-S vul.

W	N	E	S
1♣	1◇	1♠	?

♠ 9 7 5
♡ Q 10 8 7 5
◇ K Q 5
♣ Q 9

It is almost surely best to bid 2◇. The heart suit is not good enough to bid on this particular auction. You might be able to handle this hand via the snapdragon double, but for the moment, 2◇ is far superior to 2♡. More on this later.

Both vul.

W	N	E	S
1♣	1♡	2◇	?

♠ K J 8 7 3
♡ 4
◇ Q 10 8 3
♣ Q 9 8

Pass!!!! This hand is a death trap. You can make nothing. Already the opponents have announced about 23 HCP, meaning your partner has about 9. At this vulnerability, he must have a decent five- or six-card suit with a side card. There is no reason on earth for you to think he has a spade fit. On the other side of the coin, the opponents may not make much either. You should pass and see where their bidding takes them.

Neither vul.

W	N	E	S
1♣	1♡	2◇	?

♠ K J 9 7
♡ 3
◇ Q 10 8 7 2
♣ K 8 4

Pass. Do not double 2◇. Let's assume you play this double is penalty. Why double now? They are in a forcing auction and will continue bidding for at least one more round. Perhaps you can double 3◇. Even though their bidding is strong, you can tell that they have minimum values, as does your partner. When the bidding is over, they probably will go down. Double later if you must. Do not double now.

Both vul.

W	N	E	S
1♡	1♠	pass	?

♠ 9 2
♡ A 5 4
◇ J 2
♣ K Q 10 8 7 3

2♣. Nothing unusual here. You have a good suit, a moderate hand, and no fit for partner.

Neither vul.

W	N	E	S
1♣	1◇	pass	?

♠ 8 6 5 4 2
♡ 10 3 2
◇ A 8
♣ K Q 10

Bid 1♠. If your partner has a good overcall your side may find a contract you like. Your hand is too good to pass 1◇, and fortunately you have a way to enter the bidding.

W	N	E	S
1♣	1♡	pass	?

♠ A J
♡ 3 2
◇ 10 6 5 4 2
♣ K Q 10 7

Bid 1NT. When partner overcalls at the one-level he promises only 9 or so points. You should not bid 1NT with those 6- or 7-point hands that would bid 1NT in response to an opening bid. This hand is actually close to a minimum.

Both vul.

W	N	E	S
1♣	1♡	pass	?

♠ K Q 10 9 8 7
♡ K 2
◇ A 10 7
♣ 5 4

This hand is good enough that you ought to consider a game. 4♠ is a likely candidate, and 4♡ and 3NT are not out of the question. Now if 1♠ is correct on ♠86542 ♡32 ◇A8 ♣KQ107, then 1♠ is probably incorrect on the hand in question. If this was already of concern to you, full marks for thinking ahead. What should you do here? More on this later.

E-W vul.

W	N	E	S
1♣	1♡	2◇	?

♠ K J 10 9 8 6
♡ A 3
◇ 8 6 2
♣ 5 4

This is another case where you must visualize your partner's strength and distribution. While you can't work these questions out in detail, nor should you try, you can make these basic observations. The auction has told you partner's overcall is minimum. Partner won't have any extra high cards. And there is nothing in the auction to suggest any sort of spade fit in partner's hand. I don't expect anyone not to bid 2♠, but it should be clear that this is an aggressive and dangerous action. When you bid 2♠, if you do so well aware of the dangers, then you're on the right track.

It may seem that a large amount of space has been devoted to commonplace auctions, but these situations are a large part of the meat and potatoes of competitive bidding. Many small battles revolve around the one and two-levels. An understanding of when to get into and when to get out of an auction is crucial. You must know and understand when it is safe to bid and when it is not. I imagine that far more points, IMPs, or money are lost in these low-level skirmishes than anywhere else. Unfortunately, many of these losses go unnoticed because no one stops to work out that his side could have made 3◇ on a hand where the opponents have just made 2♠. What does happen is that people remember going for a number and they resolve not to do it again. It's much less emotional to lose 110 than 500. Hopefully, these principles will encourage more bidding, while at the same time cutting down on those large minuses.

N-S vul.

W	N	E	S
1◇	1♡	2◇	?

♠ J10 8 6 4 3

♡ 3

◇ A 8 6

♣ Q 9 7

At matchpoints, this is a typical aggressive 2♠ bid. All your eggs are in one basket, so to speak, and if you're wrong, you're very wrong. An important matchpoint consideration here is that the opponents are in a minor (diamonds). If they make two, they score 90. If you go one down in 2♠, you lose 100. When vulnerable, you must give thought to these things. Similarly, if the opponents stop in 1NT you might decide to let them play there rather than risk going down 100.

Admittedly, you can't often judge the exact number of tricks either side can make, let alone both sides, but in close decisions the vulnerability and the opponents' contract (1NT or 2♣ or 2◇) may sway you in one direction or another.

IMPs is much easier. Those 10-point swings don't count for anything; another case of a matchpoint top having no value whatsoever for IMPs.

In the actual hand, the opponents will frequently save you by going on to 3◇ when they could have defeated 2♠. The irony of it all is when they make 3◇ anyway, so that all your hard work was for naught.

At this stage it may occur to you that you never get a good hand. Or if you do get a good hand, you get it with "more on this later." There are two reasons for this. The first is simply that the change of suit I've been discussing applies to hands in the poor to moderate range. The second reason is that most of the examples have concerned themselves with the minimum hands falling in that already limited range. By concentrating on the minimum values required for these various actions you should be able to determine how far in that direction you can go and still feel comfortable. Once you have settled this you will find the other, better hands falling neatly into place.

In a later section I will get into the stronger responses you have available and will discuss the upper and lower ranges of these bids as well. At that time I will compare where the maximum values for a non-forcing new suit response leave off and the minimum values for the stronger invitational sequences begin.

THREE-LEVEL NEW SUIT RESPONSES TO AN OVERCALL

This section is going to be shorter and simpler than the long section heading may suggest. Once in awhile, partner will make an overcall and the auction will proceed so as to force you to bid your suit at the three-level. For example:

1◇-1♠-2♡-? You must bid 3♣.
1♠-2◇-2♡-? You must bid 3♣.
1♡-1♠-2♡-? You must bid 3♣ or 3◇.
1♠-2♡-2♠-? You must bid 3♣ or 3◇.

Once again, you have two situations. RHO has responded in a new suit, or RHO has raised the opener.

The first case is easily dealt with. The opponents have shown they hold substantial values (an opening bid facing a 2/1 response), and this guarantees it will be dangerous to start looking for a fit. You are just outgunned.

In the previous section you saw it was dangerous to bid a new suit at the two-level after the opponents had shown strength. Bidding at the three-level is correspondingly more dangerous. In practice, you will almost never have cause to do anything except raise partner or simply pass.

AUCTIONS WHERE THE OPPONENTS RESPOND IN A NEW SUIT AT THE TWO-LEVEL

Neither vul.

W	N	E	S
1♡	1♠	2♦	?

♠ J 3
♡ 8 6
◇ J 7 5 2
♣ A Q 8 6 3

Pass. Far too dangerous to act. Your best hope for a plus is to set the opponents at their final contract. You can see that partner's overcall is on some sort of minimum. The opponents have 23 or 24 HCP and you have 8. Partner has 8 or 9. Looking at it this way shows the futility of bidding. If you tried 3♣ you could easily go down a couple and likely more, and it would definitely be doubled. As the opponents don't even have a clear-cut game, –300 can be too expensive. This should be a pass in any game.

E-W vul.

W	N	E	S
1♣	1♠	2♡	?

♠ 4 2
♡ 9 6 5
◇ K Q 10 9 8 6 3
♣ 7

This is a typical 3◇ bid. Not too much in high cards, but a good suit. You should be able to get six diamond tricks most of the time, and you are guaranteed of five. If you should run into a double you could easily go for 300 or 500, but in this case it won't necessarily be bad. The opponents are likely to have a game and you have no particular reason to think you can beat it. If partner feels like saving you have the right hand for it.

You can try 3♣ without too much risk. If partner decides to save your hand is suitable, and once again, your suit is good. You would prefer partner lead a club unless his spades are so outstanding that he would lead them in any case.

Partner should be aware of the kind of hand 3♣ shows. He is not expected or encouraged whatsoever to rebid his suit. Especially, he should not try 3NT. If he does bid 3NT you should trust him to know that this is the kind of hand he should expect. Likewise, if your partner doubles something, you should feel that you have what you are supposed to have and you should pass the double.

Neither vul.

W   N   E   S
1♣ 1♠ 2♡ ?

♠ 83
♡ Q65
◇ KJ9764
♣ Q9

Pass. Your high cards are of dubious value and your suit is not good enough to bid at the three-level when you have no reason to hope for a fit.

E-W vul.

W   N   E   S
1♣ 1♠ 2♡ ?

♠ 3
♡ 87
◇ J987642
♣ AQ3

Pass is probably best. You might miss a good save, but if you bid 3◇ you run a number of risks. Partner may get off to a bad lead. Or you may take a bad save. You have some sure defense against 4♡, should the opponents try that. Your stiff spade and your ♣A suggest you would like to defend. 3◇ could work out, but it is against the odds. If partner were to bid 3NT over 3◇, you should remove that to 4◇. Partner's hand can't be good enough to stop the opponents' suits and to run diamonds. He would be expecting a better suit. Note that partner needs something in diamonds for his bid, so you are guaranteed decent support.

AUCTIONS WHERE PARTNER BIDS AT THE TWO-LEVEL AND RHO RAISES

When RHO raises, you have more reason to be hopeful and can afford to be a bit aggressive. Be aware that partner bid at the two-level. He promises more than a one-level overcall, which may change your bidding a bit.

Neither vul.

W	N	E	S
1♠	2♣	2♠	?

♠ 3 2
♡ K J 8 6 5 4
♢ Q J 6 3
♣ 2

Pass. Even though partner's overcall guarantees more than a one-level overcall would, you should quit. You need to have a super hand, a super suit, or reason to expect a fit. You have none of these. That extra trick (three-level as opposed to two-level) means you are in additional jeopardy and you have to compensate for that somehow.

Neither vul.

W	N	E	S
1♠	2♡	2♠	?

♠ 8 7 6
♡ Q 2
♢ 4 2
♣ K Q J 10 7 6

3♣ is clear. You have a good suit and a probable fit. Not only that, but your ♡Q is a huge plus.

Neither vul.

W	N	E	S
1♠	2♢	2♠	?

♠ 8 7 6
♡ K Q 9 6 4 2
♢ 4 2
♣ Q 9

This is a matchpoint-oriented 3♡ bid. Your suit is reasonable and you have hopes for a fit. The trouble with this bid is that it tends to be final in nature. If you're wrong, there's no escape. Compare this hand with the next hand.

Neither vul.

W	N	E	S
1♠	2♢	2♠	?

♠ 8 7
♡ K Q 9 6 4 2
♢ 4 2
♣ Q 9 3

Pass. The important feature of this hand is the doubleton spade, the worst possible holding in a suit bid and raised by the opponents. It says or implies nothing about partner's having a fit for you, which would be the case if you had three or four spades. And this holding starts you off with two likely losers, which is not the case if you had a singleton. With the rest of the hand being marginal, you should pass.

N-S vul.

W	N	E	S
1♠	2◇	2♡	?

♠ Q 8 2
♡ 8 4
◇ 7
♣ K J 9 7 6 5 4

This auction is one of those defined as dangerous, and if you always pass without looking at your hand you will be well off in the long run. This advice certainly holds true here. There is just nothing to recommend bidding. You should pass for all of these reasons.

1. You have the ♠Q, likely worthless.
2. You have a doubleton heart, hopeless.
3. You have a stiff diamond, partner's suit.
4. You have no reason to expect a fit.

RHO OPENS AND YOU PASS. PARTNER BIDS AT THE TWO-LEVEL

There is one last auction that is theoretically possible, but in practice, nonexistent. The auction starts with RHO opening and you passing. It goes something like this:

LHO	Partner	RHO	You
		1♣	pass
1♠	2◇	pass	2♡
		1♡	pass
2♣	2♠	pass	3◇
		1♣	pass
2♣	2♡	pass	2♠
		1◇	pass
2◇	2♡	3◇	3♠

In each of these auctions, the opening bid was on your right. You passed, and then when LHO responded and your partner overcalled, you decided to introduce a new suit of your own. Most unusual. If you were so eager to show this suit, why didn't you do so after the opening bid? Why wait and have second thoughts? There are a couple of possible reasons for this.

1. You didn't have enough strength to bid the first time.
2. You have a fit for partner.

It's easy to dispose of the first possibility. Just because partner overcalls, he does not guarantee enough strength to warrant your bidding on hands that are not worth an initial overcall, or an initial weak jump overcall.

Neither vul.

W	N	E	S
		1♣	pass
1♠	2◇	pass	?

♠ 8 7 2
♡ K Q 10 8 7
◇ K 2
♣ J 4 2

If you had passed this hand over 1♣ you might wish to bid 2♡, but you should have overcalled in the first place. Passing and then bidding does not make sense.

Neither vul.

W	N	E	S
		1♣	pass
1♠	2♡	2♠	?

♠ 4 2
♡ J 7 3
◇ A K J 8
♣ 8 7 5 4

You have the values to raise to 3♡ but you might consider bidding 3◇ instead. If you and partner wished to define this auction, you could reasonably say that a new suit guarantees a fit for partner's overcalled suit. I'll take another look at this in the section on raising partner's overcalls.

Neither vul.

W	N	E	S
		1♣	pass
1♡	1♠	2♡	?

♠ 3
♡ J 8 7
◇ K Q 10 9 7 3
♣ 8 4 2

This hand is a weak jump overcall. You will not have this situation at the table.

Neither vul.

W	N	E	S
		1♣	pass
1♠	2♡	2♠	?

♠ 10 6 5 2
♡ 3
◇ K Q 10 8 7 5
♣ Q 4

This hand could try 3◇ on the theory that a fit exists. But you can't do that if partner will expect you to have heart support. This hand is exceptional in that it is one of the very few that you might pass and then wish to bid. The reason you didn't make a weak jump overcall of 2◇ was your holding in spades. Under no circumstances should you confuse these sequences on the last couple of pages with the earlier material. Only when RHO opens, you pass, LHO responds, and partner overcalls, can a new suit by you imply a fit for partner. Be sure you discuss it. And don't wait up for it to happen. Very rare.

Neither vul.

W	N	E	S

Neither vulnerable

		1♣	pass
1♠	2♡	2♠	?

♠ 876
♡ A95
◇ AQJ4
♣ 984

If you agree that you cannot have a diamond suit, given you did not bid over 1♣, then the usefulness of playing 3◇ here to show values in diamonds and a heart raise is clear. This is a rare situation.

Neither vul.

W	N	E	S

		1♡	pass
1♠	2◇	2♠	?

♠ 843
♡ K4
◇ J3
♣ KQ10754

This hand is different from the previous hand. This time if you bid clubs, you are bidding a suit that was not convenient for you to bid the round before. In this case your bid of 3♣ is natural, showing a pretty good suit and a hand that was not able to bid clubs the round before.

Here are the rules that apply.

RULES

1. If you pass RHO's opening bid and then bid a new suit at the two- or three-level after partner's overcall, your bid is fit-showing if you could have shown your suit earlier at the one-level.
2. If you pass and bid a new suit at the two- or three-level after partner's overcall, your bid is natural if you could not show your suit earlier at the one-level.

PARTNER OVERCALLS AND YOU HAVE A GOOD HAND

So far, the only hands we've looked at are those of marginal value where you wished to compete for the partscore. Game was usually out of the question unless partner could make some forward move.

Once in a while, though, you will have a hand with near game-going values. When this happens you will want to make a stronger bid than a simple change of suit. There are many bids available and their meanings vary according to how the bidding has gone.

1. With a strong hand you can cuebid and then bid your suit.
2. On some auctions, you can jump in your suit to show an invitational hand.
3. On some auctions, you can jump in your suit to show a preemptive hand.

It may sound like you are trying to have it both ways and in fact, you can. The meaning of your jump depends on the bidding. If their bidding suggests they can be weak, your jumps in a new suit show an invitational hand. If their bidding shows strength, your jumps in a new suit show a preemptive hand. Examples to follow.

Here are some cases and examples of how your bidding varies according to what the opponents are doing.

1. Your partner overcalls and RHO passes. The possibility exists that you can have game-going values. A jump here to show an invitational hand is a reasonable treatment. If you have a stronger hand you may have to make a cuebid first and then try to describe what you have.
2. RHO makes a 1/1 response. There is still the possibility that you hold invitational strength. Using the jump as forward-going is still reasonable.
3. RHO bids 1NT. While it's barely possible for you to hold the strength to make an invitational jump, there is the more practical alternative of doubling the 1NT bidder. Note that the 1NT bidder has 7-10 HCP, while the 1/1 bidder may be bidding on distribution and can have as few as 4 or 5 HCP. This means that you are less likely to have the strength to jump after the 1NT bid. I suggest using a jump as a preemptive bid rather than a strong bid.
4. RHO raises. It's quite possible for you to have a good hand. Plus, when they have a fit, you do too. Use the jump as invitational.
5. RHO makes a negative double. This bid is not terribly threatening since the doubler can do this with some fairly weak hands. Play that a jump in a new suit is invitational.

6. RHO makes a 2/1 bid. There is no way you can have any kind of a good hand. LHO has an opener, partner an overcall, and RHO values for a two-level bid. There is little left for you. If you can't have enough to jump in a new suit invitationally, then you should find another meaning for the bid, if possible. I suggest you adopt the preemptive jump on such auctions.

EXAMPLES OF BIDDING WITH GOOD HANDS WHEN RHO PASSES OVER PARTNER'S OVERCALL

Examples of Invitational Hands

Neither vul.

W	N	E	S
1♣	1♡	pass	?

♠ A Q 10 8 7 6
♡ K 2
◇ K J 7
♣ 4 2

A normal, average 2♠ bid. This is not forcing. Partner may pass on minimum hands. Your bid shows something in the range of a good 13 to a poorish 15 points with a very good five-card or longer suit. If partner passes 2♠ you'll be in a good spot. If partner has any kind of fit he will try to raise, and you will continue accordingly.

Neither vul.

W	N	E	S
1♣	1◇	pass	?

♠ 4 2
♡ K Q 9 7 6 5 2
◇ Q
♣ K Q 4

2♡. Too many losers for a unilateral jump to 4♡. This is a good hand for partnerships with systemic understandings. You'll get to game when it's right and you'll stay in a partscore when that's right.

N-S vul.

W	N	E	S
1◇	1♠	pass	?

♠ 8 7
♡ A 5
◇ 8 7 6
♣ A K J 9 7 6

3♣. Hopefully, partner can bid 3NT. If he passes, you should be in a good spot. Your partner bid vulnerable so he rates to have a decent hand. Be sure to note the vulnerability. It pays to know what you can expect partner to have.

Both vul.

W	N	E	S
1♡	1♠	pass	?

♠ Q 2
♡ 8 7
◇ A K 5
♣ K J 10 9 7 4

Neither vul.

W	N	E	S
1♣	1♡	pass	?

♠ K Q J 8 7
♡ Q 2
◇ 4 2
♣ A J 6 5

Neither vul.

W	N	E	S
1♣	1♠	pass	?

♠ J 2
♡ A Q 8 6 5
◇ A 10 6 5 4
♣ 3

Neither vul.

W	N	E	S
1♣	1◇	pass	?

♠ Q 9 7 6 5
♡ A Q 4 2
◇ A 5
♣ 8 7

N-S vul.

W	N	E	S
1♣	1♡	pass	?

♠ J 7 6 5 2
♡ Q 2
◇ A K 8
♣ K 10 7

3♣. Typical hand. The jump does not guarantee a solid suit. It would be nice, but impractical.

2♠. Good five-card suit with game interest. Don't do this with suits like Q8743. ♠KQJ87 is on the weak side for a five-card suit.

Who knows? Some people will point to a hand like this and tell you that 2♡ should be forcing. On this hand it would be nice. But you would have problems on many partscore hands. I would bid 2♡ and hope to hear somebody bid again. I would object to 3♡. You need a fit for game in hearts to be a good spot, and if partner has a fit he will raise except with a terrible overcall. Fortunately, these hands are very infrequent.

1♠. If partner can't raise, you won't be missing much. He will raise with hands like this one: ♠K84 ♡95 ◇KQ1096 ♣A102. If he has less, he will pass and you will be in a safe partial.

I would lean toward 2NT. Spades might be your best spot, but there's no number of spades you can bid without misdescribing your hand. If you did choose 1♠, you rate to survive nicely.

Neither vul.

W	N	E	S
1♣	1♠	pass	?

♠ K 6 5 2
♡ A Q J 10 7
◇ 3
♣ K Q 7

This hand is offered as a suggestion. You can bid 4♠, but I suggest you play this bid is preemptive. If you agree, then you should make a cuebid first and then bid 4♠. This lets partner know you have a real hand. I will offer some additional ideas in a later section. If your partnership has splinter bids available, you might consider using one here. Bid 4◇ to show a game raise of spades with a stiff diamond.

Both vul.

W	N	E	S
1♣	1◇	pass	?

♠ A J 2
♡ K 10 7 6 5
◇ K J 3
♣ J 3

1♡. When you need the equivalent of 13 or more points plus three-card support to make a game, you will find it sufficient to bid only 1♡. Partner will raise on most hands containing three-card support unless he has a real dog of an overcall.

Neither vul.

W	N	E	S
1♠	2♣	pass	?

♠ 4 2
♡ 9 3 2
◇ A K Q 10 8 7 6
♣ 3

3◇. You want to hear 3NT but you don't want to force the issue. 3◇ does everything very nicely. Whatever you do, don't bid 2◇. Remember that partner bid at the *two-level*, not the one-level.

E-W vul.

W	N	E	S
1♡	2♣	pass	?

♠ J 10 9 8 4 2
♡ A K J 7
◇ 2
♣ Q 3

3♠. This suit is as bad as you will have, but your values are adequate. Note that you are counting on your ♣Q to be a valuable asset. If you did not have it, bidding just 2♠ would be enough.

If you are getting discouraged that these hands are difficult, don't be. You will be ahead of most people because you have a definition for the bids you are making. Whatever happens will at least be reasonable. Pairs who don't take the time to work out what to do with hands like these are reduced to guessing games.

Neither vul.

W	N	E	S
1♠	2♣	pass	?

♠ 8 2
♡ K Q 10 9 7 6
◇ A Q 5
♣ 10 2

3♡. Because a two-level overcall promises more than a one-level overcall, your jump can be based on a little less in hand value. On the other hand, when you are jumping to the three-level you will need a very good suit.

Both vul.

W	N	E	S
1♠	2♡	pass	?

♠ Q 2
♡ 10 2
◇ A K J 10 8 7
♣ K 5 4

The only good bid is 3◇, forcing. But it's not forcing, so you have to select from the following:

1. 2NT or 3NT (insufficient spade stopper)
2. 3♡ or 4♡ (insufficient trumps)
3. 3◇ (grossly conservative)
4. 2♠ (my choice, but awkward)
5. 4◇ (gets past 3NT)

A little bit of propaganda from the scientists

The point of this hand is that playing a new suit as forcing does have some merit. If you choose to do so, you can play that a new suit by you is forcing when your partner overcalls at the two-level. My preference is to play new suits as not forcing after a one- or two-level overcall but I am willing to tell you about a different view and offer this hand as an example for their methods.

Examples of Responding with Very Strong Hands and a Suit or Suits of Your Own

If your partner overcalls and you have a huge hand with an unbid suit such that you are sure you want to bid a game, the way to show your hand is to start with a cuebid and then bid your suit on the next round. This is such a rare circumstance that I can't recall more than one of these in the last few years. It is easier to show this idea via examples so here they are.

Neither vul.

W	N	E	S
1♣	1♠	pass	?

♠ Q 7
♡ A K J 8 7 5
◇ A Q J
♣ 9 5

Even if you play aggressive overcalls, this hand is surely worth forcing to game. The way you begin the auction is to cuebid 2♣ and then show your hearts. It is easier said than done because the bidding can take some odd twists. But in general, the idea is fine. You expect your partner to bid 2♠ (what can he have that would cause him to bid more?), and now you will bid 3♡. Your partner, no matter what he has, must keep bidding. If he rebids spades, you will bid 4♠. He may raise you to 4♡. He may bid 3NT. Anything is possible. What is important is that you have a way to show your hand.

Neither vul.

W	N	E	S
1♡	1♠	pass	?

♠ 2
♡ 7 4 2
◇ A Q 7
♣ A K Q 10 6 4

You want to explore for game even facing a minimum overcall. Bid 2♡ now and see what happens. Your partner almost always just rebids his suit when you have a hand this big. Remember, your LHO has an opening bid and you have this hand. Your partner can't have more than a 12- or 13-count. If he bids 2♠, you will bid 3♣. If he bids 2NT, you will raise to 3NT. If he keeps bidding spades, you can do little more than rebid your clubs at the four-level. Probably your partner can pass this bid. And probably you will not make it. At least you gave it an intelligent try.

Neither vul.

W	N	E	S
1♣	1♠	pass	?

♠ 8
♡ A Q 10 9 7 6
◇ A K 10 8 4
♣ 8

Your plan is to bid your red suits until you get to game. It does not pay to assume your partner has six spades and five clubs. You have to have a little optimism. Given that you decide to drive this hand to game, you have to start with a cuebid. Here is a likely auction.

LHO	Partner	RHO	You
1♣	1♠	pass	2♣
pass	2♠	pass	3♡
pass	3NT	pass	4◇
pass	4♡	all pass	

Your 2♣ bid was forcing. Partner, for now, expects you to have spade support with 11 or more points. His 2♠ bid shows a minimum hand with no game interest. Your 3♡ bid was forcing, ostensibly to game. Your partner bid 3NT, which did not show much, just that he has a club stopper and does not much like hearts. You bid 4◇, showing your second suit. This bid is still forcing. Anytime you cuebid and then start bidding new suits, your bidding is forcing. If you cuebid and then bid a suit and rebid it later, it is reasonable to play that this sequence can be passed. Your partner goes back to 4♡ and you pass. You can be sure that your partner has only two hearts. If he had three of them he would have raised 3♡ to 4♡.

As good as your hand is, game may not be cold. All you know is that your partner has a minimum 1♠ overcall and apparently a couple of hearts and a club stopper. Good luck. The big deal is that your auction is understood by the partnership.

When RHO makes a 1/1 response after your partner's overcall, your jump will be about the same as if RHO had passed. There are a few minor differences that you have to contend with.

1. RHO's bid will usually force you to jump to the three-level.

When RHO passes   1♣-1◊-pass-2♡
When RHO bids   1♣-1◊-1♠-3♡

That 1♠ bid forced you to change your bid.

2. You have more distributional information that may help with your decision.

EXAMPLES WHEN RHO MAKES A ONE-LEVEL BID AFTER PARTNER'S OVERCALL

Neither vul.

W	N	E	S
1♣	1♡	1♠	?

♠ K 8 7
♡ Q 2
◊ A Q J 9 8 3
♣ 8 7

Bid 3◊. Don't fall into the trap of bidding 2◊ and thinking that's sufficient because it's a free bid. You should bid 2◊ with no ♠K and no ♡Q.

Neither vul.

W	N	E	S
1♣	1◊	1♡	?

♠ Q J 8 7 6 2
♡ K 10 4 2
◊ A J
♣ 3

2♠. This is the only auction where RHO bids and you can still jump to the two-level. One nice thing about jump responses to show a good hand is that they remain the same for all forms of bridge; IMPs, matchpoints, etc.

Both vul.

W	N	E	S
1♣	1◇	1♠	?

♠ K J 3
♡ Q 6 5 4 2
◇ K 2
♣ A 10 3

Where's everyone else finding their bids? Someone is stretching their values. I hope it's not partner. I would try 2NT and feel a bit unhappy about losing the heart suit. On the other hand, 2♡ is an underbid and 3♡ shows a much better suit. There is a convention called the snapdragon double that may help you handle this hand. More on this in a later chapter.

The most important point in this discussion is the understanding between partners. What I'm recommending here is proven. Note that decisions are more straightforward when you have good hands than on hands where you have questionable values. On poor hands you have to ask the question, "Shall I bid at all?" as well as the question, "What shall I bid?" With good hands you have only to worry about *what* to bid, and this is frequently the easier question to answer.

When RHO raises after partner's overcall, you will have a fair number of hands worth an invitational jump. More hands, in fact, than after a 1/1 by RHO. This is because:

1. After a raise, there are two unbid suits for you to bid.
2. They have a fit, which suggests that you also have one. When good fits exist it has the effect of increasing the points around the table, so that everyone has more than his usual quota. More points, more bidding.

One problem you will encounter is that a raise by RHO is perforce at the two-level, so a jump by you must be to the three-level or higher. You can't jump to the two-level anymore. So even though you may have the values to jump, the height of the auction may make the bidding awkward.

Examples when RHO Raises After Partner's Overcall

Neither vul.

W	N	E	S
1♣	1♡	2♣	?

♠ K Q 10 8 7 6 2
♡ 3
◇ A 2
♣ J 5 4

3♠. If partner has a stiff spade and a weak hand you will be high enough. 4♠ would be an overbid and 2♠ could lead to a missed game opposite many decent minimums.

Neither vul.

W	N	E	S
1♡	2♣	2♡	?

♠ A J 2
♡ 4 2
◇ K Q 10 8 7 6
♣ Q 2

This is a difficult hand. I would bid 3◇ and feel that the alternatives were misleading. Sometimes it's better to get a sure plus when you don't have a good way to try for better things. Perhaps the responsive double can help. I will look at it more later.

Neither vul.

W	N	E	S
1◇	2♣	2◇	?

♠ K 10 9 6 5
♡ A Q J 8 7
◇ 3
♣ Q 4

You have the strength to bid and you have high hopes for a game if partner can fit either major. The solution is the responsive double, to be discussed later.

Both vul.

W	N	E	S
1♠	2♣	2♠	?

♠ 8 2
♡ K Q 10 7 6 5
◇ A 10
♣ K 6 5

Who knows? You want to bid hearts, raise clubs, and show a good hand all at once. Unfortunately, you don't have any assurance of a heart fit. That doubleton spade tells you nothing about partner's distribution and it hurts your hand as well. Best to bid a mildly conservative 3♡. Bid 4♡ if you hate the idea of bidding only three.

<table>
<tr><td>Both vul.</td></tr>
<tr><td>W N E S</td></tr>
<tr><td>1♠ 2♣ 2♠ ?</td></tr>
</table>

♠ 10 6 5 2
♡ K J 10 9 8 3
◊ 3
♣ A Q

Once again, the known fit strikes. 3♡ would be an underbid. Bid game. 4♡ should have a good play.

<table>
<tr><td>Both vul.</td></tr>
<tr><td>W N E S</td></tr>
<tr><td>1♡ 1♠ 2♡ ?</td></tr>
</table>

♠ 8 2
♡ 4 2
◊ 7 2
♣ A K Q 10 7 6 5

Bid 3♣. You would like partner to bid 3NT, but that is unlikely. Sadly, you don't have a strong bid available that is both safe and sensible. Even if 3♣ were forcing it wouldn't necessarily work. You really wish RHO had passed so your 3♣ bid would have been a jump. But it didn't go that way. So once again you just have to take the path of least resistance. Bidding 3♣ won't get you to very many games, but it will get you to a good, safe contract. Some of the time 3♣ is your maximum spot and you'll be getting the only available plus. Once again, the possibility of the responsive double being helpful appears. More later.

WHEN GAME IS UNLIKELY

When RHO bids 1NT after partner's overcall, the chances for game by your side are virtually nonexistent. The opponents have at least half the high cards and RHO has values in partner's suit. In practice, the best you can do is a partscore. If you are not likely to have the values for a strong jump, then if possible, another meaning for the jump shift should be found. One possibility is to play it as preemptive. Let's see if it works.

EXAMPLES WHEN RHO BIDS 1NT AFTER PARTNER'S OVERCALL

<table>
<tr><td>Neither vul.</td></tr>
<tr><td>W N E S</td></tr>
<tr><td>1♡ 1♠ 1NT ?</td></tr>
</table>

♠ 7 2
♡ 9 7 3
◊ 8
♣ K Q J 10 9 7 3

If you play 3♣ as a preempt, then this hand is just about right. You aren't a favorite to make it but you won't go down very many, either. With the suit as good as it is, nobody will be rushing to double you. As with most preempts, you take up a fair amount of room from the opponents. LHO can't rebid 2♡ or 2◊, and for that matter, neither can RHO. You won't have many of these preemptive jumps, but you will have some.

And when they occur, you'll do well. There are a couple of things to look out for, though.

1. RHO has made a descriptive bid and LHO will be able to double you when it's right.
2. If the opponents don't have a game, then –300 will be a bad result. To minimize the chances of this you need a fairly good suit.

Neither vul.

W	N	E	S
1♣	1◇	1NT	?

♠ 4 2
♡ Q 10 8 6 5 4 2
◇ Q 3
♣ A 4

2♡ is fine and quite enough. Your suit is too poor to jump.

Both vul.

W	N	E	S
1◇	1♠	1NT	?

♠ 10 3
♡ Q J 10 9 8 6 3
◇ —
♣ K 10 8 7

On this vulnerability you need a pretty good hand to bid 3♡. There's no reason to volunteer for a large number. When you do bid a new suit at the three-level you need a good suit, which you have. I would venture 3♡ with this hand.

E-W vul.

W	N	E	S
1♡	1♠	1NT	?

♠ 3
♡ 2
◇ K Q J 10 8 7
♣ J 6 5 4 2

I would try 3◇. Good suit, weakish hand. Clubs might be right, but with such suit disparity I'd rather bid the maximum the hand can stand. Let them guess.

N-S vul.

W	N	E	S
1♣	1♠	1NT	?

♠ J 2
♡ K Q 10 8 7 5
◇ A Q 4
♣ 9 7

It's very unlikely that you will ever have a hand this good on this sequence. If it does happen, though, you do not have an invitational 3♡ bid available. On this auction 3♡ would be weak. Your choices are a conservative 2♡ or a penalty double. Since RHO has promised spade values, you rate to have at least one spade loser. I can accept 2♡ and would accept double too.

What Should Double Mean?

A one paragraph digression:

There is a sane school of thought that says doubling when partner overcalls and they bid 1NT is a wasted effort. There is a lot of truth to this. If your experience is that using double for penalty never seems to come up, there is a valid alternative. Play that double shows the unbid suits. On this sequence, a double would be used to show at least 8 points and 5-5 in the red suits, eg:

♠ 9   ♡ A J 9 8 4   ◇ Q J 8 7 3   ♣ J 9

Continuing with the discussion.

N-S vul.			
W	**N**	**E**	**S**
1♣	1♠	1NT	?

♠ 9 7 3
♡ A K 8 7
◇ K J 7 5 4
♣ 8

If RHO had passed over 1♠ you would have made a game try. RHO's 1NT bid is bad news and you should be aware of it. RHO has a spade winner and may have two. If he has four spades this hand may play poorly. This auction has told you that your partner has a minimum overcall. I think it is enough to raise to 2♠. It is possible that they will double this. It is not out of the question. If they do, you will see why it was best not to get too high.

EXAMPLES WHEN RHO MAKES A 2/1 BID AFTER PARTNER'S OVERCALL

In this final sequence, RHO makes a 2/1 bid after partner's overcall. Everyone has a good hand. Except us. This comes with a guarantee.

So, if we don't have much to fight with, maybe we can put up a fight with what we do have. This isn't easy, though, because bidding is very dangerous in this situation. As your side does not have many high cards, your tricks will have to come as the result of a good fit or a long, strong suit.

E-W vul.			
W	**N**	**E**	**S**
1♣	1♠	2◇	?

♠ 8 6 2
♡ Q J 10 8 7 6 5
◇ 3
♣ 9 5

Bid 3♡. Opposite a spade overcall, this hand should produce six tricks rather easily. If doubled this would be –500, or perhaps less. This would not be good unless the opponents have a game. Here it seems likely that they do.

When the auction begins with a 2/1 by responder the chances of their making game are quite real, so your saves have a much wider range of success. If the opponents can do no better than a partscore, then –200, –300, or –500 will be awful regardless of the vulnerability. But against a game, these minus results can be quite rewarding.

This hand happens to have three spades, partner's suit. The problem with playing in spades is that the defenders can lead trumps, thus turning your hand into rubbish. In hearts, your hand is assured of taking five tricks. There is an old joke about not putting good seven-card suits down in dummy. There is some truth to this.

Neither vul.

W	N	E	S
1♣	1♠	2◇	?

♠ 3
♡ K J 7 6 4 3 2
◇ Q 8 7
♣ J 2

Far too dangerous to bid 3♡. Your suit is bad. You have no reason to hope for a fit. You have some defense. If you must do something, 2♡ is enough. But it's not as safe as it looks.

Both vul.

W	N	E	S
1♡	1♠	2♣	?

♠ Q 2
♡ 8 3
◇ K J 10 8 7 6 5
♣ 4 2

Just 2◇. When you don't want partner to take a save, you should content yourself with getting him off to the best lead. Your shape is too bad.

E-W vul.

W	N	E	S
1♡	2♣	2◇	?

♠ J 10 7 6 5 4 2
♡ 7 3
◇ 2
♣ K 8 7

With this defensive wonder it would not be surprising to see the opponents score a grand, let alone an assortment of various games. 3♠ is a good, practical way to make life hard on the opponents while getting to your best suit. This vulnerability is so much in your favor that you can get away with almost anything. Anything, at least, when:
1.   The opponents have a game.
2.   You have a fit or a good suit.
Here, both conditions hold. If they don't have a game on this hand, they'll never have one. And you have a fit. If not in spades, then in clubs. Note that you won't be in more than 3♠ unless partner raises them.

N-S vul.

W	N	E	S
1◇	1♠	2♡	?

♠ —
♡ Q 10 3
◇ Q 4 2
♣ K J 8 7 6 5 4

Pass. You are about to get a good score. But you won't get it by bidding. You have no suit, no fit, no tricks. Just defense. And the vulnerability is the worst.

BIDDING 1NT AFTER PARTNER'S ONE-LEVEL OVERCALL

The main thing here is that you realize your partner's overcall does not promise the same values as an opening bid. If your partner overcalls at the one-level and RHO passes, and you bid 1NT, it is a natural bid showing in the range of 8-11 points. You need to use your judgment here. You may have an 8-point hand that is full of extras and you may even have a 12-count that looks and feels like an 8-count. I will have more hands on this later.

If your RHO bids something at the one-level, that suggests their side has fair values at the least and the odds on your making a notrump contract are diminished. Importantly, when RHO bids something, you know it is a hint that your partner has less than you might hope for. If you bid 1NT after a bid from RHO, you need a nice 10- or 11-point hand. This is normal caution at work. If you have 10 points and both opponents are bidding, you know your partner won't have a good overcall and he is likely to have a minimum overcall.

BIDDING 2NT AFTER PARTNER'S ONE-LEVEL OVERCALL

If you bid 2NT in response to partner's overcall it is a natural bid and ought to show at least a good 12 or 13 points. It is not forcing. It is also extremely rare that you will have such a hand. It might happen if RHO passes, but if RHO bids something the odds are against your having a 12- or 13-point notrump hand.

It is reasonable to play 2NT as a natural and invitational bid but it is not going to happen often, as noted. For this reason, I am going to make a suggestion that I will develop later. If your partner bids at the one-level and RHO passes or bids something, a 2NT bid by you can be played as artificial, showing a raise for your partner's suit. This is one of the new tools that was not around when I wrote *Overcalls* and it is an idea with considerable merit. Look for a discussion on using 2NT as a raise in the section on modern bidding methods. Until then, a 2NT bid shows a balanced invitational hand.

PASSING AFTER PARTNER'S OVERCALL

What does pass show? If your partner overcalls and you pass, the logical thought is that you have a weak hand. This is true. Still, looking at a couple of hands is worthwhile, to see the range of hands that are included.

Neither vul.

W	N	E	S
1♣	1♡	pass	?

♠ Q9874
♡ 7
◇ J97643
♣ 3

You have a hand that rates to have a better home than 1♡, but finding that home is impossible. Should you bid 1♠ or 2◇, you are making a huge bet. If your partner does not like your suit you may be in trouble, and if he does like your suit he may get you too high. If you bid, say, 1♠ and your partner later doubled 3♣, would you be sure that you knew what to do? Some hands, tempting as they may be, should be passed for fear of starting a war you can't win.

Neither vul.

W	N	E	S
1♣	1♡	pass	?

♠ QJ7
♡ 97
◇ KQJ4
♣ 7532

You have the 9 points needed for 1NT, but they are terrible points and do not include a club stopper. If your side can make anything your partner will need at least 15 HCP, which is not likely. Pass this one out.

Neither vul.

W	N	E	S
1♣	1♡	pass	?

♠ 875
♡ —
◇ Q1086432
♣ K73

This is a pass. 2◇ is a better contract than 1♡, but only if you can stop there. If you bid 2◇, someone out there will bid again and that someone might be your partner. If you pass, opener may double for takeout and your RHO may pass for penalty. Now you can bid 2◇ and your partner will know exactly what you have.

DIFFICULT GOOD HANDS

Very infrequently, your partner will overcall and you will have enough to guarantee a game. Sometimes you can raise to game, or you may be able to bid 3NT. But on some hands the best game is unclear. It could be in partner's suit, it could be in one of your suits, or it could be in notrump. Perhaps you need partner to stop opener's suit. Perhaps you need partner to provide half a stopper in opener's suit. Perhaps you need to know if partner has a six-card suit. All sorts of questions to ask. Usually, when you have values for game and no clear route to explore, the correct action is a cuebid.

It would be logical to get into cuebids at this point, but there is a second common use for them which I wish to wait on. I have shown some examples of cuebids and will continue this discussion in a later chapter.

CHAPTER EIGHT
RAISING PARTNER'S OVERCALL WHEN RHO PASSES

ALERT #1
Before starting this chapter, I want to alert readers to the fact that this section is based on standard bidding. The methods shown here are widespread and fairly effective.

ALERT #2
In a later section, I will discuss a new structure that emphasizes many ways to raise your partner's major-suit overcall. There is some very new material and it will be valuable for you if you take a good look at it.

ALERT #3
This section deals with situations where partner overcalled in a major. When he bids 1♡ or 1♠ and you have a good hand with a fit, the usual issue is how high to go in the major. When partner overcalls in a minor, getting to notrump is a primary goal. Your bidding when partner overcalls in a major is definitely different from when he overcalls in a minor. I will discuss these situations separately for the most part.

YOUR TOOLS WHEN PARTNER OVERCALLS IN A MAJOR
When partner overcalls you will often want to raise, and depending on the auction you will have quite a few ways to do so. As there aren't enough generalities to cover first I'm going directly to the various sequences, which in turn will be broken down into:

1. Simple raises
2. Invitational or stronger raises – balanced hands – the simple cuebid
3. Invitational or stronger raises – distributional hands – the jump cuebid
4. Preemptive raises – the jump raise

The tools shown above will be discussed in this section. Note that in these discussions, sometimes RHO passes and sometimes he bids something. For now, the plan is to introduce you to these ideas in a plain, uncontested auction. Competitive bidding discussion will start shortly.

The Simple Raise

This is pretty much the same as the raise of an opening bid. The only difference is that your range changes slightly on both ends. Where you raise an opening bid on anywhere from 6 points to some 10-counts, you raise an overcall on some fives to some elevens. This range may seem excessive, but in practice it's not so bad. The main objection is that it makes game-bidding difficult, but when you are bidding defensively, game considerations are not as important. What is important is setting a firm foundation – that is, the trump suit – so your side can compete effectively.

The Preemptive Jump Raise

Even though this section discusses the simple raise, there will be hands that might qualify for a simple raise and also qualify for a preemptive jump raise. So I will define the preemptive jump raise at this time.

When your partner overcalls at the one- or two-level, a jump raise by you shows a weak hand. You promise four trumps, modest values in the 4-6 point range (along with some judgment), and some shape. You don't need a lot of shape but you should not make this bid on 4-3-3-3 hands. And, if you missed the early discussion, you never, ever make a jump raise with three trumps. I will discuss the preemptive raise later. The few hands in this section that qualify for a preemptive jump raise will be an introduction to this treatment. This treatment is one that you can use after a major-suit overcall as well as after a minor-suit overcall.

The following hands show a number of things you can do when partner overcalls and RHO passes.

Neither vul.

W	N	E	S
1♣	1♡	pass	?

♠ Q J 8 6 2
♡ K 8 7
◇ J 7 6
♣ 4 2

Bid 2♡. When you have good trumps and a major-suit fit as well, you should raise. Both 1♠ and pass would be poor.

Neither vul.

W	N	E	S
1♣	1♠	pass	?

♠ K J 8 7
♡ 3 2
♢ 10 8 6 5 2
♣ 8 7

Bid 3♠, preemptive. You have the classic requirements for this bid. You have four trumps, good ones in this case, shape, and a few points. If your partnership does not use preemptive jump raises here (it should), then at least raise to 2♠.

Neither vul.

W	N	E	S
1♣	1♡	pass	?

♠ 7 6 2
♡ K Q 8 2
♢ 8 7 3
♣ 9 6 2

Raise to 2♡. You have terrible shape but your values are sure to be welcome. Do not bid 3♡, weak, because you have 4-3-3-3 shape. Some players make jump raises with this hand but I disagree with that. Some players go the extra step and bid 3♡ without the ♡Q. Too rich for me.

Neither vul.

W	N	E	S
1♣	1♠	pass	?

♠ 8 6 2
♡ A Q 6 4 2
♢ 8 6 3 2
♣ 4

An easy raise to 2♠. Don't worry about partner having only four spades. Your hand will be good for him. 2♡ would be wrong.

N-S vul.

W	N	E	S
1♣	1♡	pass	?

♠ Q 10 2
♡ 8 6 2
♢ K J 8 3
♣ Q 5 4

It is reasonable to pass. You have three small hearts, which is adequate for a raise, but you have no shape and you have generally soft values. Another bid to avoid is 1NT. You should have a good 8-11 points for that bid. This is a poor 8. There is something you should be aware of. If your opponents are playing negative doubles (likely), RHO may have a heart stack and be hoping to double partner in 1♡. If you raise to 2♡, you will be playing into RHO's hands. If any of your values were improved, bidding 2♡ would be okay. It is just that this hand has only bad features and has nothing obvious to offer.

N-S vul.

W	N	E	S
1♣	1♠	pass	?

♠ Q 10 2
♡ 8 6 2
◇ K J 8 3
♣ Q 5 4

This is the same hand as the previous one except that partner's overcall is 1♠. Raise to 2♠. Good trump support makes up for the lack of other values. It is a common error for people to pass on this and other minimum hands. The effect of such inaction is that you lose much of the benefit of partner's having overcalled. Opener can now rebid easily if he wants to and nothing will have been gained.

Neither vul.

W	N	E	S
1♣	1♠	pass	?

♠ Q 8 3
♡ A Q 8 7
◇ Q 8 2
♣ 5 4 2

Raise to 2♠. This is about as much as you can have for a raise. If you had more, say add the ♠J, you would use one of your stronger raises. In this case the bid would be 2♣, a cuebid.

Both vul.

W	N	E	S
1♣	1♠	pass	?

♠ 9 8 7
♡ K J 3
◇ K Q 8 3
♣ Q 4 2

You wouldn't be wrong to bid only 2♠ with this hand, either. In spite of 11 HCP, the hand is not worth that much. Bad trumps and bad distribution. If you choose 1NT instead, that is probably okay.

Neither vul.

W	N	E	S
1♣	1♠	pass	?

♠ K Q J 4
♡ Q 8 7
◇ J 8 2
♣ Q 4 2

Again, bid 2♠. It is important to give partner a little room on these balanced pieces of garbage. These hands with odds and ends are not nearly as good as they look. This hand has a marginal ♣Q and the ♠J is probably not needed at all. Additionally, your ♡Q and your ◇J are only 'maybe' values. There are two areas where people frequently err. They overbid hands like this one and underbid other hands. This hand has 11 points but the shape is terrible and the actual high cards are lousy. Here is a typical North hand that shows the result of overbidding this hand to 3♠ or higher.

♠ A 10 9 7 3   ♡ A 4 3   ◇ 10 4 3   ♣ K 7

Partner has a normal 1♠ overcall but even 2♠ is not cold. There could be two hearts, three diamonds, and a club to lose. Raising too high for the wrong reasons of this kind is common.

INVITATIONAL RAISES — BALANCED HANDS — THE SIMPLE CUEBID

There will be some hands where you can hope to make a game, and the time-honored way to express this hope was to give a jump raise. The problem was that when partner had a minimum overcall, getting to the three-level was too high. Results like this one occurred all the time.

LHO	Partner	RHO	You
1♡	1♠	pass	3♠

♠Q42 ♡A865 ◇KJ87 ♣Q10

LHO opened 1♡, your partner bid 1♠, and you raised to 3♠. Partner passed and didn't make it. Partner had a 10-count and he had normal shape. It just wasn't enough. Worse, the opponents turned out to have nothing their way so your leap turned a plus score into a minus score.

Here is the modern method of handing hands with support for partner. It actually works well and is pretty much a mandatory part of a good bidding structure.

When you have a balanced limit raise the correct approach is to make a cuebid, suggesting you have a limit raise or better and a balanced hand. Your partner will bid with the awareness that you have support values but do not have a nice playing hand.

You will always be able to do this (if RHO passes) when partner overcalls at the one-level, two-level or three-level.

You may be wondering why I'm recommending a cuebid to show a good raise when I've already recommended a cuebid to show a game force with a new suit. It turns out you can do both. In this section are a number of examples showing the difference between a cuebid raise and a jump raise. In a subsequent section I'll go into how partner should respond to your cuebid.

Here are some example hands:

Neither vul.

W	N	E	S
1♣	1♠	pass	?

♠ J87
♡ 32
◇ KQ4
♣ A10976

2♣. If partner has any sort of maximum you'll make a game. When you bid 2♣ your partner will expect you to have a limit raise or better with three trumps, or with four trumps and hopeless distribution. This hand has three trumps and it has quality points plus some shape. If partner rebids 2♠ it says he has a minimum, and you will pass.

Neither vul.

W	N	E	S
1♣	1♡	pass	?

♠ K 8 6
♡ Q J 7 6
◇ K J 7
♣ Q J 7

With balanced distribution, you would prefer not to get overboard if possible. Try 2♣. If partner has a dog you will be able to stop in 2♡.

Both vul.

W	N	E	S
1♣	1♠	pass	?

♠ Q 10 7
♡ 8
◇ A K J 7 6
♣ J 9 7 4

Bid 2♣. This is a nice hand with good points and a singleton. The reason you are content to cuebid and possibly play in 2♠ is that you have just three trumps. The difference between having three-card support and four-card support often turns out to make a difference of one or two tricks. Do not lose sight of this. I am sure you have played many hands which fell apart due to insufficient trumps. If your side has a five-three fit, it will often hurt when trumps divide four-one. When you have a 5-4 fit you will seldom be run out of trumps.

Neither vul.

W	N	E	S
1◇	1♡	pass	?

♠ K J
♡ Q J 7 6 5
◇ K 8 5
♣ Q J 7

2◇. This time you have poor distribution, notwithstanding your five-card trump support. If you had a doubleton in one of the minors you would make a different bid. There is something called the Law of Total Tricks that tells you to bid 4♡ with this hand. With lousy shape, you should lean to being more conservative. If your partner has a crummy overcall, 2♡ may be your limit.

Note that without the cuebid you would have no choice but to jump-raise on your 11- or 12-point hands.

Neither vul.

W	N	E	S
1♣	1◇	pass	?

♠ K 3
♡ K 6 2
◇ A Q 8 6
♣ 8 6 5 4

Cuebid 2♣. When your partner bids diamonds, you still want to show the kind of raise you have. Note that 3NT is a possibility, something that does not exist when you are raising partner's major-suit overcalls.

Neither vul.

W	N	E	S
1◇	1♡	pass	2◇
pass	2♡	pass	?

♠ K 5 4
♡ J 10 4
◇ A 8 7
♣ K Q 7 4

Your partner overcalled 1♡ and you made a cuebid showing (usually) that you have heart support. When he rebid 2♡, he said he has a minimum hand. Should you raise? This is a function of your partnership style of overcalls. If your overcalls tend to be solid hands, you can raise to 3♡. If your partnership likes to overcall aggressively, you should just pass 2♡. Under no circumstances should you bid game with this.

INVITATIONAL RAISES – DISTRIBUTIONAL HANDS – THE JUMP CUEBID

When partner overcalls you will sometimes have a good, balanced hand, and sometimes a nice, shapely hand with support. Given that both of these types of hands will wish to invite, you need a way to tell partner which kind of hand you have. This section introduces a bid that was not around a few years ago. You have seen that the cuebid can be used to good effect. Some smart person observed that there is another cuebid available. Take this sequence.

LHO	Partner	RHO	You
		1♣	1♠
pass	3♣	pass	?

What do you think 3♣ means? Have you ever heard this sequence before? I am suggesting an excellent meaning for this jump cuebid. Play that it shows a limit raise or better with four trumps and some shape. Here are some hands. Note the difference in flavor of the jump cuebid and the simple cuebid that was discussed earlier.

Neither vul.

W	N	E	S
1◇	1♡	pass	?

♠ A 8 7 4 3
♡ K 10 8 3
◇ 9 2
♣ K 3

Bid 3◇. The jump cuebid says you have a limit raise with four trumps and shape. You may turn out to have game values and if so, you will get the partnership to game. But at this moment your partner thinks you have a hand like this one. Note that this discussion is about sequences where RHO passes. I will discuss competitive auctions shortly.

Neither vul.

W	N	E	S
1♣	1♠	pass	?

♠ K J 4 3
♡ K 4
◇ A K 6 4 3
♣ 8 7

Bid 3♣. You have enough to go to game but first you need to let partner know the nature of your hand. There are a couple of reasons for bidding 3♣ before bidding game. You may have a slam. It is unlikely, but possible. If you jump to 4♠ in response to 1♠, your partner will expect a preemptive hand. The second reason is that in the unlikely event that opener bids again, your partner needs to know what kind of hand you have for your bidding. If you show a good hand with support and shape, it will help your partner if he has to make more decisions.

Neither vul.

W	N	E	S
1♣	1◇	pass	?

♠ 9 8 7 4
♡ A 8 2
◇ A Q 8 7 4
♣ 3

Bid 3♣. The jump cuebid after partner's 1◇ overcall shows a good diamond raise with shape. If partner signs off in 3◇ you should respect that and pass. But if he has extras, knowing of your guaranteed long diamond support and good distribution, he may be able to continue on hands that would have given up had you just cuebid 2♣.

Neither vul.

W	N	E	S
1◇	1♡	pass	?

♠ A K 8 7 4
♡ K Q 8 7
◇ 3
♣ Q 10 7

This hand shows one more bidding trick. Bid 4◇. This is a splinter bid, telling partner that you insist on being in game and that you have four-card support or better along with a singleton in their suit, in this case, diamonds. Partner may be able to go on to a slam after this bid. These might be the combined hands.

♠ 9   ♠ A K 8 7 4
♡ A J 9 5 4 3   ♡ K Q 8 7
◇ J 6 5   ◇ 3
♣ A K 2   ♣ Q 10 7

Slam is cold on this layout. In fact, it would be cold (probably) if you did not have the ♡Q and the ♠K. The splinter bid did the trick, describing just about everything you have in one bid. If you had jumped to 4♡ partner would pass, expecting some kind of preemptive hand.

PREEMPTIVE RAISES

I introduced preemptive raises earlier in the discussion of simple raises. The definition of a preemptive raise is four or more trumps, 4-7 HCP (roughly speaking), and some shape. No 4-3-3-3 hands for this bid. It isn't that you won't get away with jump-raising on 4-3-3-3 hands. You may succeed on occasion. The big trouble comes when your partner bids again and discovers that you have nothing but losers and no ruffing values at all. Some examples follow.

Neither vul.

W	N	E	S
1♣	1◊	pass	?

♠ 87
♡ A875
◇ 108743
♣ J8

Raise to 3◊. Don't worry that you have four hearts. Your partner did not look for a major, and even if he has four hearts it is not likely you have a good contract there unless he can bid over 3◊. You are hoping your bid keeps them from finding spades. It is also possible that your side can make something in diamonds, and in any event, your bid informs partner of your hand type.

Neither vul.

W	N	E	S
1◊	1♠	pass	?

♠ KQ8
♡ 3
◇ 87543
♣ 8632

Raise to 2♠. Do not make weak jump raises with three trumps. When you have only three trumps the defenders can often lead trump, killing most of your ruffing tricks. If you have four trumps, as your partner will be expecting, you can't be denied getting some ruffs.

Neither vul.

W	N	E	S
1♡	1♠	pass	?

♠ AQ874
♡ 107653
◇ Q8
♣ 8

Do not bid 3♠. This hand is too good. You have to guess between 3♡, showing a limit raise with shape, or 4♠, a preemptive raise. Neither bid is accurate but both are better than a weak raise to 3♠. I would choose 4♠.

E-W vul.

W	N	E	S
1♡	2◊	pass	?

♠ J 8 7
♡ 8
◊ Q 9 8 7 2
♣ J 10 7 3

The best bid is probably 4◊, a weak raise showing four or more trumps. You might even bid 5◊. You will discover that you can use weak jump raises very effectively after one-level overcalls and after two-level overcalls. Not bidding at least 4◊ with this hand is a serious omission.

Neither vul.

W	N	E	S
1♡	1♠	pass	?

♠ 10 8 7 5 3
♡ 4
◊ K J 8 7 4
♣ J 10

Bid 4♠. The jump to game is weak, just as it is when you raise partner's opening 1♠ bid to game. You hope he can make it but you would not be surprised if he goes down. In the meantime, you are worried that they have something their way.

GAME FORCING RAISES WITH A FIT

When you have a fit for partner with game values, you can take a straightforward approach and jump to game or you can describe your hand so partner will know what to do in case there is more bidding, or in case he has an extra good hand. If you are sure there is no slam, jumping to game does have the advantage of cutting down on competitive bidding. Both the fast approach and the cuebid approach have merits.

N-S vul.

W	N	E	S
1◊	1♠	pass	?

♠ K J 7
♡ A Q 8 7 3
◊ A J 7
♣ 8 4

Bid 2◊, a cuebid. Usually you have support for partner's suit when you cuebid. With this hand you intend to go to game no matter what partner bids but by cuebidding first, you keep him in the picture. As a practical matter, raising to 4♠ right away with a hand like this is not likely to cause a problem but sometimes something funny happens. Say you bid 4♠ and opener bids 5♣. Your partner will think you have a weak hand and won't know what to do. You won't be so sure yourself. Had you cuebid first and then raised to 4♠, your partnership would be on firmer grounds. Admittedly, it is very unlikely that opener can bid over 4♠. Against that, if you cuebid, opener may be able to show a club suit and now they may find a fit that they would not have found if you had bid 4♠ instead of cuebidding.

Neither vul.

W	N	E	S
1♡	1♠	pass	3♡
pass	3♠	pass	?

♠ J 10 8 3
♡ A 8 7 4 3
◇ 3 2
♣ A K

Go ahead and raise to 4♠. You started by showing a shapely limit raise or better and this is one of the better-type hands. There are too many minimum overcalls that will make a game facing this hand.

Neither vul.

W	N	E	S
1♣	1♡	pass	?

♠ A 4 2
♡ K J 7 6
◇ A Q 8 3
♣ 4 2

Another case where bidding game rates to keep opener out of the bidding. If you think your side might have a slam you can cuebid, which might allow slam to be reached. Just be aware that if you bid 4♡ with this hand and also bid 4♡ with ♡KJxxx, a singleton, and nothing else, your partner will not know when, if ever, he should bid again. There is some cat-and-mouse to this situation. My choice on this one is to cuebid, which will bring partner's opinion into play if they keep bidding.

Neither vul.

W	N	E	S
1♣	1♡	pass	?

♠ A J 3
♡ Q 6 5
◇ K Q J 7 3
♣ J 8

2♣. You have game values, but 3NT could be your game. The cuebid will help you find out.

Neither vul.

W	N	E	S
1♣	1♠	pass	?

♠ K Q 10 7
♡ A K 8 7 6 5
◇ 4
♣ Q 3

Here you know you have a game, but slam is possible opposite two black aces. Or opposite two aces and a stiff club. Or two aces and the ♣K. I don't know how the auction will progress, but 2♣ is the way to start with this hand. With slam potential clearly there, it is right to go slow. One bid that comes to mind is 4◇, if it would be understood to show a game raise in spades with a singleton diamond. This bid would give an understanding partnership a chance to reach slam.

CHAPTER NINE
RAISING PARTNER'S OVERCALL WHEN RHO BIDS

This chapter does a lot of things that add to the previous chapter. In chapter eight I discussed raising partner's one-level overcall after a pass from RHO. In this chapter I will look at situations where your partner overcalls and your RHO does something.

Here is a list of the things that RHO can do.

1. RHO makes a negative double.
2. RHO bids a new suit at the one-level.
3. RHO bids 1NT showing 7-10 points with a stopper in your partner's suit.
4. RHO bids a suit at the two- or three-level.
5. RHO raises.
6. RHO makes a cuebid of your partner's suit.

Since there are so many things you can do, I will just touch on each case using principles already discussed.

The list of points made in these hands does not contain much new. I will show you some new stuff in the later section on modern methods.

Here is a list of the meanings of bids that are now available to you.

LHO	Partner	RHO	You
1♣	1♡	1♠	?

Pass   Nothing to show.

Dbl   Snapdragon, showing a heart tolerance and a biddable diamond suit.

Dbl   Rosenkranz, used to show a raise in hearts with or without an honor. This will be discussed briefly later.

2♣   Cuebid, as before, showing 11 or more balanced points with support.

2♢   New suit, not forcing.

2♡   Normal raise, usually with three trumps. You might have a few shapeless hands with four trumps, too.

2♠   Natural showing a six-card suit with nice spot cards. An odd bid. Probably won't come up. Discuss this one with partner.

2NT   Natural, showing 12 or 13 balanced points. In practice you won't do this very often. In the modern methods section I will show you a better use for this 2NT bid.

3♣   The jump cuebid, as usual, shows a limit raise with four trumps and shape.

3◇   Invitational jump shift.

3♡   A preemptive raise showing 4-7 points. You need to use judgment with this bid.

CASE ONE:
PARTNER OVERCALLS AT THE ONE-LEVEL,
RHO MAKES A NEGATIVE DOUBLE

You can use all of your tools here. In addition, you have another useful bid. Use redouble to show 10 or more points, exactly two of partner's suit, and no other bid that appeals. This bid helps your partner compete and it also opens up the chance that your side can double them for penalty.

Neither vul.

W	N	E	S
1◇	1♠	dbl	?

♠ J 8
♡ K J 8 7
◇ A 9 7 5 3
♣ Q 8

Redouble. You show 10 or more good high-card points and exactly two spades, partner's suit. If you had a third spade you would cuebid 2◇ instead of redoubling. The redouble denies three spades so if you later support spades, partner will know how many you have.

Neither vul.

W	N	E	S
1◇	1♠	dbl	?

♠ Q J 8 3
♡ 7 2
◇ 10 7 5 3
♣ A J 4

Bid 3◇. This jump cuebid shows a limit raise with four-card support. This may seem like a stretch and it is. Your other choices are to raise to 2♠, which would be an underbid, and to bid 3♠, a preemptive raise. This hand is not easy.

Neither vul.

W	N	E	S
1◇	1♠	dbl	?

♠ Q 8 4
♡ K 4 2
◇ 8 7 4
♣ K 7 5 2

Raise to 2♠. The simple raise shows three trumps much of the time, with values like these. If you have four trumps you tend to have a boring hand with either soft values or bad distribution.

Neither vul.	
W **N** **E** **S**	
1◇ 1♠ dbl ?	

♠ 9 5 4 3
♡ K 5 4
◇ Q 10 4
♣ K 8 4

Raise to 2♠ with this hand, too. You have four trumps but your shape is bad and you don't really like your hand enough that you want to go to the three-level or hear partner go to the three-level.

Neither vul.	
W **N** **E** **S**	
1◇ 1♠ dbl ?	

♠ K 8 4 3
♡ 9 3
◇ 8 4
♣ 10 9 7 4 2

Bid 3♠. As you may recall, I suggest that when you make a preemptive raise you have a little something. Some players will jump to 3♠ with nothing. In competition, it is acceptable to bid 3♠ with a little less than when your RHO passes.

CASE TWO:
PARTNER OVERCALLS AT THE ONE-LEVEL,
RHO BIDS ONE OF A NEW SUIT

This situation is treated almost the same as if RHO had passed. You have slightly more information to use in deciding on your bid, but the meanings are the same.

Neither vul.	
W **N** **E** **S**	
1◇ 1♡ 1♠ ?	

♠ Q J 8 4
♡ 7 2
◇ K J 3
♣ Q 8 7 3

Pass is probably best. You might bid 1NT, but given RHO has made a free bid that shows he is not broke, you suspect your partner has a minimum overcall. There is no need to get involved. When your partner overcalls, you fight to raise if you have a fit and you bid a new suit if you think it is a possible home, but when all you have is some scattered points it is not necessary to argue. Imagine that your partner has a normal 10-point hand. Where are your tricks coming from? Your diamonds are not necessarily useful given LHO's diamond bid and your hearts won't help much facing a typical suit such as ♡KQ953. You would be happier if you had a little heart help, like ♡Q4 or similar.

Neither vul.

W	N	E	S
1◇	1♡	1♠	?

♠ A9753
♡ J1074
◇ 73
♣ Q7

Using the methods I have shown so far, this is a difficult hand. 2♡ feels inadequate. 2◇, a cuebid, would be an overbid. 3♡, preemptive, is also off the mark since you have some real values. 3◇, the second cuebid, would promise even more. For now there is no accurate bid. I would choose 3♡ but nothing feels good. In the later chapter on modern methods I will introduce a method that handles hands like this one and gives you more tools in general.

Neither vul.

W	N	E	S
1◇	1♡	1♠	?

♠ KJ8
♡ Q2
◇ A10763
♣ QJ2

Firstly, let me say that you will rarely have this good a hand. Opener has 12 or more points. Your partner has at least 9. RHO ought to have 6. And any of the other three players can have just 1 or 2 more points. Theoretically you might have 13 points but in reality, it won't happen. If you do get this hand, beating all expectations, you still have to find a call. One choice is 2NT. Another is a cuebid, lying about the heart support. A conservative but probably winning call is just 1NT. Really a frustrating hand. My guess? I will opt for the big underbid of 1NT.

Neither vul.

W	N	E	S
1◇	1♡	1♠	?

♠ QJ9874
♡ 3
◇ A742
♣ 108

In the discussion about various bids, I suggested you might wish to play a cuebid of your RHO's suit as natural. On this auction, RHO bid 1♠. If he is known to have five spades you should probably pass this hand, but if he can have four of them a 2♠ bid can be used as natural, showing a hand like this one. This bid rates to be very effective. LHO will have trouble describing his hand after this bid. Note that even if RHO has five spades, your knowing in advance will help you in the play. Do not make this bid without good spade spots. Also, be sure you discuss this with partner. If he thinks you are showing support for hearts the bidding will get lost.

CASE THREE:
PARTNER OVERCALLS AT THE ONE-LEVEL, RHO BIDS 1NT

This sequence demands a touch of caution. RHO has shown moderate values and, of more importance, he has a stopper or more in partner's suit. This means you shouldn't be raising on some of the minimum hands, and especially not those with three small trumps.

Neither vul.

W	N	E	S
1♣	1♠	1NT	?

♠ 872
♡ K8654
◇ KJ3
♣ 42

Best to pass. Minimum and poor trumps. While it is true that 2♠ could work out, it is tempting fate. When your side overcalls aggressively you give the opponents problems. Here, RHO seems to have solved the problem. There is no need to continue putting pressure on the opponents when they have completed a satisfactory description of their values. After RHO bids 1NT you should be raising when you *expect* to have a play for the contract, not when you *hope* to have a play for it. When RHO bids 1NT, a raise by you will be doubled whenever you are too high. It is one of the easiest auctions for the opponents to clip their coupons when you get out of line.

Neither vul.

W	N	E	S
1◇	1♡	1NT	?

♠ 87
♡ 10654
◇ A87
♣ Q654

Bid 2♡. You have a moderate playing hand with a fourth trump. There is almost no hand where partner will be bidding toward game and he's not too likely to be competing for a partscore unless he has something extra. Partner knows the trump suit will be offside and his bidding will take that into consideration.

N-S vul.

W	N	E	S
1♡	1♠	1NT	?

♠ KJ87
♡ 8
◇ 7642
♣ 9632

2♠. Good trumps plus good distribution means anything goes. RHO probably has something like ♠Q103 and will be disappointed when he takes no trump tricks. Only when you have exceptional trumps such as these can you expect to negate RHO's holding. Note that if RHO had done something else, like raise to 2♡, you would have bid 3♠, preemptive.

E-W vul.

W	N	E	S
1♣	1♠	1NT?	

♠ Q8654
♡ KQ3
◇ A76
♣ 106

In spite of your good hand a raise to 2♠ is sufficient. Game prospects are dim. One alternative is to double, but a general rule in bridge is to take the path of least resistance. You have a safe partscore and a speculative double. Perhaps some people didn't overcall with your partner's hand. If this is the case, you will be in the auction on hands where others did not compete. I said that game was unlikely. Almost *a priori*, when the bidding goes something like the example auction you will never have a game on the basis of high cards. Game will succeed as the result of distribution and working cards. This hand has good HCP, but in spite of the fifth spade the distribution is somewhat pedestrian.

Neither vul.

W	N	E	S
1♣	1♠	1NT?	

♠ 963
♡ AK432
◇ 7653
♣ 4

Three small for a raise should be avoided on this auction. The rest of this hand is so good, though, that you can raise to 2♠. Everything is working overtime. Even the opening lead will be in your favor. RHO will lead a club, which is exactly what you would have asked him to lead had it been possible.

Neither vul.

W	N	E	S
1♣	1♠	1NT?	

♠ K4
♡ J1097652
◇ Q987
♣ —

Bid 3♡. The issue here is what 3♡ should mean. When RHO makes a weak bid over your partner's bid, a jump shows an invitational hand. If RHO bids 1NT or makes a 2/1 bid, a jump in a new suit shows a preemptive hand. The bids by RHO that are classified as weak are pass, a negative double, one of a new suit, and a raise. If RHO had made one of these bids, your jump would be invitational.

Neither vul.

W	N	E	S
1◇	1♠	1NT?	

♠ 4
♡ AJ9853
◇ 983
♣ K74

Bid 2♡. A new suit is mildly forward-going in that you hope to make your bid. It does not force partner to bid.

Neither vul.

W	N	E	S
1◇	1♠	1NT	?

♠ 8 3
♡ K Q 7 5 4
◇ Q J 4 3
♣ K 9

Pass. LHO has an opening bid, RHO has 9 points, you have 11 points. Your partner has a minimum overcall. RHO says he has a spade stopper and he may have two. I can tell you that one of the hardest things to do is to double that 1NT bid and then set it. Accept that they have their values and then realize that their values are probably better placed than your values. If you double and they make it, your partner will get gun-shy about making aggressive bids. Do not discourage him. If they go down, be happy with that.

Neither vul.

W	N	E	S
1♣	1♡	1NT	?

♠ A 8 7 6 5 4
♡ J 8 4 3
◇ 3
♣ 4 2

3♡ is just about right. Four fair trumps, excellent shape, and useful high cards. If you bid 2♡ they will surely keep bidding. If you bid 3♡ they will have a tougher time of it.

Both vul.

W	N	E	S
1♣	1♠	1NT	?

♠ J 10 6 5 4
♡ A J 4
◇ 7
♣ 8 5 4 3

3♠. You would bid 4♠ normally, but after RHO's 1NT bid that would be excessive. This is the sort of hand where 4♠ could depend on a spade finesse for the king. But the auction has told you that won't work.

N-S vul.

W	N	E	S
1♣	1♠	1NT	?

♠ K J 8 7
♡ A 4 2
◇ K J 8 7
♣ Q 3

This hand does not exist. Someone is playing games with you, probably LHO. No way can everyone have his bid. I suggest bidding 4♠, although making a cuebid might be best. Be sure you reach game.

In practice, when the bidding starts 1♣–1♠–1NT, any leap to game by you will usually be dependent on shape and trumps, unlike the previous hand, which is close to being a fantasy. Your hand will normally be along the lines of these four examples.

Hand One	Hand Two
♠ 8 6 5 4 2	♠ K 10 6 5
♡ A 10 6 5 4 3	♡ A J 8 6 5 4
◇ 7	◇ 7 4
♣ 6	♣ 6

Hand Three	Hand Four
♠ K J 6 5 4	♠ J 9 5 4
♡ K 2	♡ 3
◇ 8 6 5 4 3 2	◇ 4
♣ —	♣ A J 9 7 5 4 2

CASE FOUR:
PARTNER OVERCALLS AT THE ONE-LEVEL, RHO BIDS A NEW SUIT AT THE TWO- OR THREE-LEVEL

You have seen warnings throughout this book about the dangers of bidding when they make a 2/1 response. Those dangers exist here as well.

LHO	Partner	RHO	You
1♡	1♠	2♣	?

If you have a fair hand, you can tell that your partner has a minimum hand. If you play the hand you will be outgunned in high cards. Your source of tricks, if any, will come from trumps and distribution. If you and your partner have balanced hands you will lose a lot of side tricks and will go down in flames. To combat a 2/1 sequence you need to have shape that will allow your trumps to work.

Here is a list of possible bids you can make. Some show support, some show a suit. Some show weak hands. It is important to show partner what you are fighting with. After the sequence above, your options include:

Pass Nothing to show. Do not forget this bid.

2◇ A new suit. It does not promise much; just a competitive bid with a fair suit.

2♡ A cuebid. You won't have this bid on this sequence.

2♠	Just a raise but with useful values. After a 2/1 bid, you should not waste your time raising with boring hands and only three ordinary trumps.
2NT	This bid does not exist. At least not yet. More on this later.
3♣	A cuebid. Again, you won't have any use for this cuebid.
3◇	A jump in a new suit after a 2/1 shows a preemptive hand with a long suit, usually seven cards like QJ108532.
3♠	The jump raise is always preemptive. Do not be foolish, though, when the opponents have shown strong hands. You can bid this with weak hands but they must have good trumps and shape.

CASE FIVE:
PARTNER OVERCALLS AT THE ONE-LEVEL,
RHO RAISES OPENER'S SUIT

When partner overcalls and RHO makes a 2/1, you should feel constrained to be very careful. When partner overcalls and RHO raises opener, you should feel free and empowered. The sky is the limit in terms of what you are allowed to do.

What important bidding tool do you lose when partner overcalls and RHO raises to the two-level?

When RHO raises it is not a threatening bid, but it does take away some of your bidding room. Barring extreme science, you will have this problem. Say you have this auction.

LHO	Partner	RHO	You
1♣	1♡	2♣	?

That innocuous 2♣ bid took away your 2♣ cuebid. That cuebid would have been nice for those ordinary 11- or 12-point hands that have support but nothing much in shape. When they bid 2♣, you would like to find a way to show which kind of limit raise you have; with shape or balanced. Frankly, there is no easy solution and I am going to suggest that for now, you just cuebid and hope it works out.

There is a bid that I will show you in the modern methods chapter that is a partial solution but for now, the cuebid is the answer.

Note that one of your new tools will be the responsive double. I have not discussed it yet but will show a few examples which touch on it. Consider its inclusion in these hands as an introduction to it.

Both vul.

W	N	E	S
1♡	1♠	2♡	?

♠ 4
♡ 8 4
◇ Q J 8 7 3
♣ A Q 10 5 3

Double. This hand is an introduction to the responsive double. It is often used on sequences where your partner bids and they raise. In essence, if your partner doubles for takeout or overcalls and they raise, a double by you asks partner to bid as follows.

If he has made a takeout double of a major, a double by you asks for the minors.

If he has made a takeout double of a minor, a double by you asks for the majors.

If he overcalls and they raise, a double by you asks for the unbid suits.

This hand has 5-5 in the unbid suits and decent values. You are asking partner to pick one of the two unbid suits. Be aware that he is likely not to have a four-card suit on the side so you do need good suits to make this bid. More on the convention, along with lots of example hands, later.

Both vul.

W	N	E	S
1♡	1♠	2♡	?

♠ A K 7 4
♡ 7 3
◇ 9 8 7 3
♣ 10 8 3

Bid 2♠. This is a difficult hand since you have lots of nice things. 2♠ is an underbid. 3♠ is preemptive. And you do not have enough for a cuebid. Later in the section on modern bidding I will show you a new convention that helps with a hand like this.

Both vul.

W	N	E	S
1♡	1♠	2♡	?

♠ Q 10 8
♡ J 8 4 3
◇ K Q 3
♣ K J 4

If RHO had passed you would have bid 2♡ yourself, saying you have (probably) a limit spade raise with balanced values. RHO got there first and you do not have the same options as before. There are three things you can try.

You can raise to 2♠ and hope there is no game. Actually, in practice this is not a bad idea.

If you are enamored of your hand you can cuebid 3♡, which says you have a limit raise. On this auction you can't tell partner you have shape or a balanced hand.

There is an optional treatment you can use with care. You can double, asking partner to show a minor suit, after which you will bid 3♠, telling partner you have a balanced limit raise. By using the cuebid to show a shape limit raise and the responsive double to show a balanced limit raise, your partner gets in on the news in time to use it. This responsive double sequence followed by support is generally used only after RHO raises.

Both vul.

W	N	E	S
1◇	1♠	2◇	?

♠ 8 3
♡ Q J 6 4 3
◇ Q 8 4
♣ J 3 2

Pass. Nothing to say. You can have a wide assortment of hands ranging from a zero-count up to a 9-count with no convenient bid.

Both vul.

W	N	E	S
1◇	1♠	2◇	?

♠ 5
♡ K 10 8 7 5 3
◇ 9 4 3
♣ A J 5

2♡. A new suit. Not forcing, but not hopeless either.

Both vul.

W	N	E	S
1◇	1♠	2◇	?

♠ J 4 3
♡ A 7 4
◇ Q 8 4
♣ Q 9 6 4

2♠. The raise says that you have three trumps or an uninspiring hand with four trumps. Your range is 5-9 points. Partner is welcome to bid again but he should not expect a 'good' hand.

Both vul.

W	N	E	S
1◇	1♠	2◇	?

♠ 10 9 7 3
♡ A 8
◇ 9 7
♣ K 10 7 4 3

2♠. Sadly, this hand and the previous hand are 2♠ bids. But look at the differences. This hand has quality points and shape and four trumps. Surely it is better than the previous hand. I will show you a way to differentiate between these two hands in a later chapter on modern methods.

Both vul.

W	N	E	S
1◇	1♠	2◇	?

♠ 8 3
♡ K 3
◇ 8 5 4
♣ A Q 10 8 7 6

Bid 3♣. Not forcing, but something to show. Since you are at the three-level, you owe partner a bit more than if you were able to bid at the two-level.

Both vul.

W N E S
1◇ 1♠ 2◇ ?

Bid 3◇. The cuebid after RHO raises is ambiguous. It shows limit or better values but it does not say if you have shape or just a balanced hand with points.

♠ Q954
♡ A10975
◇ 73
♣ A7

Both vul.

W N E S
1◇ 1♠ 2◇ ?

Bid 3◇ with this one, too. Not perfect at all since partner won't know if you have this hand or the previous hand.

♠ A95
♡ KQJ
◇ 874
♣ Q954

CASE SIX:
PARTNER OVERCALLS AT THE ONE-LEVEL,
RHO MAKES A CUEBID

RHO's cuebid can mean many things but the meaning most in use today is that RHO has a limit raise or better for his partner. Since there is an opening bid on your left and a good hand on your right, you won't have much to say. Still, there are one or two things you can do. Here they are.

Both vul.

W N E S
1♡ 1♠ 2♠¹ ?

1. Limit raise or better

Double. The double of RHO's cuebid says you would have raised to 2♠. Do not double with hopeless 5-7 point raises if you do not want your partner to keep bidding. He often will. This hand has four trumps, but three is just as likely.

♠ J432
♡ 843
◇ KQ
♣ J754

Both vul.

W N E S
1♡ 1♠ 2♠¹ ?

1. Limit raise or better

♠ K 10 8 7
♡ 8 6
◇ K Q 7 3
♣ 9 6 3

3♠. You don't have a way to show this hand and the next hand. This one has some values. I suggest you just bid 3♠, realizing that the hand belongs to them.

Both vul.

W N E S
1♡ 1♠ 2♠¹ ?

1. Limit raise or better

♠ K 8 7 4
♡ 8 7
◇ J 8 5 4 3
♣ 9 2

I would bid 3♠ with this hand, too. If my partner bids 4♠ he will almost surely be sacrificing, and that is okay. Look in the later chapter on modern methods for a way to distinguish between this hand and the previous hand.

Both vul.

W N E S
1♡ 1♠ 2♠¹ ?

1. Limit raise or better

♠ K 8 5 4 3
♡ 8
◇ Q J 7 6 4
♣ 8 3

Bid 4♠. Don't let yourself get immersed in precision science when the old-fashioned blunderbuss is available. Don't go slow when you know you are going to bid 4♠ no matter what. Let them decide where they are going. Note that their meaning for the cuebid is silly. Opener does not know if his partner has 10 or 11 points or a game hand. Opener will not be happy guessing what to do here.

When Partner Overcalls 1◇:
Partner Overcalls 1◇ and RHO Passes

When partner overcalls with 1◇ and RHO passes, things do not change much. You can bid a new suit. Nothing has changed here. You can bid notrump. Nothing has changed here. You can raise diamonds. You have the usual choices of how to do that.

Here are some examples of hands showing these methods.

Neither vul.

W	N	E	S
1♣	1◇	pass	?

♠ A J 8 7
♡ 8 3
◇ K 8 3
♣ 8 7 4 3

Raise to 2◇. No other bid makes sense. If your side can make something, your partner will continue.

Neither vul.

W	N	E	S
1♣	1◇	pass	?

♠ 9 8 5
♡ 7 4
◇ K Q 7 4
♣ J 10 8 3

Raise to 3◇, preemptive. You probably won't make it but it will help keep the auction to yourselves. If partner does continue, you don't mind since you have good diamonds.

Neither vul.

W	N	E	S
1♣	1◇	pass	?

♠ K 4
♡ A K J 4
◇ 10 9 8 4
♣ 8 6 3

Bid 2♣. The cuebid usually shows a balanced limit raise such as this. Note that if partner signs off, you will respect that. Also note that you would much prefer to reach game in notrump as opposed to game in diamonds.

Neither vul.

W	N	E	S
1♣	1◇	pass	?

♠ A 9 4
♡ A J
◇ K 8 7 6 4 3
♣ 9 4

Bid 2♣. Usually partner will rebid 2◇. Given the opening bid and your hand, there isn't a lot left for partner. If he does bid 2◇, you have to decide if your hand is worth another bid. Is it? If so, what should it be? My suggestion is to bid 3♣. The first cuebid showed a good diamond raise. The second cuebid shows extras and strongly implies interest in 3NT. Partner, if he has a club stop, should bid 3NT now unless he has absolutely no interest in it. Your hand should provide eight tricks. All you need is one more from partner.

Neither vul.

W	N	E	S
1♣	1◇	pass	?

♠ Q 8 4
♡ K 10 9 4
◇ Q 8 3
♣ A J 3

If your partner likes to overcall with lousy hands, cuebidding 2♣ and passing if partner bids 2◇ is probably okay. If your partner adheres to a sound 10-point minimum, bidding 2NT is acceptable. You would feel better about this if you had another point, though.

Neither vul.

W	N	E	S
1♣	1◇	pass	?

♠ 9 7 4 3
♡ A 8 4
◇ K Q 8 7 5
♣ 8

Bid 3♣. This shows a nice, shapely limit raise. You happen to have a singleton club. This is an accident. You do not promise any specific shape, just a nice limit raise with playing shape.

Neither vul.

W	N	E	S
1♣	1◇	pass	?

♠ 9 4
♡ J 10 9 8 5
◇ Q J 8 6 4
♣ 7

Bid 4◇. This bid is preemptive and shows a more extreme hand than a preemptive jump to 3◇. If you were vulnerable, you might want to have a tad more. Make the diamonds KJ864 and 4◇ feels about right.

Neither vul.

W	N	E	S
1♣	1◇	pass	?

♠ A 4 3
♡ Q 10 8 7 6
◇ K
♣ J 8 7 5

Bid 1♡. You are making a mildly constructive bid. This is not an escape.

Neither vul.

W	N	E	S
1♣	1◇	pass	?

♠ K 10 8 7 4 3
♡ 10 7 5 3
◇ 3
♣ J 8

Pass. Perhaps you can back into spades later. If you bid 1♠ your partner will be entitled to expect more. Add the ♡K to your hand and 1♠ would be okay.

PARTNER OVERCALLS 1◇ AND RHO BIDS SOMETHING

You have choices here which include passing, raising, bidding a new suit, doubling, bidding notrump, and cuebidding. Here are some examples of bidding when RHO raises.

LHO	Partner	RHO	You
1♣	1◇	2♣	?

You can do some things as before, but that raise takes away some of your tools.

2NT shows eleven or twelve balanced points with clubs stopped. I can virtually guarantee that you won't have the right hand for this bid. You may have noticed that bidding 2NT in response to an overcall is rare, especially when RHO bids something.

A raise to 2◇ shows normal values for a raise.

A raise to 3◇ shows a weak hand.

Two of a major is natural and not forcing.

3♣ shows a limit raise or better and does not promise shape or a balanced hand. The raise hurts you in this regard.

You do have a responsive double to show both majors. You might wish to say that a double followed by a diamond raise shows a balanced hand, which means a cuebid implies a shapely hand.

Using this scheme of things, your bidding will be something like this.

Neither vul.

W	N	E	S
1♣	1◇	2♣	?

♠ K 4 3
♡ A 8 7 4
◇ Q 10 6 4
♣ 7 4

An irritating hand. 2◇ is probably right but it leaves you with a feeling that you are missing something. 3◇ is preemptive, which means your partner won't know you have this much.

Neither vul.

W	N	E	S
1♣	1◇	2♣	?

♠ A K J
♡ 8 7
◇ K 9 7 5 3
♣ 8 5 3

Bid 3♣. You show a limit raise or better. Partner can't tell if you have shape or balanced points.

Neither vul.

W	N	E	S
1♣	1◇	2♣	?

♠ Q J 3
♡ K J 3
◇ A J 5 3
♣ 7 6 3

One solution is to double. Partner will think you have the majors. He usually bids 2♡ or 2♠. You will return to 3◇, which says you do not have the majors; you have a balanced limit diamond raise. Note that if you bid this way, you might have one major. If so, you accept the major and if not, you return to 3◇. Hands like ♠AK104 ♡94 ◇K874 ♣J54 are otherwise hard to bid.

A second solution is to bid 3♣, showing an unspecified limit raise.

WHEN BOTH OPPONENTS HAVE BID AT THE ONE-LEVEL BEFORE YOUR SIDE OVERCALLS

There is more to think about.

When opener passes

LHO	Partner	RHO	You
		1♣	pass
1♡	1♠	pass	?

You have a lot of tools to consider. Which ones should you use? As before, you have the case where opener passes and you have the case where opener rebids something. It may be a raise, a rebid of his original suit, it may be notrump, it may be a support double.

When opener passes (as in the above auction) you can use the basic method, using normal raises, preemptive raises, and 2♣ and 3♣ as your cuebids. You might think of bidding 2♡ or 3♡ but this is a bit esoteric so I won't delve into these bids.

When opener rebids his suit

LHO	Partner	RHO	You
		1♣	pass
1♡	1♠	2♣	?

When opener rebids his suit, you will find that you do not have as many tools as you need.

Double is penalty.

2◇ is one of those odd bids that makes your partner wonder why you did not overcall earlier. Here is a thought. If you could have bid this suit at the one-level, the reason you are bidding it now is to show a nice holding but you also are raising your partner.

2♡, a cuebid of responder's suit, shows your balanced limit raise for partner's spades.

2♠ is a normal raise.

2NT probably does not exist but if it comes up, it shows 11-13 notrump-type points. This bid is going to be the focus of the modern methods bidding section.

3♣, a cuebid of opener's suit, shows a limit raise with flavor and four or more trumps.

3♠ is preemptive.

When opener raises his partner

LHO	Partner	RHO	You
		1♣	pass
1♡	1♠	2♡	?

It gets a little sticky when opener raises. Here are some ideas.

2♠ is a normal raise.

2NT is a natural, non-forcing bid.

3♣ shows a limit raise with shape.

3♠ is preemptive.

This leaves you with a boring, balanced limit raise. How do you show that? You can do it in one of two ways. You can bid 3♣, which means that the cuebid shows all limit-raise hands. Or you can play that double shows the balanced limit-raise hand. I am inclined to play that double shows the balanced raise because it keeps the bidding at the two-level when partner has a minimum facing your balanced raise. Whatever you do, you must discuss these situations. Keep this one thing in mind. It is impossible, in the real world, to want to double 2♡ for penalty. There has to be a better meaning for double.

CHAPTER TEN
PARTNER OVERCALLS AT THE TWO-LEVEL

When partner overcalls at the two-level you have less room for exploration. You can make a single raise or a game raise, whereas after a one-level overcall you can raise to the two-level, three-level, or higher. Even with the inclusion of the cuebid, you still have fewer options. This means you have to give something up. In practice, a structure like the following works well.

A raise is mildly encouraging and a cuebid is highly encouraging. But whereas after a one-level overcall the cuebid showed a good, balanced raise, after a two-level overcall it shows a good raise but with no distributional requirements. It can be balanced *or* distributional. Note that because partner is bidding at the two-level and therefore promising a good hand, a 2NT bid by you is not that rare anymore.

When Partner Bids at the Two-level and RHO Passes

Neither vul.

W	N	E	S
1♠	2♡	pass	?

♠ Q 2
♡ A 4 3
◇ K J 4 2
♣ 8 7 5 4

Just about right for 3♡. You discount the ♠Q somewhat as being of dubious value. You would raise with or without it.

Neither vul.

W	N	E	S
1♠	2♡	pass	?

♠ 9 7 6 5 4
♡ 10 7 6
◇ A Q 4 2
♣ 7

3♡ again. After a two-level overcall, three small is not nearly as questionable support as after a one-level overcall.

N-S vul.			
W	N	E	S
1♠	2♦	pass	?

♠ 7 2
♡ A 4 3 2
♦ K Q 7
♣ Q 5 4 2

2♠. This is much too good for a simple raise. Note that 3NT is a possible contract.

N-S vul.			
W	N	E	S
1♠	2♡	pass	?

♠ 8 6 5 4
♡ A 6 5 2
♦ Q 10 7 6
♣ 5

Anything could be right. I do think this is too good for a simple raise to 3♡. I suggest going to 4♡.

N-S vul.			
W	N	E	S
1♦	2♣	pass	?

♠ Q 6 5 4 2
♡ 8 6
♦ A 7 3
♣ K 5 4

3♣. It would be a clear error to introduce spades. This hand is about as good as you will have for a raise.

Neither vul.			
W	N	E	S
1♦	2♣	pass	?

♠ 8
♡ A 8 4 2
♦ 10 6 5 4
♣ K 10 7 3

3♣. You would like to bid a little more. But if you cuebid and partner veers off into notrump, your hand will be a disappointment. If after 3♣ partner tries 3NT, you can be content.

Both vul.			
W	N	E	S
1♠	2♡	pass	?

♠ A 3
♡ J 7 5
♦ A 8 6 5 4 2
♣ 7 6

This is quite a good hand. Anything less than a direct 4♡ would be poor. 3♦ is terrible and runs the risk of inducing a pass from partner. 3♦ down one instead of 4♡ making would be a likely result. Not best. You have the values for a cuebid, but there is no reason to clutter up the auction when you know what the final contract should be.

Both vul.	This is an okay 2NT bid. The range is subject to your judgment.

Both vul.

W N E S
1♠ 2♡ pass ?

This is an okay 2NT bid. The range is subject to your judgment. With nothing much in hearts, you need a fair hand to suggest notrump.

♠ Q 8 7 4
♡ 9 7
◇ Q J 7
♣ A K J 2

Both vul.

W N E S
1♠ 2◇ pass ?

Bid 2NT with this hand, too. You have the very nice ◇KJ so you hope there are six tricks there. You are not sure where the last couple of tricks will come from but this hand is a good start.

♠ K 8 7 5
♡ A 8
◇ K J
♣ 10 8 7 4 3

When Partner Bids at the Two-level and RHO Raises

PARTNER OVERCALLS AT THE TWO-LEVEL IN A MAJOR, RHO RAISES

This is easy, sort of. The decisions themselves aren't easy, but that raise by RHO has taken away so much room that you don't have many options. Look at a typical auction.

LHO	Partner	RHO	You
1♠	2♡	2♠	?

Partner overcalled at the two-level, which shows a distinctly better hand than when he overcalls at the one-level. Given partner has a good hand for his two-level bids, you do not have to be as delicate in your bidding.

Here are my thoughts.

Given the bidding above, this is how you can respond to partner's 2♡ overcall.

2NT is unlikely to come up in the natural meaning. (See later discussion for more on this one.)

3♣ and 3◇ are new suits and are encouraging but not forcing.

3♡ is a normal raise of modest consequence. Your partner can continue but he should not expect too much.

4♡ is bid on many hands, including preemptive hands and ordinary limit raise hands.

3♠ is a cuebid for hearts. You are making this bid not so much to get to game, but to help partner know what to bid when they go on to 4♠. This bid will not come up very often.

Some Examples of Bidding After Partner's 2♡ Overcall and RHO's Raise to 2♠

Neither vul.

W	N	E	S
1♠	2♡	2♠	?

♠ J 4 2
♡ K 4 2
◇ Q 10 3 2
♣ 7 6 5

When you have the ace or king of partner's suit plus adequate length, you should raise on any excuse. This hand just barely makes it. If RHO had passed, you wouldn't have raised.

E-W vul.

W	N	E	S
1♠	2♡	2♠	?

♠ Q 10 7
♡ 8 6 4 2
◇ K 5 4
♣ Q 10 7

At matchpoints only, you could try 3♡. You're hoping the opponents will continue to 3♠. In fact, at matchpoints 3♡ will get you 3♠ or 4♠ from opener about 70% of the time. Half of these times your opponent will have made a bad bid. Bidding 3♡ is not all stars and twinkles. It has a downside. They may double 3♡, which would be bad. Or your partner may lead a heart, thinking you have something in hearts. Or your partner, thinking you have something useful, might bid to 4♡ and go down, perhaps doubled. I do not recommend bidding this at IMPs.

Note that had RHO passed, you would have had no excuse for bidding. It is curious that in competitive auctions the strength of the free bid is reversed from the usual concept. On hands where you would normally pass, you take action only when RHO takes action. He passes, you pass. He raises, you raise.

Neither vul.

W	N	E	S
1♠	2♡	2♠	?

♠ 8 7 6
♡ K J 7
◇ A Q 6 2
♣ 7 3 2

Had RHO passed you would have cuebid 2♠. Over RHO's raise you have another choice. 4♡ is a possible bid, and so is doubling, with the intention of showing heart support next. Ideally you can do this at the three-level. The one bid that you should avoid is a raise to 3♡. Your hand is just too good for that, given partner bid at the two-level.

PARTNER OVERCALLS AT THE TWO-LEVEL IN A MINOR, RHO RAISES

In general, I have said that when your partner overcalls and they raise, you will not have 3NT. If there are going to be exceptions to this rule it will be when partner overcalls at the two- or three-level, showing a good suit, often six cards long. When you have a source of tricks you may be able to make 3NT.

If you agree with this, your methods will be as follows.

LHO	Partner	RHO	You
1♡	2♢	2♡	?

Dbl is responsive and can be used to show a limit raise as well.

2♠ is natural, invitational, and passable.

2NT is natural, showing 10-12 points.

3♣ is natural, invitational, and passable.

3♢ is just a raise.

3♡ is a cuebid, most likely looking for 3NT. This is a rare choice.

Some Examples of Bidding After Partner's 2♣ or 2♢ Overcall and RHO's Raise

N-S vul.

W	N	E	S
1♢	2♣	2♢	?

♠ A Q 3
♡ 9 7 3 2
♢ 8 7 3
♣ A Q 2

Double. When partner overcalls in a minor suit and RHO raises, if you have potential game strength or better you may wish to explore for 3NT as well as five of a minor. Your double will at this point sound like the majors. You intend to correct to clubs to clear up your intent. It is sad that you can't cuebid but that bid forces your side to the four-level if partner can't bid notrump. If you had the ♠K instead of the ♠Q you could bid 3♢, making a pretty emphatic statement about your hand.

Neither vul.

W	N	E	S
1♡	2♢	2♡	?

♠ A 8 7
♡ 4 2
♢ Q 10 7
♣ A J 6 4 2

Double. 3NT, 4♢ or 5♢ could be good contracts. The cuebid is the only action that expresses the strength of the hand and leaves all options open.

Raising to 3♢ would probably end the auction. You have at least an ace more than that. Another choice is to bid 3♡. That will determine if partner has a heart stopper, but it might also get you too high.

Neither vul.

W	N	E	S
1♡	2◇	2♡	?

♠ 7 4 2
♡ 4 2
◇ Q 10 7
♣ K J 6 4 2

Don't forget the simple raise. Bid 3◇.

PARTNER OVERCALLS AT THE TWO-LEVEL, RHO BIDS A NEW SUIT

As usual, when RHO has enough values to bid a new suit at the two- or three-level the hand does not belong to your side. The only reason for raising is to get partner off to a good lead or to suggest a save. This means you will have good trumps (an honor) or distribution.

Neither vul.

W	N	E	S
1♠	2♣	2♡	?

♠ 8 6 5 4
♡ 8 6 2
◇ Q 5 4
♣ K J 7

3♣. When the opponents show strength a raise by you is not particularly forward-going. It is more of a small noise. A little squeak. A squeak with a purpose, but a squeak nonetheless.

E-W vul.

W	N	E	S
1♠	2◇	2♡	?

♠ 7 2
♡ 9 8 4 2
◇ K Q 6 2
♣ J 7 3

You could bid 4◇ if it would be understood as preemptive. Note the good things that can come of it.

1.   LHO can't rebid 3♡ or 3♠.

2.   If LHO chooses to bid 4♡ or 4♠, there will be much ambiguity as to his values. Does he have a strong hand taking a slight underbid? Or does he have a weakish hand just accepting the push, as so many players will?

You can be sure that your opponents will misjudge their values frequently on auctions like this one. Sometimes they will misjudge their fits as well. LHO might have six spades and three hearts and decide to raise hearts. Maybe spades was the right spot. When you bid 4◇ you create guessing games. When the opponents do the right thing, you get about average. When they do the wrong thing, you get a top. Not bad odds.

Neither vul.

W	N	E	S
1♠	2♣	2◇	?

♠ 8 2
♡ J 7 6 5 4 2
◇ 3
♣ Q J 7 2

A good 4♣ bid. If the opponents were vulnerable, a jump to five would be reasonable.

N-S vul.

W	N	E	S
1♠	2◇	3♣	?

♠ 3
♡ K 6 5 4 2
◇ K 7 5 3 2
♣ 8 3

This vulnerability does not suggest you do anything rash. 5◇ would be right any other time. Vulnerable versus not, however, dictates second thoughts. Bid only 4◇. Partner will realize you have a good playing hand and will bid accordingly.

When partner overcalls at the one- or two-level and RHO bids a new suit at the two-level or higher, it is very important to accept that the hand belongs to the opponents. It follows that there won't be room for constructive bidding by your side.

PARTNER OVERCALLS AT THE TWO-LEVEL, RHO BIDS 2NT

Don't bother over-thinking. It's so dangerous to bid anything at all that if you're wondering whether you should bid, you clearly shouldn't. If you think you should be bidding, then you probably shouldn't. Only when you know for sure that you have a bid is it likely to be right. The one thing that is clear here is that you will never be bidding from strength. You will be bidding from shape and fits. Nothing you bid can be construed as forward-going. The only thing by you that partner will bid over is a cuebid, and I have no idea what that would mean.

Neither vul.

W	N	E	S
1♠	2♡	2NT	?

♠ 8 6 5 4 2
♡ J 6 5 4
◇ 2
♣ K 9 7

Bid 3♡. Not because you expect to make it, but because it might cause LHO slight embarrassment. LHO can't rebid 3♣ or 3◇. You have an excellent supporting hand for partner. You should have no less.

E-W vul.			
W	N	E	S
1♠	2♣	2NT	?

♠ 8 6 5
♡ 9 8 6 4 2
◇ 3
♣ K 6 4 3

I lean toward bidding 3♣. But pass may work. If you bid 3♣, your partner will know you are bidding with shape and not a few scattered points. Perhaps your raise will help him in some way.

Neither vul.			
W	N	E	S
1♠	2◇	2NT	?

♠ Q 8 2
♡ 4 2
◇ 3
♣ K Q 10 9 7 6 5

Pass. The opponents are not likely to have game values. 2NT may end the auction. 3♣ would offer them 300 or more on a hand where you might actually have gone plus.

PARTNER OVERCALLS AT THE TWO-LEVEL, RHO MAKES A NEGATIVE DOUBLE

This is treated much as after a one-level overcall and negative double. With a minimum raise, you raise. With a maximum raise, you cuebid. Good hands with no fit can redouble. But be sure your cards will be useful to partner in the unlikely event your redouble gets passed out. Jumps are preemptive. If partner overcalled in a minor suit, 2NT is rare, but natural.

Neither vul.			
W	N	E	S
1♠	2◇	dbl	?

♠ 8 6
♡ K 8 6 2
◇ K J 4
♣ 10 7 6 5

3◇. It's important to bid when you have something worthwhile to say. And when that something is a raise of partner's overcall, passing with the intention of bidding later just isn't bridge. Why let the opponents have an unobstructed discussion? Perhaps your partner will be able to compete further after your help. It's so bad to hide your head in the sand. You just get your head kicked and you don't even see it coming.

E-W vul.			
W	N	E	S
1♡	2♣	dbl	?

♠ A 8 7 6
♡ 8 6 5
◇ K 5 4
♣ K J 7

Cuebid 2♡. In spite of RHO's double, game isn't out of the question. Probably not 5♣, but perhaps 3NT.

Neither vul.

W	N	E	S
1♠	2♣	dbl	?

♠ 8 5 4 2
♡ 10 6 3
◇ 9
♣ K 10 6 5 4

A jump to 4♣ is reasonable. Partner should play you for something in this family. If the opponents were vulnerable you could give thought to jumping to 5♣.

Both vul.

W	N	E	S
1♠	2♡	dbl	?

♠ A 8 7 6 5
♡ K J 8
◇ Q J 4 2
♣ 3

Jump to 4♡. On this one specific sequence your jump is not necessarily preemptive, although it could be. You intend to bid 4♡ in any event and do not need to leave the opponents room for discussion. Mind you, if you wish to bid 2♠, that is a sane alternative, although it runs the risk that they discover a big club fit.

Neither vul.

W	N	E	S
1♠	2♡	dbl	?

♠ A 8 6 2
♡ 4 2
◇ K J 8 7
♣ Q 5 4

Redouble. You hope partner can do something knowing you have a good hand but with no fit. Be sure to have exactly two cards in partner's suit.

Neither vul.

W	N	E	S
1♠	2◇	dbl	?

♠ A J 8 7 3
♡ K J 5 4
◇ —
♣ Q 10 7 3

Pass. The danger in redoubling is that it might be passed out. When you pass, LHO will almost always bid and you can start doubling. When you redouble, partner will depend on you for a balanced hand of some sort.

CHAPTER ELEVEN
1NT AND 2NT RESPONSES TO AN OVERCALL

I described these earlier. Here are examples with more details. The hands where it is right to bid some number of notrump are usually self-evident. They include a rational point range with appropriate stoppers or near stoppers. The difficult hands to handle are those where you have the values to do something and nothing seems clear-cut. Here are some examples. Note that there are serious concerns about bidding notrump if your RHO has shown any values.

Neither vul.

W	N	E	S
1♣	1♡	pass	?

♠ K J 7 2
♡ 8 3 ·
◇ K 10 8
♣ Q J 8 2

A clear-cut 1NT. Your range starts at an excellent 8-count and can go to 11 or a terrible 12 so this hand is average. As your values approach the top of your range, your stopper may become suspect. With minimums, though, you must have a full stopper in LHO's suit.

Neither vul.

W	N	E	S
1♡	1♠	pass	?

♠ J 2
♡ 9 7 5
◇ K Q 5 4
♣ A 10 6 3

Pass is likely best. If you had a fourth heart 1NT would make sense. If you had ♡J84, that would be okay too if you had a maximum. Note that when you do not have a stopper, you do have a maximum hand.

N-S vul.

W	N	E	S
1◇	1♡	pass	?

♠ K Q 6 2
♡ 8 3
◇ Q 5 4
♣ 8 6 5 4

With a minimum, no spots, a marginal stopper, and vulnerable besides, I would pass. Add the ♣J and I would still suggest a pass.

Neither vul.			
W	N	E	S
1♣	1♡	1♠	?

♠ Q J 8 7
♡ 8 3
◇ K Q 10 7
♣ Q J 4

1NT. When RHO bids a suit you shouldn't bother bidding with minimum hands. Also, while your stopper in opener's suit may be questionable, your stopper in RHO's suit must be for real.

Another thought with hands like this one; you can pass and see what happens. If opener rebids 1NT, you can double it if you wish. Passing requires good bidding judgment later so if you prefer to bid 1NT right now, that is okay. Among other things, it gets partner back into the bidding if he has the hand for it.

Neither vul.			
W	N	E	S
	pass	1♣	pass
1♡	1♠	pass	?

♠ 8
♡ Q 10 8 3
◇ K Q 3 2
♣ K Q J 7

Normally you would jump to 2NT, showing an invitational hand of 12-14 HCP. Here, though, partner is a passed hand. This plus your stiff spade suggests a conservative 1NT. Perhaps one of your opponents will try again and your underbid will reap a different reward. If you had a second spade you could jump to 2NT in spite of partner's original pass.

Neither vul.			
W	N	E	S
1♣	1♡	2♣	?

♠ K 8 7
♡ Q 2
◇ J 9 6 5
♣ A 10 9 3

Your possible bids include raising to 2♡, a fair bid. 2NT is not a good choice because you need a better hand to bid notrump at the two-level. Doubling is not a hot idea because your partner will expect you to have spades and diamonds, which you do not have. It is rare to raise with two trumps and if you hate the idea, then just pass.

Both vul.			
W	N	E	S
1♡	1♠	2♣	?

There is no hand worth a 2NT bid on this auction. Only when you have such an incredibly good hand that you know someone has psyched could you have a hand worth some number of notrump. On this auction you will have 6 or fewer HCP about 98% of the time. You can, if you wish, use 2NT in some artificial way. (See later section for more on this.)

Neither vul.

W	N	E	S
1♠	2♣	2♡	?

As above. If you miss the one hand in a hundred where you should have bid 2NT as a natural bid, you will save a fortune on the other ninety-nine where you shouldn't. Again, using 2NT as a raise is a possible idea. More later.

Neither vul.

W	N	E	S
1♠	2♣	pass	?

♠ Q 10 7
♡ Q 8 2
◇ A J 9 7 5
♣ Q 3

2NT. This sequence does guarantee a stopper. It shows 10-12 points, with allowances for good spots and the fit for partner's suit. When RHO passes, as he did here, it is possible that you will have a good enough hand to bid 2NT.

Neither vul.

W	N	E	S
1♠	2♡	pass	?

♠ Q 8 6 5 2
♡ —
◇ K Q 8 2
♣ K Q J 2

Even with this full 13 points, 2NT is sufficient. Your spade spots are weak and you don't have fast tricks on the side. Your heart void is so bad that a pass could be best, although I wouldn't expect anyone to do this.

Both vul.

W	N	E	S
1♠	2♣	2♠	?

♠ J 10 8 3
♡ A 8 6 5
◇ A 4 2
♣ Q 9

3NT. This is the perfect hand. A fit for partner's suit. A stopper. And sure tricks on the side. 2NT would be quite conservative.

CHAPTER TWELVE
THE RESPONSIVE DOUBLE

During the early part of this book I made references to a number of conventions. One of these, the negative double, is used only by the side that opens the bidding. Nothing has been said about using it, only defending against it.

The defending side uses other conventions, which we'll be looking at in more depth. For the most part, though, the discussion will be how to use these conventions in general rather than how to use any one in particular. There is one convention that stands out, however, and I am going to go much further in describing it than any other. If you get the impression that I am recommending it, I am. Of all the many conventions out there today this one, like few others, stands on merit. It is the responsive double.

The responsive double takes many forms, but two of them account for over 90% of its usage. Here are the two situations.

1. LHO opens. Partner overcalls. RHO raises. You double.
2. LHO opens. Partner doubles. RHO raises. You double.

THE RESPONSIVE DOUBLE AFTER PARTNER OVERCALLS

Before showing examples, it is necessary to know what a responsive double is. On auctions where partner has overcalled and RHO has raised, a double shows the two unbid suits. On auctions where partner doubled and RHO raised, you show two suits. Since there are three suits to choose from, you use this rule. If their side bids a minor a double by you shows the majors. If their side bids a major a double by you shows the minors. These ideas will be developed extensively in the next few pages.

Usually the auction looks like this:

LHO	Partner	RHO	You
1♣	1♠	2♣	Dbl
1◊	1♡	3◊	Dbl
1♡	2♣	2♡	Dbl
1♡	2♣	3♡	Dbl
1◊	1♡	4◊	Dbl

Note that partner's overcall is not a jump overcall. After a jump overcall your double is for business. Note also that RHO's bid is a raise.

These auctions are *not* responsive:

LHO	Partner	RHO	You
1♣	2♠	3♣	Dbl

Partner's bid was a jump.

LHO	Partner	RHO	You
1♣	1♠	2◇	Dbl

RHO did not raise. He bid a new suit.

It would not be unreasonable to include the following auctions as responsive as well, against weak two-bids and weak three-bids.

Versus a weak two:

LHO	Partner	RHO	You
2♡	2♠	3♡	Dbl
2♠	3♣	3♠	Dbl
2◇	2♡	3◇	Dbl

Versus a weak three:

LHO	Partner	RHO	You
3♡	3♠	4♡	Dbl
3♣	3♡	4♣	Dbl

What is the responsive double?

Basically, the responsive double is a takeout double which announces sufficient strength to enter the auction and which shows length in the unbid suits.

Neither vul.

W	N	E	S
1♣	1♠	2♣	?

♠ 8
♡ K J 8 7 2
◇ A 10 5 4 2
♣ 8 3

This is the usual example quoted to show the responsive double. You have enough values to compete but no idea which suit is best. Double shows interest in both hearts and diamonds and guarantees finding the best fit. Should partner persist with spades, he will probably have six or seven of them. If he has only five spades he should have at least three cards in one of the red suits. Only if he is 5-2-2-4 will you be in trouble. This is a small price to pay for the ability to compete successfully on most other occasions.

How important is the responsive double?

Extremely! The important point of the convention is that it is used when the opponents have a fit. When they have one, you have one. If partner's overcall fails to locate a fit, then the fit will exist elsewhere. Some of the time you will have a suit to bid, but frequently you will have a hand similar to the example hand. You know a fit exists. It is merely necessary to determine where.

How safe is the responsive double?

Very safe. As long as no one forgets the bid and as long as no one goes crazy, you will incur only average to good results. Only when you suffer the occasional fix will you get a poor result. Everything is in your favor. Remember. When RHO raises, that creates the safest of all auctions and you really need a bad hand before it's right to pass.

What do you lose by using the responsive double?

What you lose is the penalty double. In theory. In practice, I submit this is no loss at all. In fact, it is more likely to be a blessing. The one thing you are not likely to have is a penalty double when partner overcalls and RHO raises. Even on those rare occasions where you do have a sound penalty double partner sometimes yanks the double; or more likely declarer, warned by your double, plays the hand very well.

You just don't have a sound trump holding often enough to want to play the double for penalties when there is a much better alternative available.

Another huge gain, incidentally, is that you will not be able to make any bad penalty doubles and you won't be losing 670 or 280 when you should be going plus. You will also find that the responsive double will come up ten to twenty times as often as a penalty double, and it will be far easier to use. One result of the responsive double is that your side will play more hands, which by definition is easier than defending them.

Does this mean you can never double them for penalties?

Not at all. In fact, the contrary is true. Some of the time your partner can pass your responsive double for penalty. When this happens, his trump holding will be well located for your side (over the bidder). And sometimes when you would like to make a penalty double you pass instead, and partner may be able to reopen with a takeout double. You can pass for penalties and the result will be the same.

How does the responsive double differ from other takeout bids such as the takeout double, the unusual notrump, and the Michaels cuebid?

The major difference is that this is the only defensive takeout bid you can make where you can expect some values from partner. Partner has overcalled (or doubled), guaranteeing a foundation to build on. When the opponents open and you make a takeout double or an overcall, you are faced with the possibility that partner is broke. You haven't a clue as to his shape or values. But when partner has made a contribution and RHO raises, everything is different. The auction is now safe, you know partner has some values, and you know you have a fit. You are very well placed to estimate your side's potential. Optimism is the password.

Neither vul.

W	N	E	S
1◇	1♡	2◇	?

♠ K J 10 3
♡ 8
◇ 8 6 5
♣ A 10 9 3 2

Double. You do not promise five cards in each unbid suit. Even if partner bids a three-card spade suit, as he should on some hands, your support will be fine.

Neither vul.

W	N	E	S
1♣	1◇	2♣	?

♠ Q J 6 5 4
♡ K 10 6 5 2
◇ 3
♣ 6 5

Double. You have two five-card suits and partner can bid one at the two-level. Hands like these are duck soup for the responsive double. What would you do without it? You'd guess. Between 2♠, 2♡, and pass.

Neither vul.

W	N	E	S
1♡	1♠	2♡	?

♠ 8
♡ 3 2
◇ Q 9 7 6 5
♣ K 8 6 5 4

Pass this one. Double forces partner to the three-level, unlike the previous hand.

N-S vul.

W	N	E	S
1◇	2♣	2◇	?

♠ A Q 9 5
♡ K J 10 3
◇ 8 6 5
♣ 3 2

Double. In spite of only four-card support for the unbid suits, your hand is otherwise good enough. Opposite a vulnerable overcall you have plenty to compete.

E-W vul.

W	N	E	S
1♣	1◇	2♣	?

♠ 8 6 5 4
♡ J 6 4 2
◇ 3
♣ A J 6 5

No need to go to extremes. Your values are inadequate and your suits are poor. You should pass.

Neither vul.

W	N	E	S
1♡	1♠	2♡	?

♠ 8 2
♡ 8 7 5
◇ K J 4
♣ K 10 6 5 4

Pass. You need at least four-card support for each unbid suit. Five is more or less expected. Remember that partner may innocently bid a three-card suit, expecting support from you. Don't disappoint him.

Neither vul.

W	N	E	S
1♣	1♡	2♣	?

♠ Q 10 8 7
♡ Q 5 4
◇ A 7 6 5 2
♣ 2

Bid 2♡. Don't overlook the raise. As a general rule, a responsive double denies support. The purpose of the bid is to find a fit. When one exists (and a major-suit fit at that) there is no reason to look elsewhere. If you double and partner bids 2♠, you will have gone past what may be your optimum spot; that is, 2♡. Or, if you double and LHO bids 3♣, passed back to you, you won't be on firm grounds bidding 3♡ and you'll likewise feel awkward about passing.

N-S vul.

W	N	E	S
1◇	1♡	2◇	?

♠ A Q 10 8 7
♡ J 2
◇ 3
♣ A J 8 5 3

Here you can hope for a game contract, but there's no clear route to bidding it. Until now, the only forcing bid available would have been the cuebid. But this is a case where the responsive double can help with the strong hands as well. Double, showing clubs and spades, will help you get your suits into the game and you can catch up on your strength later. This principle will come up frequently later in the book. Note the difficulties you would incur if you cuebid. Now try to get all your suits in and still stop in 3NT if that is the best spot. Not easy.

Neither vul.

W	N	E	S
1♣	1♡	2♣	?

♠ A Q J 7 5
♡ 3
◇ 10 7 6 5
♣ J 5 4

With such suit disparity and the expectation of a fit, try 2♠.

Neither vul.

W	N	E	S
1♣	1◇	2♣	?

♠ J 10 7 5
♡ J 9 5 4
◇ Q 2
♣ A K 3

This is a matchpoint responsive double. Hardly ideal suits, but sufficient to offer one little oomph. I've seen people make penalty doubles on hands like these, which is good reason to take that bid away from their arsenal. After the responsive double a typical result would be 2♡ or 2♠, making 110 or –50. Equally likely would be one of your opponents continuing on to 3♣. For whatever it's worth, I wouldn't care to double that either, which shows you what I think of a penalty double of 2♣. Don't hang partner.

Both vul.

W	N	E	S
1♣	1♠	3♣	?

♠ Q 2
♡ J 10 8 7 5
◇ A Q 6 4 2
♣ 3

You are unlikely to hold this hand if 3♣ is a game force. But many players play 3♣ as either weak or merely invitational. In such circumstances you might well hold this hand and the responsive double is the perfect answer. The fact that partner must bid at the three-level suggests you need a reasonable hand. But otherwise, it's the same as if RHO had bid 2♣.

N-S vul.

W	N	E	S
1♡	1♠	3♡	?

♠ 3
♡ J
◇ A J 10 7 6
♣ K 10 9 6 5 4

Double is still responsive. Here you are vulnerable and partner must bid at the four-level, so you need a useful hand. This one is not much over a minimum. Without the responsive double, anything would be a guess. Does partner have one of these two hands?

Hand One

♠ A Q 6 5 4	♠ 3
♡ 8 6 2	♡ J
◇ K 8 5 4	◇ A J 10 7 6
♣ 3	♣ K 10 9 6 5 4

Hand Two

♠ A Q 6 5 4	♠ 3
♡ 8 6 2	♡ J
◇ 3	◇ A J 10 7 6
♣ A 7 3 2	♣ K 10 9 6 5 4

The first hand offers a play for 5◇ and the second could make 6♣. Happy guessing.

Neither vul.

W	N	E	S
1◇	1♠	4◇	?

♠ Q 3
♡ A 10 7 3
◇ 8 6 2
♣ K J 9 3

Double. When RHO makes an extreme leap like this, your double is no longer responsive by definition. But inasmuch as you are unlikely to have good trump on this auction, your double will tend to show something like this hand; that is, a balanced hand with scattered values and no particular interest in partner's suit.

Some thoughts

When the auction begins with a weak two bid, your partner overcalls, and RHO raises, there is some merit to playing responsive doubles. My preference in this area is not to play them, though, for a simple reason. I can't remember the last time one came up. There have been a few times where a penalty double was in order, but those have been rather rare as well. I don't think there's much to make of this. Flip a nickel and choose. Whatever you decide will be fine.

If you do decide on responsive doubles, you should be aware of the level of the auction and will need values to match. 2♠-3♣-3♠ is much more difficult to contend with than 2◊-2♡-3◊, so you will require a better hand. Errors to avoid are doubling for takeout when you should be supporting partner instead, and forgetting that your double is for takeout. One last admonition. Don't let the fact that they are using weak two-bids cause you to bid for the sake of bidding. RHO can easily have a good hand for his raise. Tricks don't come out of air. They come from high cards and distribution.

THE RESPONSIVE DOUBLE AFTER PARTNER MAKES A TAKEOUT DOUBLE

These doubles are always responsive.

LHO	Partner	RHO	You
1♣	Dbl	2♣	Dbl
1◊	Dbl	2◊	Dbl
1♡	Dbl	2♡	Dbl
1♠	Dbl	2♠	Dbl
1♣	Dbl	3♣	Dbl
1◊	Dbl	3◊	Dbl
1♡	Dbl	3♡	Dbl
1♠	Dbl	3♠	Dbl

These doubles after a weak two-bid should be responsive too.

LHO	Partner	RHO	You
2◊	Dbl	3◊	Dbl
2♡	Dbl	3♡	Dbl
2♠	Dbl	3♠	Dbl

These doubles ought to be responsive if your partnership agrees.

LHO	Partner	RHO	You
1♣	Dbl	4♣	Dbl
1◇	Dbl	4◇	Dbl
2◇	Dbl	4◇	Dbl
3♣	Dbl	4♣	Dbl
3◇	Dbl	4◇	Dbl

These doubles are usually played as penalty, although usually the doubler just has some high card points, not necessarily a big trump holding.

LHO	Partner	RHO	You
1♡	Dbl	4♡	Dbl
1♠	Dbl	4♠	Dbl
2♡	Dbl	4♡	Dbl
2♠	Dbl	4♠	Dbl
3♡	Dbl	4♡	Dbl
3♠	Dbl	4♠	Dbl

This can all be summarized fairly simply. After partner's takeout double, your double of any raise to the three-level is responsive. If you wish you can include the double of a raise to 4♣ or 4◇ as well. Initially, I would suggest limiting your range to the three-level until you feel comfortable with the convention. Whatever you decide, you will run into the law of diminishing returns. Four-level decisions aren't that frequent and the convention doesn't help that much. In fact, you could make one further reduction in the range by limiting it to doubles of 3◇ or lower. But this would be trimming it to the maximum. For the purposes of the example hands, I will assume the responsive double is being used through 4◇.

To give you a cross section of opinions, there are some players who play the responsive double as high as 7♡. I think this is a bit too much of a good thing and some of the discussions following a bad result have been sillier than the result itself. But I've seen them get outstanding results as well. This is in no way a recommendation to play responsive doubles on all auctions, but it is a strong recommendation that you do play them on some auctions. Very few partnerships have tried them and rejected them.

Neither vul.

W	N	E	S
1♣	dbl	2♣	?

♠ J875
♡ Q865
◇ K654
♣ 3

Double. This hand is clearly worth a competitive effort. But which suit should it be? Your double shows the majors and the fact that you have diamonds too is a coincidence.

Neither vul.

W	N	E	S
1♣	dbl	2♣	?

♠ K876
♡ A1054
◇ 42
♣ 753

Again, double. You are asking partner to bid hearts or spades. He made a takeout double so he ought to have a four-card major. If he does not have one, he can often bid 2◇. If you happen to have diamond support you can pass.

Both vul.

W	N	E	S
1♣	dbl	2♣	?

♠ QJ32
♡ 42
◇ K10653
♣ 86

Bid 2◇ or 2♠. Whichever suits your fancy. Double would show hearts and spades. You are missing one of those suits. Note that you are placed exactly as you would have been without the responsive double. It helps often, but not always.

N-S vul.

W	N	E	S
1♣	dbl	2♣	?

♠ KQ87
♡ KJ107
◇ Q54
♣ 32

Double. The responsive double is not a weak bid at all. Here you will raise either major to three. Game is a strong possibility.

Both vul.

W	N	E	S
1♣	dbl	2♣	?

♠ K8765
♡ Q9542
◇ 3
♣ 87

It's probably better to bid 2♠. You will follow with 3♡ if the auction permits. Double implies 4-4 in the two suits you are bidding. 5-5 is unexpected.

Both vul.

W	N	E	S
1♣	dbl	2♣	?

♠ K Q 7
♡ K J 9
◇ 8 7 5 4
♣ 9 7 4

Double. Whatever partner bids will be fine. Partner may be playing in a 4-3 fit, but your high cards will make that a better proposition than defending 2♣. If you had better diamonds, you could bid them instead.

Neither vul.

W	N	E	S
1♣	dbl	2♣	?

♠ Q 2
♡ K Q 9
◇ J 6 5 4
♣ 8 6 4 2

2◇. Even with bad diamonds it is right to bid them. Your values are fine but your doubleton in spades precludes a responsive double.

Neither vul.

W	N	E	S
1◇	dbl	2◇	?

♠ Q 9 7
♡ K J 3
◇ 5 4 2
♣ Q 5 4 3

Double. Something to say, but no clear suit. Typically, the responsive double can be used on hands where you just wish to compete at the two-level. You may have no interest in doing more than pushing the opponents up one more. With this hand, you know you have some sort of fit and it remains only to find it. But without the responsive double any action is committal and dangerous. Consider how you would feel about bidding 2♡, 2♠, 3♣, and pass. I know I would feel nervous about any of them.

Neither vul.

W	N	E	S
1◇	dbl	2◇	?

♠ K Q 8 7
♡ 8 6
◇ 4 3 2
♣ J 7 6 2

Just 2♠. A decent suit in a minimum hand.

Neither vul.

W	N	E	S
1♡	dbl	2♡	?

♠ K 8
♡ 8 7 5
♢ Q 5 4 2
♣ A J 3 2

Double. When the opponents are bidding and raising a major, that leaves only one major suit for you to bid. When you can do so, you should. Therefore, a responsive double should emphasize the minors. Partner will be very wary about bidding a major.

Both vul.

W	N	E	S
1♡	dbl	2♡	?

♠ Q 8 7 5
♡ 3 2
♢ Q 8 7
♣ A 10 5 4

2♠. It's almost always right to bid the missing major when the opponents are competing in the other.

Neither vul.

W	N	E	S
1♡	dbl	2♡	?

♠ J 8 7
♡ 4 2
♢ K 6 5 2
♣ K J 8 3

Double again. The issue is whether you have enough. In support of either minor you have 8 useful high-card points, which rate to be worth more than 8 since they are in the suits your partner is interested in. The responsive double makes miscellaneous hands like this easy to handle. I feel like saying it after each example. With much difficulty I will try to restrain myself and will ask instead that you imagine on each hand what you would do without the responsive double. If you find that you would be passing some of these hands because you didn't know what to do, then you are probably losing a lot of partscore battles that you should be winning. If you find that on hands like this one you are selecting a suit, then you are probably losing a lot of partscore battles because you miss the best suit. I have the feeling that I'm going to lose my resolve and will be repeating this again, and soon.

Neither vul.

W	N	E	S
1♡	dbl	2♡	?

♠ 4 2
♡ 8 6 5 3
♢ A J 10 7
♣ K 10 2

Bid 3♢. This does not promise five. Passing would be wrong at any game or vulnerability and double would be a misdescription.

Both vul.

W	N	E	S
1♡	dbl	2♡	?

♠ J 3
♡ K J 7 5
♢ J 10 2
♣ A 10 6 3

Whatever you do, you can't double. This hand is typical of bad doubles that you can no longer make. A popular bid with this hand is 2NT. I suggest you do not do that. If you play in 2NT, LHO will lead a heart. You may get the first trick but when RHO gets in (he usually does) the defense will then take four heart tricks. Here's a rule you can count on. When the bidding goes as shown here, a notrump bid by you is often ineffective because they have a suit they can set up. Your ♡KJ75 is likely to be compromised. If you are silent, they may misjudge the hand and go down a trick or two.

Important note: If you pass you won't miss a good contract because if partner has extra values he can double again.

One last thought. You do have a fair hand. A 3♣ bid could be the winner, but your hearts are worthless in the play and might be useful on defense. I would pass this one.

E-W vul.

W	N	E	S
1♡	dbl	2♡	?

♠ 3
♡ Q J 10 8 2
♢ A 5 4
♣ Q 10 5 4

Pass. This is the good penalty double you have to give up. If you pass, partner may be able to double again. If not, 2♡ down two may be a good result anyway. And for the really greedy, you can try 3♣. You'd be surprised how often someone competes. Now you can double 3♡!

Neither vul.

W	N	E	S
1♡	dbl	2♡	?

♠ 9 6 5 4
♡ 2
♢ Q 10 6 5
♣ K 9 6 3

Bid 2♠. I once suggested doubling with this hand. No longer. The only bad things that can happen are that you play in 2♠ and go down because partner has only three of them, or that they bid 3♡ and your partner makes a bad spade lead. The good things outweigh these possible bad things.

WHEN THE OPPONENTS BID AND RAISE SPADES

LHO	Partner	RHO	You
1♠	dbl	2♠	?

The spade suit is difficult to overcome. The responsive double will help you on many hands and the only change is that you should have a little extra value in recognition that partner will be bidding at the three-level.

Neither vul.

W	N	E	S
1♠	dbl	2♠	?

♠ 10 2
♡ 9 8 7
◇ A Q 8 4
♣ A K 10 5

A super responsive double. You have lots of values, but that is not an issue since you will bid again when partner shows his better minor. Say he bids 3♣. You will bid 3♠, asking for a notrump stopper. It is hard to fathom where everyone is getting their bids from, but they have done so and you have to come up with a solution. 3NT is very possible. You can offer a possible eight tricks in the minors and if partner has a spade stopper, there may be an easy game.

Important note: You do not bid 3♣ first because you want to show the minor suits. After establishing you have the minors, then you can look for notrump.

Both vul.

W	N	E	S
1♠	dbl	2♠	?

♠ 4 2
♡ 4 2
◇ A K 8 2
♣ 8 6 5 4 2

Double. Either minor could be right. This lets partner help decide.

Neither vul.

W	N	E	S
1♠	dbl	2♠	?

♠ 8 6 5 4
♡ A J
◇ Q J 8
♣ J 10 8 5

A difficult hand. Double is possible. If partner bids clubs, all is well. If he bids diamonds, it still might be okay. Or, you can bid 3♣. Finally, if you hate these choices you can pass. Pick one. My choice by a slim margin is double.

Neither vul.

W	N	E	S
1♠	dbl	2♠	?

♠ 8 6 5 2
♡ K 2
♢ 5 4 3
♣ A Q 9 3

With a good suit and values, 3♣ is fine. Your hand is good enough that you will have a play for 3♣, and perhaps more. Here is a possible layout to show you the strength of your hand.

♠ 8 6 5 2	♠ 7
♡ K 2	♡ A 8 7 3
♢ 5 4 3	♢ A J 10 8
♣ A Q 9 3	♣ K 10 4 2

Your partner has a 12-count and it is enough that it should make 3♣ a winning contract. Note that you may not have to play it there. They may continue to 3♠.

Neither vul.

W	N	E	S
1♠	dbl	2♠	?

♠ 4 2
♡ K J 8 2
♢ Q 3 2
♣ K 10 5 4

Bid 3♡. If you double, partner will respond in a minor. Your hand is quite good enough to bid 3♡ if you decide to play that a direct 3♡ bid shows a decent hand. (See the next hand.)

Neither vul.

W	N	E	S
1♠	dbl	2♠	?

♠ 8 7 2
♡ J 10 8 4 3
♢ K J 7
♣ 10 5

This is just barely good enough to compete with 3♡. If you play that the responsive double followed by 3♡ is a weak, competitive hand, you should do that. If not, then this is a very minimum 3♡ call. Both of your ten-spots are working toward making a bid. (See following discussion.)

A NICE DISTINCTION

You can, in fact, make a very nice distinction here if you wish to take the trouble. You can play as follows.

LHO	Partner	RHO	You
1♠	dbl	2♠	3♡

Shows a decent hand.

LHO	Partner	RHO	You
1♠	dbl	2♠	dbl
pass	3♣	pass	3♡

Shows a weak, competitive hand. This is quite reasonable and only lack of frequency dictates not bothering with it.

E-W vul.

W	N	E	S
1♠	dbl	2♠	?

♠ 7 6 5 4
♡ 2
◇ Q 10 8 6
♣ K J 4 2

The shape tells you there is a very good fit available. The hand will play quite well for you. Double, looking for a minor-suit fit. This hand is light but the alternative is to let them swipe the hand for 2♠, always a bad idea.

Both vul.

W	N	E	S
1♠	dbl	2♠	?

♠ 3
♡ 2
◇ A Q 8 7 6
♣ K 10 8 5 4 2

It is usually best to show your suits and subsequently catch up on your values. Double first and then make whatever slam try you feel like. If opener bids 3♠ and your partner passes, you will continue, perhaps with 5♣.

Neither vul.

W	N	E	S
1♣	dbl	3♣	?

♠ Q 8 7 4
♡ K Q J 3
◇ 4 2
♣ 9 7 3

A minimum responsive double. The important point is to resolve to get into the auction whenever possible. Note that if you do not bid, they will steal the hand in 3♣. Double will get you to the right major.

Neither vul.

W	N	E	S
1♣	dbl	3♣	?

♠ 8 2
♡ K 10 7 6
◇ A J 4 3
♣ 9 7 3

3♡. You need both majors to double. With one, you have to decide if it is worth a bid. I would say yes.

Both vul.

W N E S
1♣ dbl 3♣ ?

♠ K J 9 7
♡ A Q 6 5
◇ Q 9 4
♣ 4 2

Double. When partner bids a major, raise it to game. Don't expect it to be cold, however.

Neither vul.

W N E S
1♣ dbl 3♣ ?

♠ K 10 7 4
♡ A Q 3 2
◇ 10 7 5
♣ J 6

Double, showing the majors. This bid is easy. The bigger decision will come when partner bids a major. Say he bids 3♡. Should you go to game? The answer is no. Your double promises around 9-11 support points, which is about what you have. Partner is expected to jump to game if he has 15 or more. If he bids 3♡ he has less than that and your bidding again will be too much.

E-W vul.

W N E S
1♣ dbl 3♣ ?

♠ J 5 4
♡ K 5 4
◇ J 10 8 7 4
♣ K 3

3◇. This bid is not quite as clear as it appears because your ♣K is probably worthless. Still, you have five diamonds and that is a vote for bidding.

Neither vul.

W N E S
1◇ dbl 3◇ ?

♠ J 7
♡ K 4 2
◇ 4 3 2
♣ K 10 7 5 3

If it was legal to bid 3♣, you would. Bidding 4♣ is too much. Pass.

Neither vul.

W	N	E	S
1♡	dbl	3♡	?

♠ Q 5 4
♡ 3
♢ K J 7 5
♣ Q J 5 4 2

The first thing that meets the eye is that this auction is getting pretty high and getting there pretty fast. Very annoying. At least everyone else is holding these cards and hopefully they are having the same problem. Or does it just happen to you? Oh, well. Be assured that things will get worse. Just wait. In the meantime, your solution to this hand depends on whether you use the responsive double, and your definitions. If you play that 1♡–dbl–2♡–dbl is responsive, then I suggest you extend that to this auction as well. It's convenient for memory purposes and it's logical bridge-wise as well. The only question is whether this hand is good enough to compete at the four level, and the answer's easy. Yes. Double to show the minors. In fact, you have extras. It is possible that your partner has five of one minor and three of the other. Your double will find the best fit.

Both vul.

W	N	E	S
1♡	dbl	3♡	?

♠ K 10 7 5
♡ 3
♢ Q J 4 2
♣ K 9 6 3

3♠. Double would imply the minors and no interest in spades. If you had a fifth spade and one less club or diamond, you would be entitled to bid 4♠.

Neither vul.

W	N	E	S
1♡	dbl	3♡	?

♠ 3
♡ 8 2
♢ K 10 8 7 6 4
♣ A 8 7 5

Bid 4♢. With such suit disparity, give up on clubs. Note that two small hearts is a very poor holding, suggesting two fast losers. You would far prefer to have any other number of hearts.

N-S vul.

W	N	E	S
1♡	dbl	3♡	?

♠ K 2
♡ 8 3
♢ Q J 8
♣ Q 10 6 5 4 2

Very tough. If not vulnerable, I'd go for 4♣. Perhaps at matchpoints it would be okay anyway but those two small hearts are a big, big minus. I'd rather have a third heart. Whatever you decide, this is not a double.

LHO	Partner	RHO	You
1♠	dbl	3♠	?

The auction gets higher yet. Once again, double should be for the minors but with the extra values needed to justify four-level action. Watch out for auctions where they have the spade suit and be happy when you are the one with the spades.

Neither vul.

W	N	E	S
1♠	dbl	3♠	?

♠ 8 4 2
♡ K J 7 3
◇ 8 2
♣ A Q 8 5

4♡. Double would deny hearts so you can't do that. Your spade length is good and your values should provide a play.

Neither vul.

W	N	E	S
1♠	dbl	3♠	?

♠ 8 6 2
♡ K J 6 5 2
◇ J 10 3 2
♣ 7

4♡. This is a guess of sorts. Experience shows that when you have values like these (a good five-card major and good shape) it is okay to overbid a bit. Just to show you that this is an okay bid, I am providing a typical minimum hand for partner.

♠ J ♡ Q 9 8 4 ◇ A Q 8 5 ♣ Q J 10 4

In hearts, you have a play for ten tricks. If partner had a little more game might be cold. Your hand has good ingredients. You should be aware of these.

E-W vul.

W	N	E	S
1♠	dbl	3♠	?

♠ K Q J 10
♡ 3 2
◇ A Q 2
♣ K 9 7 6

Well? The biggest number in history and you can't get it. Double is takeout! What you can do is bid 3NT, getting a decent but unspectacular result that way, or you can pass. If it gets passed out, you will beat them a lot. Someone has psyched and offhand I'd say it was opener. Of course, if your partner is prone to indulgences, he might be the guilty one. Who knows. Perhaps everyone is for real. In any case, if they go down five or more you get a reasonable score. If you have a slam, you just got fixed.

LHO	Partner	RHO	You
1♣	Dbl	4♣	Dbl
1◇	Dbl	4◇	Dbl

These auctions can both be treated as responsive or penalty at your pleasure. If you play the double as responsive, it should show a hand with both majors and 10 or so support points. Some liberties may be taken occasionally if you have maximum values and 4-3 in the majors. Note that if your partner has a balanced takeout double he may elect to pass your double and try to get a penalty. Here is an example from his point of view.

Neither vul.

W	N	E	S
		1♣	dbl
4♣	dbl	pass	?

♠ A K 5
♡ Q 7 6 5
◇ Q 8 7 4
♣ K 4

You doubled 1♣ with this hand. What should you do when the next player bids 4♣ and partner makes a responsive double?

You can't be 100% sure your partner has four hearts, and in any event you have some defense along with the ♣K, which rates to be more useful on defense than on offense. You know partner has 10 or so points so their side will be way outgunned in 4♣, doubled. You can and probably should pass.

Neither vul.

W	N	E	S
1♣	dbl	4♣	?

♠ K 10 7 5
♡ J 7 6 4
◇ A Q 2
♣ 3 2

Double. Partner will bid a major and that will be fine. In the unlikely event he doesn't have a four-card major, he can choose to bid a diamond suit or he can choose to pass. Your high-card points and his should produce a penalty against 4♣, doubled.

Neither vul.

W	N	E	S
1♣	dbl	4♣	?

♠ K J 7
♡ A 5 4 2
◇ Q J 7 3
♣ 9 7

Double again. You may end up in a 4-3 spade fit, but it may make. What you can not do is pass with this fine a hand.

Neither vul.

W	N	E	S
1♣	dbl	4♣	?

♠ K 4 2
♡ J 9 6 4 2
◇ K 10 7 6
♣ 3

4♡. No reason to double. You know hearts are right and you have adequate minimum values.

Both vul.

W	N	E	S
1◇	dbl	4◇	?

♠ K J 3
♡ A 5 4
◇ 7 3
♣ Q 5 4 3 2

Double. Even though you have only three-card support for both majors, there is a chance that:
1.   Your high cards will permit partner to make 4♡/4♠.
2.   Partner may pass for penalty. This is a fair chance.
3.   They may save.
The biggest reason for doubling is that letting them play in 4◇ feels terrible. One can only hope that double will improve matters.

Neither vul.

W	N	E	S
1◇	dbl	4◇	?

♠ K 2
♡ A Q 4
◇ 8 5 3
♣ J 6 5 4 2

Awful. You can bid 4♡ as an experiment in terror. You can bid 5♣ and go down. You can double and wonder what to do when partner bids 4♠. Or you can pass. And you have to do it in tempo or everyone calls for the cops and complains about your incredible huddle. No one said bridge was easy. And if you were wondering, I am unhappy too. I think I would pass, feeling this was our best chance for a plus score.

Does the fact that they preempted make it safe for you to bid?

When the opponents start with a weak two- or three-bid and RHO raises after partner's double, you still need sane values to use a responsive double. LHO's preempt does not mean you can bid with nothing. If you are forcing the bidding to the four level, your side still needs around 24-26 support points to be safe there.

How high should our responsive doubles be played after partner makes a takeout double?

However high you decide to play responsive doubles, you should play them to that level regardless of whether partner doubles a one-bid or a two-bid or a three-bid. I offer that the bulk of your decisions will come at the two- and three-levels. Something like:

60% two-level	30% three-level	10% four-level

Whatever you choose, make sure partner knows it.

SOME OPTIONAL VARIATIONS (ROSENKRANZ DOUBLES AND SNAPDRAGON DOUBLES)

If you wish, you can add some extra refinements to competitive doubles. Here are two of the more common additions. The long quiz following discusses responsive doubles and only alludes to the two doubles shown below.

1. Rosenkranz doubles

When partner overcalls and RHO bids a new suit you can raise partner on hands containing an honor in his suit and you can double to show a raise with no honor.

Neither vul.

W	N	E	S
1♣	1♡	1♠	?

♠ 8 2
♡ K 10 7
♢ A 9 5 4
♣ 8 6 4 2

2♡. You have the ♡K.

Neither vul.

W	N	E	S
1♣	1♡	1♠	?

♠ 8 2
♡ 10 6 5
♢ K J 5 4
♣ A 10 7 3

Double. A raise with no ♡A, ♡K, or ♡Q.

Note that this is not the same as when you double a raise. Here you are doubling a new suit. Note also that this treatment could apply to two-level new suits as well.

LHO	Partner	RHO	You
1♡	1♠	2♣	dbl

or

LHO	Partner	RHO	You
1♠	2♣	2♡	dbl

Make sure that if you add this weapon to your repertoire, you know when it applies. For instance, do you want to play the convention after 1♠–2♡–3♢–? I suggest you play it after new suits by RHO at the two-level or lower.

2. Snapdragon doubles

These were discussed earlier. The snapdragon double uses the same double as the Rosenkranz double. You can have one or neither of these conventions, but not both. In the case of the snapdragon double, when you double responder's new suit you show a decent holding in the fourth suit and at the same time you have a tolerance for partner's suit.

Neither vul.

W	N	E	S
1♣	1♡	1♠	?

♠ 8 7 3 2
♡ Q 2
◇ A Q 10 8 7
♣ J 2

You could double to show a good diamond suit and the ability to play in hearts.

A suggestion that lets you use the best of each double:

Neither vul.

W	N	E	S
1◇	1♠	2♡	?

♠ J 2
♡ 8 7 5
◇ 10 9 5
♣ A Q 10 4 2

On this sequence, as we've seen, there isn't much chance that you'll have a club suit worth playing at the three-level. When you double, you're involved in the auction and you better have some safe escape. Let's say you double 2♡. If partner doesn't like clubs, you'll be stuck in 2♠, and I would not like to get doubled. On this sequence you are offering partner a choice between 2♠ and 3♣. Note that on this auction you know partner has a minimum overcall.

When the bidding has gone 1♣–1◇–1♠–dbl, you offer partner the choice of 2◇ or 2♡, and there is no reason to believe that partner has the worst hand possible. He may well have something extra.

Snapdragon and Rosenkranz together

I suggest you consider doing this. Treat doubles at the one-level as showing the fourth suit plus a tolerance for partner's suit. Treat doubles at the two-level as showing a raise with no honor and the raise itself as the good trump raise. And I would forget about three-level doubles. Risk versus gain is not worth it. Personally, I think the one-level double to show the fourth suit plus a semi-fit is reasonable. I think the Rosenkranz double at the two-level is okay. Both of these doubles are prone to being forgotten. For the record, I don't use these doubles unless requested to do so. Many excellent players swear by them so they do have merit. It's your choice.

Complete Responsive Double Auctions

This is an important convention, thus the examples that follow are extensive and worth a serious look. You will note that there is a bidding trick at the very end of this list. Give it some consideration.

West	East
♠ K J 8 7 6	♠ 3 2
♡ K 10 5	♡ A J 8 2
◇ K 6	◇ Q J 4 3 2
♣ Q 4 2	♣ 9 7

West	North	East	South
			1♣
1♠	2♣	dbl	pass
2♡	all pass		

Under no circumstances should either player find another bid if the opponents compete further. West does not have much of a fit and East has a minimum hand with a minimum number of hearts.

West	East
♠ K 2	♠ 8 7 3
♡ A Q J 7 6	♡ 4
◇ A 2	◇ K J 10 8 7
♣ 7 6 5 4	♣ A Q 9 3

West	North	East	South
			1♠
2♡	2♠	dbl	pass
3♣	all pass		

If they compete to 3♠, it would be fine to defend. West might even double it. If either player does choose to bid 4♣, incorrectly I think, it should be West. He is the one that knows he has real club support.

West	East
♠ A J 7 4	♠ Q 10 8 2
♡ K J 9	♡ A 8 5 4
◇ K 8 7 2	◇ Q 10 6
♣ 4 2	♣ 10 6

West	North	East	South
			1♣
dbl	2♣	dbl	pass
2♠	all pass		

A routine responsive double sequence. The value of the double is shown on this hand. It got East-West to their best major suit fit, something that might not happen if East tried to guess the major suit.

West	East
♠ K J 8 7	♠ Q 10 6 4
♡ A 9 8 5	♡ K Q 10 2
◇ Q J 3	◇ A 10 4
♣ K 3	♣ 9 6

West	North	East	South
			1♣
dbl	2♣	dbl	pass
2♡	pass	3♡	pass
4♡	all pass		

Note that a free bid by East would likely lead to a missed game, as West should pass. A jump by East would risk missing the correct suit, and a cuebid would leave East with a guess after West chooses a suit. The double allowed East to show the majors and to raise later.

West	East
♠ K 10 7	♠ Q 6 5
♡ 8 2	♡ Q 4
◇ A 6 5 4 3	◇ J 10 8 2
♣ A Q 2	♣ K 10 7 4

West	North	East	South
			1♡
dbl	2♡	dbl	pass
3◇	all pass		

East's double is stretching things. Having the responsive double does ensure that you reach the proper minor. Diamonds is much superior to clubs. Finding them is easy after East's marginal double.

West	East
♠ Q J 10 7	♠ A 2
♡ 3 2	♡ 10 5
◇ A J 8 5	◇ K Q 9 2
♣ A Q 9	♣ J 8 6 5 4

West	North	East	South
			2♡
dbl	3♡	dbl	pass
4◇	all pass		

On this hand East used the responsive double at the three-level. He needs this good a hand to commit the partnership to the four-level. I will show you another bidding trick at the end of these examples.

West	East
♠ K Q 9 7	♠ J 8 4 2
♡ A Q 8 6	♡ K J 7 3
◇ 3	◇ 4 2
♣ A 10 6 5	♣ K Q 9

West	North	East	South
			1◇
dbl	3◇	dbl	pass
4◇	pass	4♡	all pass

East makes a responsive double and West, knowing there should be a game, bids 4◇ to locate East's best major. East might have a five-card major and a four-card major so finding the right one is important.

West		East	
♠ 8 2		♠ 9 3	
♡ K J 8 7		♡ Q 2	
◇ Q 5 4		◇ K 10 9 6 2	
♣ A Q 10 7		♣ K 9 6 4	

West	North	East	South
			1♠
dbl	2♠	dbl	pass
3♣	all pass		

Another routine sequence. East doubles to show the minors and West bids his longer minor. East's hand is close to minimum. Note that East likes his ♡Q so correctly counts it as a useful card.

West		East	
♠ Q 8 7 5		♠ K 10 3 2	
♡ K J 9		♡ Q 10 5 3	
◇ K 2		◇ J 4	
♣ A 6 3 2		♣ J 9 7	

West	North	East	South
			1◇
dbl	2◇	dbl	pass
2♠	3◇	all pass	

East should not make the error of raising to 3♠. That would be forward-going and runs the risk of West continuing to game. If West has something extra he can bid again. Note that the responsive double helped you find your best suit. There is no need to push further except when you have suitable values.

West		East	
♠ A 10 8		♠ K 9 3	
♡ K 10 4 2		♡ Q J 6	
◇ A Q 3 2		◇ K 7 6 4	
♣ 4 2		♣ 9 8 5	

West	North	East	South
			1♣
dbl	2♣	dbl	pass
2♡	pass	pass	3♣
3◇	all pass		

This is a good sequence. East-West would have been content to play in 2♡, but when pushed were able to find a superior fit. East has no reason to take any bid other than his original double.

West	East
♠ Q 8 7 6	♠ K J 10 3
♡ A J 9 5	♡ K 7 6 4 3
◇ K Q 4	◇ 8 6 2
♣ 3 2	♣ 7

West	North	East	South
			1♣
dbl	2♣	dbl	pass
2♡	pass	pass	3♣
pass	pass	3♡	all pass

This is a rare hand where East may compete to the three-level when he wasn't earlier worth a raise. Sequences like these invite penalty doubles so it is useful to have good trumps, as in this hand.

West	East
♠ A K J 8 7	♠ Q 2
♡ 10 5 4	♡ A K J 7
◇ Q 6 5 4	◇ K J 10 3
♣ 3	♣ 8 6 2

West	North	East	South
			1♣
1♠	2♣	dbl	pass
2◇	pass	3♣	pass
3◇	pass	3♠	pass
4♠	all pass		

Getting to 4♠ or 5◇ should be a good result. 5◇ is nominally cold, but 4♠ will be okay. Note that East doubles first to show his approximate shape, followed by a cuebid to catch up on his strength. At the end East bid 3♠, implying two-card support (else he would have approached the hand differently), and that allowed West to make the final decision. West chose spades because he had a fine suit. Had he overcalled on ♠K10864, he would have returned to diamonds.

West	East
♠ Q 8 7 6 5	♠ J 2
♡ K 2	♡ Q 9 7 5 4
◇ K J 7 6	◇ A Q 10 8
♣ K 2	♣ 7 3

West	North	East	South
			1♣
1♠	2♣	dbl	3♣
3◇	all pass		

When partner makes a responsive double you should compete very strongly when you have a fit in either of his suits. When both sides have fits you have to fight for what's yours. Don't give up quietly. Note East's awkward hand. He has imperfect shape but he does have values for a bid at the two-level. 2♡, another possibility, is rejected because of the poor suit.

West	East
♠ A K 8 7 6 5	♠ 3
♡ 3	♡ Q 5 4
◇ J 10 8 7	◇ K 9 6 5
♣ Q 2	♣ A 9 8 5 4

West	North	East	South
			1♡
1♠	2♡	dbl	pass
3◇	all pass		

With good support for one of partner's suits, it would be bad practice to rebid spades. Note that if either opponent continues to 3♡, you can bid 3♠. Partner can pass with a doubleton or return to diamonds as he wishes.

West	East
♠ A 7 6 5 4	♠ J 2
♡ K 6	♡ 3
◇ K Q 7 5	◇ J 10 8 6 4
♣ 3 2	♣ A Q 7 5 4

West	North	East	South
			1♡
1♠	2♡	dbl	pass
3◇	3♡	pass	pass
4◇	all pass		

West should not sell out. With a heart lead 4◇ will make, possibly with an overtrick. The key is that West has a good fit and is willing to compete further. If West had a bunch of garbage he might decide to give it up.

West	East
♠ K J 7 6 5	♠ 9
♡ K 5 4	♡ A 7 6 3
◇ 3 2	◇ K Q 10 8 7 5
♣ K 7 6	♣ 5 3

West	North	East	South
			1♣
1♠	2♣	2◇	all pass

With great diamonds and so-so hearts, East just bids his diamonds. If East had ♡AQ10x and ◇K107654, doubling would be a sane choice.

West	East
♠ A J 3	♠ K Q 7 6
♡ 2	♡ Q 9 8 7 6 4
◇ A 10 9 7 6 3	◇ K 2
♣ Q 5 4	♣ 8

West	North	East	South
			1♣
1◇	2♣	dbl	3♣
pass	pass	3♡	pass
3♠	all pass		

Each player had to make some decisions here. East chose to double because the spades were so good and the hearts somewhat attenuated. But he wasn't willing to sell out to 3♣. Thus the 3♡ bid. West knew East had four spades to go with longer hearts and decided to play in the 4-3 fit. Note that East wasn't even close to raising 3♣ to four. If West had a good enough hand for game he would have bid over 3♣. This is a difficult hand which was reasonably resolved.

West	East
♠ A 10 8 7 6	♠ J 2
♡ 8 7	♡ 9 2
◇ K 5 4	◇ A Q 8 7
♣ K 5 4	♣ A J 9 7 6

West	North	East	South
			1♡
1♠	2♡	dbl	pass
3♣	pass	pass	3♡
pass	pass	dbl	all pass

This is not a penalty double in the sense that East has a vicious trump stack. Rather, East is announcing a hand with shape consistent with the responsive double and which includes good defense. Note that East can't be too short in hearts or he would have enough spades to raise West's spades or enough shape to raise West's clubs.

West	East
♠ Q J 9 7 6	♠ 4 2
♡ 4 2	♡ A 3
◇ A 8 7	◇ K J 9 4
♣ Q J 5	♣ A 9 6 4 3

West	North	East	South
			1♡
1♠	2♡	dbl	3♡
pass	pass	dbl	all pass

This might make, but at matchpoints at least, the risk should be taken. Note also that East could count on a better hand from West at IMPs. From East's point of view, West will sit for this only when he expects to beat it, or if he has no reasonable escape suit. In the first case, they will go down. And in the second case, the reason partner doesn't know what to bid is that he has no suit of appropriate length to bid, which in turn means he doesn't have a singleton heart.

West	East
♠ A 10 8 7 5	♠ Q 2
♡ Q 6 2	♡ K J 9 7
◇ 4	◇ 10 8 2
♣ K 10 8 7	♣ A Q 9 3

West	North	East	South
			1◇
1♠	2◇	dbl	pass
3♣	pass	pass	3◇
pass	pass	dbl	pass
3♡	pass	4♣	all pass

East knows West has exactly 5-3-1-4 and a weak hand. If West's hearts were equal to or longer than his clubs he would bid hearts before clubs, and with a good hand he would have bid over 3◇.

West	East
♠ K Q J 10 7 6	♠ 8 2
♡ 8 7	♡ J 9 4
◇ K 5 4	◇ A Q 10 6
♣ 4 2	♣ K Q J 9

West	North	East	South
			1♡
1♠	2♡	dbl	3♡
pass	pass	dbl	pass
3♠	all pass		

West has no problem running to 3♠. East's auction usually shows around 11-13 points. Inasmuch as West's overcall is based on playing strength and not defensive strength, he should move it out to 3♠. West couldn't do this earlier over 3♡ as that would show a much better hand.

West		East	
♠ K J 8 7		♠ Q 10 6 2	
♡ K 10 6		♡ A J 8 2	
◇ A 5 4 2		◇ K J 3	
♣ 9 3		♣ 10 7	

West	North	East	South
			1♣
dbl	2♣	dbl	3♣
pass	pass	dbl	pass
?			

East's second double here is very much the same as if West had overcalled, rather than doubled. West can pass or bid 3♠. West's choice is unclear. For the record, East-West have seven potential defensive tricks.

West		East	
♠ Q J 6 2		♠ K 10 5 3	
♡ K 5 4		♡ A J 6 2	
◇ A J 8 7 5		◇ Q 6	
♣ 3		♣ Q 10 4	

West	North	East	South
			1♣
dbl	2♣	dbl	3♣
pass	pass	dbl	pass
3♠	all pass		

East's double of 3♣ showed that he has a good 10 or more points. It is not a penalty double. Essentially, East is saying he has 4 or more points than he showed with his original double. West bids 3♠ and East passes. East knows that West has a minimum hand since he did not bid over 3♣ and a well-judged sequence finishes in 3♠.

West	East
♠ A Q 9 6 2	♠ K 10
♡ A Q 5 4	♡ J 10 7 6 3
◇ 5	◇ A 9 7 6 2
♣ 10 8 3	♣ 4

West	North	East	South
			1♣
1♠	2♣	dbl	3♣
4♡	all	pass	

West has a huge hand once East shows the red suits. West expects East to have two clubs at most and perhaps only one. With good hearts, West bids game, not leaving East to make a decision that West is able to make himself.

West	East
♠ Q 10 3	♠ K J 6 5
♡ A J 8 7 6	♡ Q 9
◇ K 2	◇ Q J 10 9 8
♣ 10 6 3	♣ 4 2

West	North	East	South
			1♣
1♡	2♣	dbl	pass
2♠	pass	pass	3♣
all pass			

East made a responsive double and later sold out to 3♣. East's hand is nothing special since West did not promise four spades. There might be no real fit. East tried and West never showed much interest. Defending is best. Note that if West happened to have four spades he could compete with 3♠ if he had any kind of extra values. He has only three trumps so that should cause him to retire.

A SPECIAL DOUBLE

West	East
♠ J 10 5 3	♠ 9 4 2
♡ A 9	♡ 7 6
◇ Q 7 6	◇ A K J 10 9 8
♣ A K 7 4	♣ J 9

West	North	East	South
			2♡
dbl	3♡	dbl	pass
3NT	all pass		

Here is a bidding trick that deserves your attention. West doubles a weak two in a *major*, 2♡ in this case, and finds East with a good hand. How should East bid over 3♡? If East bids 4◇ that will be too high and the best spot, 3NT, will be lost. Can East get to 3NT or is that too difficult?

A very acceptable answer is to play that a double by East on this sequence asks for 3NT. On this hand West can bid it. If West cannot bid 3NT, he has to find a bid and East will show his hand. This treatment works well if West has a stopper in their major. It does not work so well if West does not have a stopper. My feeling is that this is a good double because the prize is so worthwhile.

Be aware that you lose the ability to make a responsive double showing both minors. You must decide which hand type is most important for you to show. Both have value.

CHAPTER THIRTEEN
HANDS WHERE RESPONDER HAS GOOD BUT UNCLEAR VALUES
VARIOUS CONTINUATIONS BY THE OVERCALLER

Here is another face of the cuebid.

So far there have been several examples of cuebids by the overcaller's partner. There have been cuebids with intention to show a game force in a new suit. There have been cuebids to show a raise of partner's suit. And there is the cuebid to show a good hand where you have no idea what to do.

You've also probably noted that partner won't have any idea which cuebid you are making and his first response will somehow have to cater to all the possibilities. So. First let's look at the "I have a good hand and don't know what to do" cuebid, and then we'll see what partner should do.

Neither vul.

W	N	E	S
1♣	1♠	2♣	?

♠ K 2
♡ A Q 3
◇ K Q J 9 2
♣ 10 6 3

Who knows? The usual criteria. Good hand. Game is possible. But where? 3♣ starts the dialogue. This is a rare hand where you wish that a new suit, 2◇, would be forcing. The later auction may be difficult and the only comfort I can offer is that this hand is almost impossible to have.

Neither vul.

W	N	E	S
1♣	1♠	pass	?

♠ Q 2
♡ A K J 7
◇ K J 10 4
♣ 8 6 2

2♣. You could have game in anything except clubs. It will often be the case that when you have a good hand with no clear direction, it will include two or three cards in the opener's suit with no stopper. If you had a stiff or void you would probably have a fit or a suit of your own. With a stopper, you might have been able to bid some number of notrump. Here is how the bidding might continue.

If partner bids 2◇, you will raise to 3◇. This rates to be not forcing since you can cuebid 3♣ at this juncture if you choose.

If partner bids 2♡, raise to game.

If partner bids 2♠, you have a tough hand indeed. Raising to 3♠ is a possible bid, although it won't have lots of fans. Another possible bid is to pass since your partner did show a minimum.

Neither vul.

W	N	E	S
1♠	2♣	pass	?

♠ J 8 7
♡ K Q 4
◇ A 10 9 6 5
♣ Q 3

2♠. Game is possible but not guaranteed. If partner shows no interest you can stop in a partscore.

N-S vul.

W	N	E	S
1♠	2♣	2◇	?

♠ 8 6 2
♡ A Q 3
◇ K 9 7
♣ K J 4 2

Well? The only explanation for all this bidding is that someone has psyched. Probably the opener. If it's partner you should get a new one, and if it's RHO it would be unusual. Psyching a 2/1 is an infrequent strategy at best. Identifying the problem, though, doesn't provide the answer. Should you jump to 5♣? Should you try 2NT or 3NT? Should you cuebid, and if so, which suit should you cue?

Two bids can be eliminated rather easily. 2NT, because it's a gross underbid. And 5♣ because:

1. 3NT could be the right game.
2. You could be missing a slam. Partner will expect a highly distributional hand rather than this balanced one. It's unlikely he could continue.

3NT is not such a bad bid as it may seem. LHO, who has psyched, may well not lead a spade, or partner might have a stopper, or the suit might be only four cards long. But it will end the auction and 5♣ or 6♣ could be best.

This leaves 2♠ and 3◇ as your strong, exploratory bids. Either can lead to complications. Partner should be able to determine there has been a psyche and cooperate in untangling this somewhat messy affair, but it will be awkward. Here are some questions for which I have no answers.

1. Should you cuebid your stopper? That is, your ◇K as opposed to three small spades.
2. Should you automatically make the cheapest cuebid, 2♠?
3. If you cuebid 2♠, should partner bid notrump with a spade stop or does he need a diamond stop as well?

I would try 2♠, but I have no idea what will happen. The questions are valid, however, and you might find it worthwhile discussing them in your partnerships.

Neither vul.

W	N	E	S
1♣	1♡	1♠	?

♠ 982
♡ Q 3
◇ A K Q 10 3
♣ K 6 5

Here is a more realistic problem with many of the considerations of the previous problem. This hand came up and everyone had his bid. Each bidder had minimum values, but they were for real. Once again you have a number of potential games ranging from 3NT to 4♡ to 5♢. On the other hand, your limit could be 2♢, or even 1♢. Partner could have something like:

♠ K 7 3   ♡ A J 10 6 4   ◇ J 2   ♣ 10 7 3

in which case the defense may take three spades and three clubs. Unlucky, but possible. With good luck, though, you might be able to make as many as eleven tricks. Not bidding a game, or at least trying for one, is a bit conservative.

So the best bid is? I vote for 2♢, a bid that looks really feeble but which rates to get us a plus score. If partner passes, we do not rate to have a game. If partner rebids 2♡, I will raise to 3♡. If he bids 3♢, unexpected, I have another guess. One point of this hand is that you have a potentially wasted ♣K and any spade honor partner has may be wasted too. This hand serves as a warning to anyone who is listening.

Overcaller's Rebids After Partner Makes a Cuebid

To cover all possible cuebidding sequences would require an encyclopedia, let alone a chapter. In the interest of space, I'm going to look at a few cuebidding auctions and the basic considerations that make them work.

When partner cuebids, there are three likely hands he may have. A game force in another suit, some sort of raise for your suit, or some good hand with no clear bid available. Your rebid should cater to all these possibilities.

RULE

When partner cuebids you should assume partner has the weakest hand possible; that is, a raise of your overcall. If partner has a better hand than that, then he will bid again and clarify.

Neither vul.

W	N	E	S
		1♣	1♠
pass	2♣	pass	?

♠ K Q 10 7 5
♡ A J 4
◇ 3 2
♣ 9 7 5

With the example hand here I would not wish to be higher than 2♠ if partner has the 11-point raise, and would rebid 2♠. Partner is allowed to pass this. Here is the auction so far:

West	North	East	South
		1♣	1♠
pass	2♣	pass	2♠
pass	?		

If partner raises to 3♠ I would pass, feeling my three little clubs were a big warning plus my hand is barely more than a minimum. Note that 3♠ is not forcing.

If partner bids 3♡, it is a new suit and a game force. Raise to 4♡.

If partner bids 3◇ it is a game force and I would rebid 3♡. This can't be a suit or it would have been shown earlier. If partner goes back to 3♠, I would go on to 4♠. If he rebids diamonds I would give some consideration to passing. There is a lot to be said for defining game-forcing cuebids as being forcing to 3NT or four of a suit. This would allow you to stop in four of a minor if other games were not viable.

And finally, partner may pass 2♠ if he has a minimum cuebid with a spade raise of 11 or 12 points.

Neither vul.

W	N	E	S
		1♣	1♠
pass	2♣	pass	?

♠ A 10 8 7 5
♡ 4 2
◇ K J 9 4 3
♣ 9

2◇. Partner's cuebid is forcing to 2♠, so you can afford to make a descriptive bid. 2◇ does not imply any extra values at all. If partner returns to 2♠ it shows a strong but passable raise, which I would pass. If partner bids 3♠, continue to four. If partner bids 2♡, game forcing, rebid 2♠. I think I would want a bit more to try 3◇. If partner bids 2NT, rebid 3◇. When partner cuebids 2♣ and then bids 2NT he is showing a slightly better hand than a direct 2NT response. Both auctions are invitational only.

Neither vul.

W	N	E	S
		1♣	1♡
pass	2♣	pass	?

♠ 8 7
♡ A Q 10 8
◇ 3 2
♣ A J 9 4 3

2♡. This does not guarantee a five-card suit. It simply says you have some sort of minimum hand which does not have another minimum bid available, such as the preceding hand. This hand is actually good enough to go on to game if partner raises to 3♡. If partner instead bids 2♠ or 3◇, you should bid some minimum number of notrump. Note that you do this in spite of an unstopped suit.

N-S vul.

W	N	E	S
		1♣	1♠
pass	2♣	pass	?

♠ A Q 8 7 6
♡ Q 2
◇ A K 7 3
♣ J 7

2◇. You have a fine hand and will make sure of reaching some game eventually. Note that partner's cuebid is forcing to 2♠, so you can begin by showing some distributional feature without fear of being dropped. You can catch up on your strength later.

Neither vul.

W	N	E	S
		1◇	1♡
pass	2◇	pass	?

♠ A 7 6
♡ K Q J 9 5
◇ 4 2
♣ K 7 6

The one thing you must not do is rebid 2♡. Partner could pass this. I would try 2♠ and hope partner doesn't get enthusiastic about them. If he raises hearts or introduces notrump, raise to game.

Neither vul.

W	N	E	S
		1♠	2♣
pass	2♠	pass	?

♠ Q 10 7
♡ 4 2
◇ A J
♣ A Q 10 9 7 3

2NT. You are hardly embarrassed about your values and as such should show your stopper. Don't worry about the lack of a heart stopper. You can't have everything. If you feel that your hand is worth 3NT, there is nothing wrong with that. You have slightly more than a minimum and your clubs are excellent. Definitely do not rebid 3♣ with this hand. A question you will run into is whether 2NT by you is forcing. You do show more than a minimum so it is reasonable to play it as forcing. Your decision.

Neither vul.

W	N	E	S
		1♡	2♣
pass	2♡	pass	?

♠ 4
♡ Q J 7 2
◇ 4 2
♣ A Q J 10 8 7

3♣. True, you have a heart stopper, but your hand is a bit weak in terms of notrump. Plus, you are looking at two unstopped suits, not one.

N-S vul.

W	N	E	S
	1♣	1♠	
pass	2♣	pass	?

♠ Q J 10 8 7
♡ K 8 7
◇ 4 2
♣ A 6 5

2♠, in spite of the club stopper. You need in the neighborhood of opening bid strength to bid 2NT. A balanced hand does not qualify per se. If over 2♠ partner cuebids again, or if he bids 3◇, you can bid 3NT. Partner will assume a weakish hand and should not get unduly excited.

N-S vul.

W	N	E	S
	1◇	1♠	
pass	2◇	pass	?

♠ A Q J 8 7 6
♡ 3
◇ 8 7 5
♣ A J 5

3♠. This shows extra values, a good six-card suit, and is a game force. You could have a much bigger hand for this bid. The important point is that opposite any minimum cuebid you want to be in game. You are not jumping because you have a six-card suit. You are jumping because you have a six-card suit plus a good hand.

A Pair of Tricks to Help You Locate a Stopper in Opener's Suit

The two bidding tricks following apply when you overcall and partner makes a cuebid. In this specific situation, you have two very useful tools that will help sort out which game to play in. If notrump is an option, this bidding trick will help.

Trick One: Cuebidding to show a partial or full stopper

N-S vul.

W	N	E	S
	1♣	1♠	
pass	2♣	pass	?

♠ A Q 10 8 6
♡ A 2
◇ K 6 3
♣ J 8 7

For starters, you can't bid 2♠, as this could be passed. You could bid 2◇, intending to catch up on values later, but you do have a balanced hand suited to notrump. The only drawback is no club stopper. For partnerships wishing to devote a little discussion to system you can try this convention. Cuebid 3♣. This is a cuebid response to a cuebid, and it means the following. "I have values to be bidding at this level and I have a half stopper *or better* in the cuebid suit." It also tends to show a balanced hand, as you would prefer to show your distribution if holding a second suit. With suitable values, you would cuebid on any of these holdings:

♣ Q x
♣ J x x
♣ K x x
♣ A x x   etc.

When partner has a half stopper himself, he can bid notrump if he wishes. This means you can untangle stoppers like Qx opposite Jxx, and you can play notrump from the right side when you have combined holdings like these:

A x x   opposite   Q x
K x x   opposite   Q x
K x x   opposite   J x x

Note that when you have a full stopper you can always bid notrump later if partner can't do it himself.

Trick two: Redoubling to show a partial or full stopper

An extension of this convention can be used when RHO doubles partner's cuebid. When holding something in their suit you can redouble. This is an excellent understanding to have as it affords you a descriptive bid with no loss of bidding room. Do remember, however, that you need a goodish hand for this action. A stopper or a half stopper does not of itself warrant a redouble.

Neither vul.

W	N	E	S
	1♡	2♦	
pass	2♡	dbl	?

♠ 8 7
♡ A 6 2
♦ A Q J 10 8 3
♣ Q 10

Redouble, showing half a stopper or better. This is a good hand with interest in hearing partner bid notrump if possible. If he can not bid notrump, you will bid it yourself. By redoubling, you get partner to bid it if he has a partial heart stopper. 3NT will play better from his side if he has Qx or similar in opener's suit.

Neither vul.

W	N	E	S
		1♣	1♦
1♠	2♣	pass	?

♠ 8 2
♡ A 6 5
♦ A K Q 10 8 5
♣ 4 2

While you could consider 2♡, 3♦ is a more natural and descriptive bid. This jump is forcing to 3NT or four of something, so it's possible to quit short of game. This is only the case when your suit is a minor.

Neither vul.

W	N	E	S
		1♠	2◇
pass	2♠	pass	?

♠ 8 7 3
♡ A 2
◇ K Q J 10 8 7
♣ K 5

Sometimes it is impractical to jump when partner cuebids because it will get you past 3NT. If this is the case, you may wish to manufacture some other call. I would try 3♣ here. If partner bids 3◇, I'll try 3♡, looking for 3NT.

Neither vul.

W	N	E	S
		1♠	2◇
pass	3◇	pass	?

♠ Q 4
♡ A 2
◇ A Q J 10 8 3
♣ Q 7 5

When partner has raised, as in this auction, you can consider a cuebid as an effort to look for 3NT. Due to the fact that you are running out of room, you can't assign more than one possible meaning to the cuebid. I suggest you do this:
1. Notrump equals a full stopper.
2. A cuebid equals a half stopper.
3. Another suit equals no stopper.
    With this hand, you could bid 3♠ as your search for 3NT. If you had the ♡Q instead of the ♠Q you could bid 3♡.

Note that this treatment only works when you have room to make your various bids.

Neither vul.

W	N	E	S
		1♡	2◇
pass	3◇	pass	?

♠ J 10
♡ 8 6
◇ A Q 10 8 7
♣ A K Q 9

In keeping with the guidelines of the previous hand, your bid here would be 3♠. This isn't intended as a psyche. It's just the only bid left to explore the possibility of 3NT. Cuebidding 3♡ would imply a half stopper in hearts.

I hardly guarantee any of this. But you will find that some reasonably concise definitions will work far better in general than a go-as-you-please guessing game.

The next section is offered with an apology. I would like to present a number of hands on cuebids with complete auctions. This part I can do. But because of space considerations there won't be nearly room enough for the discussion each hand deserves. Some discussion, yes. But not as much as I would like. Nonetheless, this is an important section as the many faces of the cuebid will be in evidence.

CHAPTER FOURTEEN
QUIZ ON RESPONDING TO OVERCALLS

The hands in this extensive section show many examples of responding to partner's overcall. The tools include various raises and also include the responsive double. This is an important section. Many of the hands have little tidbits that you would do well to note. Skimming these hands is not a good idea.

Neither Vul.				**West**	**East**
W	N	E	S	♠ J 8 7	♠ A Q 10 9 5 2
			1♣	♡ K Q 10 9 4	♡ J 3
1♡	2♣	3♠	all pass	◇ K 6 3	◇ A Q 7
				♣ 4 2	♣ 10 5

East's 3♠ bid is invitational. West has a fit but he has a minimum, aceless hand otherwise. I suggest he pass 3♠. Game is against the odds since South rates to have the missing ♠K.

Neither Vul.				**West**	**East**
W	N	E	S	♠ Q 2	♠ A J 10 8 7 3
			1♣	♡ A Q 6 5 4	♡ 8
1♡	pass	2♣	pass	◇ K 10 3	◇ A Q J 4
2♡	pass	2♠	pass	♣ 5 4 2	♣ K 3
3♠	pass	4♠	all pass		

East has too much to bid 2♠, which would be invitational. Cuebidding 2♣ and then bidding 2♠ creates a forcing auction. When East shows his spade suit, West raises and East goes on to game. East needs a little luck with this approach. If West has no fit at all, game may be too high.

Neither Vul.				**West**	**East**
W	N	E	S	♠ A Q 10 8	♠ K 7 6 5
			1◇	♡ 3 2	♡ A 5
1♠	pass	3◇	pass	◇ A J 8 7	◇ 10 5
4♠	all pass			♣ K 5 4	♣ A 10 8 6 2

East uses the jump cuebid to show at least a limit raise with four or more trumps. West does not have to worry that he has only four spades because East promises four at least. West, with a maximum hand, is happy to bid game.

N-S Vul.				West	East
W	**N**	**E**	**S**	♠ K J 8 6 5	♠ Q 10 2
			1◇	♡ 4 2	♡ A 8 6 5 3
1♠	pass	2◇	pass	◇ A J 3	◇ 10 5 2
2♠	all pass			♣ 10 6 5	♣ A J

East cuebids, showing at least a balanced limit raise. West has a minimum and rebids his suit. He does not bid 2NT, which would promise more. East knows West is minimum and passes it out. A nice partnership sequence.

Neither Vul.				West	East
W	**N**	**E**	**S**	♠ K J 8 6 5	♠ A 9 2
			1◇	♡ 4 2	♡ A 8 6 5 3
1♠	pass	2◇	pass	◇ A J 3	◇ 10 5 2
2♠	pass	3♠	all pass	♣ 10 6 5	♣ A J

East has a better hand than in the previous example. He cuebids and West shows a minimum. East has excellent values and is entitled to raise to 3♠. West has close to a real minimum and passes 3♠. Note that West knows East has three-card support. East would have responded 3◇ if he had four.

Neither Vul.				West	East
W	**N**	**E**	**S**	♠ 8 7 2	♠ Q J 4
			1♣	♡ A Q 10 9 8	♡ K 7 5 2
1♡	pass	3♣	pass	◇ A 6 5	◇ 8 3
3♡	pass	4♡	all pass	♣ 4 2	♣ A K 8 5

East might just raise to 4♡ but the route he takes is fine. East's 3♣ bid shows a limit raise or better with four trumps. When West signs off, East goes on to game since he has so many extras.

Both Vul.				West	East
W	**N**	**E**	**S**	♠ J 2	♠ Q 10 8 3
			1♣	♡ K Q J 8 7 5	♡ A 6 4
1♡	pass	2♣	pass	◇ A Q 8	◇ 4 2
3♡	pass	4♡	all pass	♣ 10 5	♣ A 9 8 7

East has a minimum 2♣ cuebid but his two aces count for a lot. West's 3♡ bid is forcing so East bids game. On some layouts, West's bid might lead to better things.

Neither Vul.				West	East
W	**N**	**E**	**S**	♠ 7 2	♠ Q 8 5
			1◇	♡ A Q 9 6 3	♡ K 2
1♡	pass	2◇	pass	◇ K Q 4	◇ 8 7 5
2NT	pass	3NT	all pass	♣ Q 9 7	♣ A K J 4 2

East has a good hand with no good bid. He chooses 2◇ and hopes the auction does not get out of hand. Really a tough hand. West has more than a minimum and is just within range of his 2NT bid. East goes on to game. A spade lead may set this but that is just unlucky. In the event that West rebids 2♡, East should probably pass even though it risks playing in a 4-2 fit.

Neither Vul.				West	East
W	**N**	**E**	**S**	♠ K Q 10 7 6	♠ 8
			1♡	♡ 4 3 2	♡ 10 6 5
1♠	pass	2♡	pass	◇ 8 6	◇ A K Q J 9 5
2♠	pass	3◇	pass	♣ A J 4	♣ K Q 3
3♡/♠	pass	4◇	all pass		

This is a very difficult hand. West correctly overcalls 1♠ and East cuebids 2♡. East is thinking of 3NT, and a 3◇ bid now would not show these values. West rebids 2♠ to show a minimum overcall. East bids 3◇ showing a good hand with diamonds. 3◇ is forcing, which means West must bid again. What that bid should be is the hard part of this auction. West can choose from 3♠, which implies another spade, or he can bid 3♡, which more or less asks East for a heart stopper. East does not have one and he rebids diamonds. West can pass this and does. Down one. Unlucky, but more or less unavoidable. It is better than 3NT down two.

EW Vul.				West	East
W	**N**	**E**	**S**	♠ K 4	♠ Q 5 3
			1♣	♡ A 10 7	♡ K J 8 4
1◇	pass	2♣	dbl	◇ K Q J 8 4	◇ A 10 9 3
rdbl	pass	2NT	pass	♣ J 3 2	♣ Q 5
3NT	all pass				

West overcalls 1◇ and East cuebids 2♣. East intends to pass if West rebids 2◇. South doubles 2♣ and West redoubles to show a good hand with either half a stopper or a full stopper in clubs. East's hand is pretty good now that West has shown extras, so East bids 2NT, knowing that East-West have a club stopper. West raises and a good 3NT is reached. East has some guessing to do but the contract is worth bidding.

Both Vul.				West	East
W	**N**	**E**	**S**	♠ A Q 10 7	♠ K 6 5
			1♡	♡ A 6 5 4	♡ Q 2
1♠	pass	2♡	pass	◇ K J 2	◇ A 9 8 7
3♡	pass	3NT	all pass	♣ 8 7	♣ Q 9 4 2

This auction is similar to the previous hand. West overcalls 1♠ and East cuebids. South passes and West bids 3♡, showing a good hand with something in hearts. East knows his ♡Q is worth something in notrump and bids it.

Neither Vul.				West	East
W	**N**	**E**	**S**	♠ Q 10 8 7 5	♠ J 9 6 2
			1♣	♡ A Q 5 4	♡ 3
1♠	pass	3♣	pass	◇ 4	◇ K 10 9 5 3
4♠	all pass			♣ K 8 7	♣ A 4 2

West overcalls (better than doubling) and East makes the jump cuebid of 3♣. West knows that East has four trumps and some shape and goes to game. Considering how much better West's hand is than it has to be, West is on sound ground with this bid.

Both Vul.				West	East
W	**N**	**E**	**S**	♠ A 9 7 6 5	♠ 4
			1♣	♡ A Q 2	♡ 10 8 5 4
1♠	2♣	2◇	pass	◇ K J 3	◇ A Q 10 6 4 2
3♣	pass	3NT	all pass	♣ 4 2	♣ K 5

West overcalls 1♠ and East bids 2◇. This bid is natural. It shows modest values. West does something that is often overlooked. He likes diamonds and he is not ashamed of his hand. West can choose 3♣ here, or perhaps a conservative 3◇ bid. I like 3♣ because West has solid side cards along with his diamond fit. For this cuebid to show half a stopper requires that your side both know about the diamond fit. Note that using a cuebid to show half a stopper or better comes only after partner's cuebid.

Both Vul.				West	East
W	**N**	**E**	**S**	♠ 8 2	♠ K 5 3
			1♠	♡ 8 2	♡ A Q 7 3
2◇	pass	3NT	all pass	◇ A Q J 10 8 7	◇ K 9 4 2
				♣ A J 4	♣ 8 3

West overcalls 2◇ and East has a choice of bidding 2NT or even 3NT. I agree with East's choice of 3NT. West made a vulnerable two-level overcall so he ought to have a sound hand.

Neither Vul.				West	East
W	**N**	**E**	**S**	♠ 4 2	♠ K 7
			1♠	♡ K 2	♡ J 9 5
2◇	2♠	3◇	pass	◇ A Q 8 7 6 5 2	◇ K 4 3
3♡	pass	3NT	all pass	♣ A 8	♣ Q 6 5 4 2

West overcalls 2◇ and is very pleased to hear East raise. West tries for 3NT by bidding 3♡. If West chooses 3♠, that is acceptable. The issue is that West sees that 3NT is a good contract if East has a spade stopper.

Neither Vul.				West	East
W	**N**	**E**	**S**	♠ A Q 8 4 3	♠ J 2
			1◇	♡ J 5 4	♡ A Q 9 8
1♠	2◇	dbl	pass	◇ K 8	◇ 7 3 2
2♡	all pass			♣ 5 4 2	♣ K Q 10 9

East makes a responsive double and West shows his three cards in hearts. Since East needs West to have a full opening bid along with four hearts, I think passing 2♡ is okay.

N-S Vul.				West	East
W	**N**	**E**	**S**	♠ Q J 10 7 5	♠ 6 2
			1◇	♡ K J 2	♡ A 9 8 7
1♠	2◇	dbl	pass	◇ K 8	◇ 7 4
2♡	pass	3◇	pass	♣ 8 7 2	♣ A K Q 9 3
3NT	all pass				

East makes a responsive double and West again shows a heart holding. It is as likely as not that West has only three hearts, something East should keep in mind. East has a good enough hand that he can make a game try. His 3◇ bid suggests West consider 3NT. Note that if East had five hearts he would raise hearts. As it is, if West had a different hand, it is possible for him to return to 3♡ or 4♡. A 4-3 fit is a real possibility here. The tools used in this auction were necessary to find 3NT.

EW Vul.				West	East
W	**N**	**E**	**S**	♠ A Q 7 5 2	♠ 8 4
			1◊	♡ K J 3	♡ A Q 8 7
1♠	2◊	dbl	pass	◊ 4 2	◊ 10 7 3
3♡	pass	4♡	all pass	♣ A 6 2	♣ K Q 9 8

West has an interesting decision. He bids 1♠ and North raises. East's responsive double shows the two unbid suits, hearts and clubs. Note that East needs a fairly good hand to make a responsive double with 4-4 shape after West's overcall. If West had doubled, a responsive double routinely shows 4-4 shape because a fit is known to exist. Having said all of this, West does well to bid 3♡. He expects East to have five hearts so his ♡KJ3 is a fine holding and the rest of his hand is excellent. East has maximum values so continues to game, not really concerned that he has only four hearts.

Neither Vul.				West	East
W	**N**	**E**	**S**	♠ 8 6 5	♠ K 7 4 2
			1♣	♡ A Q 10 8 4	♡ J 9 7
1♡	dbl	2♣	dbl	◊ K 9 7	◊ A J 5
2♡	all pass			♣ Q 2	♣ K 5 4

West overcalls 1♡ and East cuebids 2♣. South doubles this. What should West bid? His choice of 2♡ was intended to show a minimum hand with five hearts and a reason to bid. In other words, West has a nice minimum. East is happy to pass this.

EW Vul.				West	East
W	**N**	**E**	**S**	♠ A Q 8 7 5	♠ K 6 4
			1♣	♡ J 2	♡ K Q 5 4
1♠	pass	2♣	pass	◊ A K 9	◊ J 7
2◊	pass	2♠	all pass	♣ 4 3 2	♣ Q J 8 5

East cuebids in response to West's 1♠ bid. West has too much to bid 2♠ so he makes a waiting bid of 2◊. East has only what he promised, no extras, and bids 2♠, which confirms his general values. West has a good hand but his ♣432 are a big worry. Expecting East to have 10-12 support points and discounting a little for his own barren shape, West settles for a plus score. 3NT by East is a good spot but I think it is too hard to bid.

Neither Vul.				West	East
W	N	E	S	♠ Q J 10 7 5	♠ K 6 4
			1♣	♡ K 2	♡ A 8 6 3
1♠	pass	2♣	pass	◇ A K 8 5	◇ J 6 4
2◇	pass	2♠	pass	♣ 4 2	♣ K 7 5
3♠	all pass				

This hand is all about how West views his hand. He overcalls 1♠ and East cuebids. West has a good hand and temporizes with 2◇. East correctly bids 2♠. In support of spades, West has a sound overcall. He has 13 useful HCP and he has good shape along with the nice ♠10. West does well to bid 3♠, asking if East likes his hand in light of the bidding. East is not pleased with his ♣K and with balanced shape, he chooses to pass.

EW Vul.				West	East
W	N	E	S	♠ A Q 8 7 5	♠ K 6 4 2
			1♣	♡ K J 4	♡ A 7 2
1♠	pass	2♣	pass	◇ A Q 10 2	◇ K J 3
2◇	pass	2♠	pass	♣ 3	♣ 9 7 2
4♣	pass	4♡	pass		
4NT	pass	5♡	pass		
6♠	all pass				

This sequence shows some ideas that I have only alluded to before. West overcalls 1♠ and East cuebids. West bids 2◇, clearly intending to bid a lot later. East returns to 2♠, thinking he has a minimum hand. Note that East has four spades. This is not expected. Only because East is 4-3-3-3 does he bid this way. After 2♠, West bids 4♣, a splinter bid. East looks at his hand this way. Given he is known to have a minimum hand, he has as good a hand as possible. He has important cards and he knows West is short in clubs so all of his other high cards are working. East cuebids and West continues to slam via Keycard Blackwood.

Neither Vul.				West	East
W	**N**	**E**	**S**	♠ K 10 7 6	♠ 4 3
			1♠	♡ 4 3	♡ K 10 7
2◇	pass	2♠	pass	◇ A Q 10 8 6	◇ K 7 5 4
2NT	pass	3◇	all pass	♣ A 6	♣ K 5 3 2

This is a quiet, well-judged sequence. West overcalls 2◇ and East cuebids. West shows a good hand with 2NT and East shows he has a minimum raise. He bids 3◇. West, with just five diamonds, accepts and it is passed out. Interestingly, 3NT has a play. The defense will lead a spade and after winning the ♠K West may be able to negotiate a heart trick. It is possible. This hand shows the edge that declarer has when he knows where the high card points are.

EW Vul.				West	East
W	**N**	**E**	**S**	♠ A J 8 7 5	♠ Q 2
			2♡	♡ K 5 4	♡ 9 3
2♠	pass	3♡	pass	◇ K Q 7	◇ A 10 8 5
3NT	all pass			♣ J 5	♣ K Q 4 3 2

West makes a thin overcall after South's weak 2♡ bid. East has a decision. With 11 good points he ought to bid, and he chooses 3♡. When you overcall over a weak two and your partner cuebids, it is usually looking for notrump. West has a heart stopper and bids 3NT. If West ducks the first heart lead and is lucky thereafter, he may make it. The importance of this hand is the mechanics of the bidding for East-West after South's 2♡ call.

Neither Vul.				West	East
W	**N**	**E**	**S**	♠ A 10 8 6 5	♠ 3
			1♡	♡ A 7 6	♡ J 2
1♠	pass	2◇	pass	◇ K 5 4	◇ A Q 9 7 6 3 2
3◇	pass	3♡	pass	♣ 10 7	♣ Q J 4
3NT	all pass				

West overcalls 1♠ and East bids 2◇. West makes a well-judged raise to 3◇ and now East can see the potential for a lot of tricks. He bids 3♡ and West bids 3NT.

Both Vul.				West	East
W	**N**	**E**	**S**	♠ A K J 6 4	♠ 8
			1♣	♡ 7 6 3	♡ A 8 5
1♠	2♣	2◇	pass	◇ K Q 6 3	◇ A 10 8 7 5 4
4♣	pass	4♡	pass	♣ 7	♣ 8 6 3
4NT	pass	5♡	pass		
6◇	all pass				

West overcalls 1♠ and East has just enough to bid 2◇, not forcing. West's hand has grown a lot. One choice, the one shown here, is a jump to 4♣, a splinter bid. East's hand just got bigger. He cuebids 4♡ and that is enough for West to check on aces before bidding slam. East has to play carefully but slam should make barring bad breaks.

Neither Vul.				West	East
W	**N**	**E**	**S**	♠ K Q 10 8 7	♠ J 2
			1♣	♡ 9 8 7	♡ A K 5
1♠	2♣	?		◇ A 10 4	◇ K Q J 8 3
				♣ 8 3	♣ 10 6 4

This is a hard hand. Good players would not agree on the best auction. Given West's 1♠ bid and North's raise to 2♣, East's choices are all over the place. His bids range from a quiet 2◇ bid, a 3♣ cuebid, and a jump to 3◇. I am showing this hand to demonstrate that not all hands are neat and tidy. 4♠ is the only game that has a chance, but if spades divide 4-2 it is in trouble. 5◇ is down off the top and 3NT has no play at all. Stopping in a partscore with these cards is probably best. Can you do it?

N-S Vul.				West	East
W	**N**	**E**	**S**	♠ 8 5	♠ J 4 2
			1♠	♡ 9 5 4	♡ A Q J 10
2◇	pass	2♠	pass	◇ A Q J 9 7	◇ 8 2
3◇	all pass			♣ A Q 5	♣ K J 10 7

Another hand with unclear resolution. West makes a scary 2◇ overcall. Definitely not a good bid if vulnerable. East once again has choices. If he tries for game with 2♠, West will rebid his diamonds. East should pass but the contract is potentially too high. Another possible choice by East is 2♡, a bid that would get some votes on a bridge panel of experts. West probably would pass that and the contract would be okay, but this doesn't prove anything. Any other ideas out there?

Both Vul.				West	East
W	**N**	**E**	**S**	♠ K 3	♠ 9 5
			1♠	♡ 9 4 2	♡ A J 3
2◊	pass	2♠	pass	◊ A Q J 8 7 6	◊ K 10 3
3◊	pass	3♠	pass	♣ 8 7	♣ A Q J 4 2
3NT	all pass				

West makes a sane 2◊ overcall and East starts thinking of game. His 2♠ cuebid didn't encourage West, who just rebid his diamonds. East bid 3♠, saying that he was extra strong and still interested in 3NT. This time West admitted a spade stopper and game was reached.

Neither Vul.				West	East
W	**N**	**E**	**S**	♠ K 2	♠ A 8
			1♠	♡ A 8 7	♡ 6 4
2◊	pass	2♠	pass	◊ K J 10 7 6 5	◊ A 4 3 2
3◊	pass	3♠	pass	♣ 4 2	♣ A K J 5 3
3NT	pass	4◊	pass		
4♡	pass	6◊	all pass		

West bid 2◊ and East started with a 2♠ cuebid. West signed off in 3◊ and East cuebid spades again. This time West bid 3NT. East's 4◊ bid indicated that he had been cuebidding toward a possible slam. West, having overcalled and then shown minimum values, decided that as minimum hands go, this was a good one. He cuebid 4♡ and East bid a slam. Not perfect since a grand slam is reasonable, but still, a well-judged sequence.

Neither Vul.				West	East
W	**N**	**E**	**S**	♠ 7 2	♠ A K 9 8 4
			1♣	♡ Q J 8 7 6 4	♡ 10 5 3
1♡	1♠	2♣	pass	◊ J 2	◊ K 7 6 5
2♡	all pass			♣ A Q 7	♣ 4

A good stop. West overcalls 1♡ and North bids 1♠. East doesn't waste time thinking of ways to defend against 1♠. East has heart support and cuebids to show it. West is content to stop in 2♡ and East respects it.

Neither Vul.				West	East
W	**N**	**E**	**S**	♠ K Q 8 7 5 2	♠ J 9 6 3
	pass	pass	1◇	♡ 7 3	♡ A K J 5
1♠	2♣	3◇	pass	◇ 3	◇ 10 9 4 2
4♠	all pass			♣ A 10 8 6	♣ 7

East uses the jump cuebid to show his hand and West, holding good values and excellent shape along with a sixth spade, goes on to game. This auction is one of the few cases where East can use a cuebid after the opponents make a 2/1 response. On an auction like this, there can be no meaning other than a good fit for partner's overcall. Note that after 2♣, 3♠ by East would be preemptive.

Neither Vul.				West	East
W	**N**	**E**	**S**	♠ 9 2	♠ 10 8 5 3
			1♠	♡ K Q 7	♡ A J 9 5
2◇	pass	2NT	all pass	◇ A J 10 9 7 5	◇ 4
				♣ J 10	♣ A Q 8 6

This hand offers another perplexing choice. West overcalls 2◇, finding East with an opening bid of sorts. East can choose from 2♡, which lies about the length of his suit; 2NT, which lies about a spade stop; and pass, which is a nothing bid. I lean to 2NT for the reason that it is closest to showing my hand. Hopefully, West will have a spade honor. Note that East should not cuebid because he won't have any idea what to do if partner rebids 3◇. Better to make a sensible misdescription, which keeps the auction simple.

N-S Vul.				West	East
W	**N**	**E**	**S**	♠ 9 2	♠ 10 8 5
			1♠	♡ K Q 7	♡ A J 9 5
2◇	pass	3♣	all pass	◇ A J 10 9 7 5	◇ 4
				♣ J 10	♣ A Q 8 6 5

This hand is exactly like the previous except that East has one less spade and one more club. These cards do not warrant a 2NT bid so East tries 3♣ instead. Not perfect at all but a sensible try.

PART THREE

CONTINUING THE AUCTION

CHAPTER FIFTEEN
OVERCALLER'S REBIDS

So far in this book we have looked at two areas of bidding. These are:

1. The overcall.
2. The response to the overcall.

With a few exceptions, the auction has gone no further. The subsequent bidding remains to be discussed.

Why was so much time devoted to the initial overcall and partner's response? Quite aside from the fact that overcalls are important are the following more subtle distinctions.

1. The overcall is one of the most dangerous actions you can take in bridge. This is because the overcaller knows less about the hand than at any other time. Why not wait for more information? Because the auction may be too high to risk entry or the information acquired may not sufficiently clarify the situation.
2. In a lesser way, responder has similar considerations. If responder raises the overcall there is no problem, as a fit has been found. But introducing a new suit is still speculative in that the information available is too limited for an accurate appraisal. That first decision, by either defender, as to whether or not to introduce a suit is very delicate. Well worth all the space devoted to it.

The subsequent bidding is much easier. Each defender has had a chance to express certain values and suits, and a rapport of sorts has been established. The opponents have been able to bid more too, and you can draw further inferences from their actions as well. Your bidding will no longer be based so much on fiction as on fact. It's much easier to judge things when you have heard from partner.

This hardly means that once you survive the first round of bidding the rest of the auction is a cakewalk. Isn't so. Once in a while you will be able to have an uncontested auction after you overcall, but most of the time your opponents are going to resent your intrusion into their hand and they are going to contest the issue quite actively. As well they should. It is a basic premise that the side that opens the bidding owns the hand, or at least they think they do, and they do not like having you steal from them.

By the time opener has made his first rebid the auction will have acquired a distinct flavor. Ownership of the hand may have been established, in which case an uneventful auction will follow. Or both sides may have claims, in which case the typical dogfight ensues. Sometimes, who owns the hand is unclear and fits are still being explored, leading to delicate pussyfooting by both sides. Sometimes this flavor is so distinct that the auction can be accurately predicted. And when the opponents play the hand, you can predict the result by looking at your hand to see if suits break well or poorly for declarer. It is very important to have a constant grasp on the state of the auction. An understanding of this will help immensely in your competitive judgment.

Remember when the auction went 1♣–pass–2♣ and I told you to bid almost regardless of your hand?

Remember when the bidding went 1♠–pass–2◊ and I told you to pass almost regardless of your hand?

These two auctions represented the extremes of safety and danger, other auctions falling somewhere in between. Being aware of the status of the auction was the key to deciding what to do on any given hand, and it remains so.

Now that the auction has progressed, you have much additional information to help you make your decision. You should use it thusly.

When the hand belongs to the opponents, you should give up on most hands. The only reason you can justify further bidding is on the basis of a good fit or an exceptional playing hand. High cards aren't enough.

When no one seems to be sure of whose hand it is, you should hope to find a fit but you must use some sense in the search. The reason for this is that it is far easier for them to double you than for you to double them. This is because they have the sound foundation of an opening bid while you are working on the more nebulous basis of an overcall. Of more importance is that on hands where no game seems to exist, –200 or –300 will be sure zeros. On partscore hands you can't afford any kind of numbers.

If they have a fit and you do not, your hunt for one has to be cautious.

If both sides have a fit, there may be a lot of bidding by both sides. If they do not have a fit and you do, that is good news because you may pressure them into indiscretions. The key is in knowing how hard to look for a fit, and then judging what to do with it.

When everyone has a fit, you may press on or you may retire, according to many factors. You may press on rather energetically with the fit you have found or in search of the one you hope to find. If this seems difficult, let me assure you of one thing. A good 70% of your decisions will consist of whether to overcall or whether to respond to partner's overcall. Once you are comfortable with that initial decision, those same deciding factors will help you greatly with the rest of the auction. Decisions remain, to be sure, but the feeling of bidding with a bag over your head is over. If your first bid is accurate you will have an excellent start on the auction. And the things which helped you with your first bid will help you with your later bids.

By the time the second round of bidding starts the number of possible considerations has risen astronomically and it is no longer feasible to inspect all the cases. Fortunately, the things which were important during the first round of bidding remain important during the next rounds as well. It only remains to determine what is happening and which rules to apply.

Introducing the Michaels cuebid

It may feel like an odd moment to introduce the Michaels cuebid. The reason I am doing so is that if you or your partner are playing Michaels cuebids and you fail to make this bid, it offers important inferences in the later part of the auction. You will find that if your partnership uses this convention, many of the hands where you do not use it will become easier.

First, a short discussion on what the bid shows and how it works. The inferences will be discussed in the quizzes following.

THE MICHAELS CUEBID

A convention that is almost universal today, but which was barely coming on the scene when *Overcalls* was first written, is the Michaels cuebid. I do not have the pages to go into this convention but can offer a few suggestions.

Typically, you need 5-5 shape to bid Michaels. The point range starts at 8 useful points for a not vulnerable overcall and 10 for a vulnerable overcall. This is my own personal perception and I promise you that lots of players have their own ideas on what you need for a Michaels cuebid.

If you cuebid a minor suit, you show both majors. This is the basic treatment but it has some twists that are recommended. For instance, if you cuebid a major, you show the unbid major and one of the minors. Which minor suit is not known at this point.

Important: Some players use something called a split-level range. This means that they bid Michaels on minimum-strength 5-5 hands and maximum-strength 5-5 hands. I, and many other players, am on record as hating this treatment. The consensus is that Michaels is better used on all 5-5 hands as long as they have the required minimum values. The reasons for this are substantial.

1. You get to use more Michaels cuebids.
2. You never get shut out of the bidding when you have a middle-range Michaels hand.
3. When you have the middle-range Michaels hands your partner can bid more accurately since he knows of your shape. If you just overcall, you may not be able to show your shape if the auction gets out of hand.
4. Say you have spades and hearts and they bid 1♣. If you bid 1♠ and later bid 2♡, your partner knows for sure that you have five spades and four

hearts. If you had 5-5 shape, you would have used Michaels. Partner's knowing when you have 5-4 is an important piece of news that he can use.

Here are some hints on responding when your partner bids Michaels.

When partner bids Michaels and RHO passes

LHO	Partner	RHO	You
1♣	2♣	pass	?

Pass   You wish to play in clubs. This is possible but not likely. Your partner will not be amused initially but when he sees your hand he will find some humor in it.

2◇   You can play this as natural or as asking for partner's choice of majors.

2♡   You want to play in 2♡. You must be careful to bid the full value of your hand when given the chance.

2♠   You want to play in 2♠.

2NT   This bid is artificial. It does not ask to play in notrump. What you usually have is a hand with three-card support for a major and game interest, and you wish to tell partner that you have three trumps and not four. Your partner bids as follows.

If not vulnerable:
> 3♣   A minimum hand (about 8-12 points).
> 3◇   A goodish hand with around 13 or 14 points.
> 3♡   A maximum hand with 15+ points.

If vulnerable:
> 3♣   A minimum hand (about 10-12 points).
> 3◇   A goodish hand with around 13 or 14 points.
> 3♡   A maximum hand with 15+ points.

Mind you, some judgment has to be used in evaluating your hand. For the sake of simplicity, you can play that 3◇ and 3♡ are forcing to game.

3♣   A cuebid. Very rare. It usually shows a game-forcing hand of some kind, perhaps looking for notrump, perhaps about to show a strong hand with diamonds.

3◇   A jump in the other minor is natural and not forcing. A good preempt is about right.

3♡   Invitational with four-card support. You are able to tell partner when you are inviting with three trumps and when you have four, which will help his judgment.

3♠   Invitational with four-card support. Partner can pass a jump to 3♡ or 3♠.

3NT   Extremely rare. This is natural and partner will pass most of the time.

When partner bids Michaels and RHO bids something

When RHO bids something, your bids can change. If RHO makes a weak bid such as a raise, your bids still have some constructiveness to them. If RHO makes a strong bid such as double, a cuebid, or a notrump bid, your bids now become competitive, not constructive.

LHO	Partner	RHO	You
1♣	2♣	2♡	?

Pass   A hand that does not want to compete. It is important that if you do have something to say, you say it now. Use this opportunity to get into their bidding.

Dbl   It is likely that the 2♡ bid is artificial. Many players use it to show a limit raise of partner's minor. If you double one of these artificial bids, you are saying you wanted to bid two of that major but do not have enough to bid three.

2♠   Wishing to compete to 2♠. Not a strong bid at all.

2NT   As always. This is artificial, asking what range of Michaels your partner has. You might have to bid 2NT on a hand with four trumps because the jump is no longer constructive.

3♣   Bidding their suit is a cuebid. Rare. You may have a huge hand with the unbid minor, in this case diamonds. You may be looking for notrump. I have seen this bid come up once in ten years so you do not need to discuss it beyond the fact that it is forcing.

3◇   Bidding the unbid minor is competitive. Your partner usually passes.

3♡   Competitive with four hearts. RHO showed some values so your bids are more competitive, even preemptive, and not invitational.

3♠   Competitive with four spades. When your RHO shows values, it is more likely that you will have a weak hand with a fit than a strong hand with a fit.

Following is a selection of Michaels hands.

Neither vul.

W	N	E	S
		1♣	2♣
pass	2♡	3♣	?

♠ KQ875
♡ KJ1072
♢ 75
♣ 3

Pass. You showed your shape and partner bid only 2♡. He had ways to show a good hand and didn't. You have a minimum hand and show it by passing. If your side can compete to 3♡, it is up to your partner to do it.

Neither vul.

W	N	E	S
		1♣	2♣
pass	2♡	3♣	?

♠ KQJ107
♡ AQJ32
♢ 97
♣ 4

This is an improved hand. You have enough to compete to 3♡. If your partner has something useful, he is entitled to go on to game. Your 3♡ bid is not a sign-off.

N-S vul.

W	N	E	S
		1♢	2♢
pass	2NT	pass	?

♠ KQ875
♡ AJ872
♢ 3
♣ K3

Partner is asking you what your range is. You have better than a minimum hand and not quite a maximum so you bid 3♢, telling partner that you have a king or so more than a minimum. The important thing is that you know what partner is doing. Usually he has an invitational hand with three cards in one of the majors. Your bid shows extras so you are going to game.

N-S vul.

W	N	E	S
		1♣	2♣
pass	pass	pass	

♠ AKJ72
♡ KQ875
♢ A5
♣ 3

How do you feel? In fact, you should be happy, relatively speaking. Your partner knows you have the majors and he said he has no interest in them. He does not have three cards in hearts or spades and he might not even have a doubleton. Here is a hand that he might have that would pass 2♣:

♠ 8   ♡ 104   ♢ Q874   ♣ Q109764

Neither vul.

W	N	E	S
		1◇	1♠
2◇	pass	pass	?

♠ Q J 8 7 4
♡ A Q 8 5
◇ 3 2
♣ A 5

Bid 2♡. You did not use Michaels so your partner will play you for a fair hand with 5-4 in the majors. This is an important inference.

Neither vul.

W	N	E	S
		1◇	2◇
dbl	3♣	pass	?

♠ J 8 7 6 5
♡ A Q J 10 5
◇ 9 3
♣ Q

Pass. You have a minimum and you did not find a fit. Your partner is escaping to clubs. Be glad your minimum values include an ace and the ♣Q, two cards you are sure will be appreciated.

Neither vul.

W	N	E	S
		1◇	2◇
dbl	3♠	pass	?

♠ K Q 7 6 5
♡ K Q J 10 5
◇ Q 3
♣ 8

Pass. You have a fair hand but the key is that your partner's bid is preemptive (competitive) after a strong bid by LHO. LHO showed some values, which means that your partner's jump is an effort to muddle their bidding. What might partner have? ♠J982 ♡83 ◇94 ♣KJ973. He doesn't have much but he does have a fit and a willingness to compete.

Neither vul.

W	N	E	S
		1♣	1♠
2♡	pass	3♡	?

♠ A Q 9 7 5
♡ 4
◇ A J 9 8 6
♣ K 5

This is a tough decision. Regrettably, you were not able to show both suits at once. If you wish to bid diamonds now, you have to do so at the four-level. Given that your partner did not raise spades and given that their side should have most of the missing high cards, passing 3♡ is sane. Mind you, if you pass, there is a chance that your partner will have ◇Kxxxx and you will miss a game. The main thing here is that your methods kept you from showing your hand on the first round.

Neither vul.

W	N	E	S
		1♡	2♡
pass	2NT	pass	?

♠ A Q 9 7 5
♡ 4
◇ 8 3
♣ A 10 7 6 5

You bid 2♡, showing spades and a minor. Partner's 2NT bid asks which minor you have. You have clubs so you bid them. If you had a bigger hand you might bid 4♣. If you happened to have a huge hand you would consider cuebidding and then bidding clubs. These Michaels cuebids are helpful but you will discover that when you have really strong hands, the Michaels cuebids can make life difficult for you.

Down to cases. Remember that the Michaels convention is in use and will be referred to in the following problems.

CASE ONE
YOU OVERCALL. PARTNER PASSES.

The first thing that should occur to you is that partner is either broke or his values are such that he could not adequately express them. You can make an educated guess as to which case exists by noting the nature of the opponents' auction. Is it strong or is it weak? Or is it unclear? If it's weak, then you can reasonably infer that partner has some values that were not suited to bidding, and if that's all you need, you can compete further. On the other hand, if the opponents' bidding is strong or unclear, you would do well to pass except on those hands where you yourself have the necessary values to continue. Should you rebid your own suit? Perhaps, but there are distinct dangers.

1. If LHO bid 1NT over your overcall, then there is a good chance he can double you if you continue.

Neither vul.

W	N	E	S
		1♣	1♠
1NT	pass	pass	?

♠ K J 7 6 5 4
♡ A Q 8
◇ K J 4
♣ 3

It looks easy to rebid 2♠, and many would. But with poor spade spots, the knowledge that LHO has a spade stop should turn you off. Your dummy rates to have 1¼ spades and 4½ points. This is the sort of hand of which –300's and –500's are made. At matchpoints you could survive 2♠ against conservative opponents because they might not double when they should, or because they might defend poorly, or because someone might decide to raise clubs. At IMPs you should clearly pass. To get this up to a 2♠ call would require better spade spots, or perhaps change the diamonds to ◇AJ10. You need something worth another trick.

    I can't imagine a hand where it would be right to rebid a five-card suit after LHO bid 1NT.

2. If LHO has made a 2/1 response, you don't have much reason to rebid your suit because the opponents are going to bid on anyway and you will merely be offering them the extra option of doubling you. Only because some people make very light or even ridiculous 2/1 bids should you bother to rebid your suit.

E-W vul.

W	N	E	S
		1♡	1♠
2♣	pass	2♡	?

♠ Q 10 8 7 6 5
♡ A 4 2
♢ K Q
♣ K 10

This is a fine 1♠ overcall. It is an equally fine pass over 2♡. The auction screams that partner is broke. If he is short in spades as well you will go for a ride.

E-W vul.

W	N	E	S
		1♡	1♠
2♣	pass	2♡	?

♠ K Q J 9 7 6
♡ 3
♢ A 10 7 5
♣ 4 2

2♠ would be okay here. You have a good suit and distribution. If partner wants to save, that's fine. Perhaps he can raise to 3♠ and you will save.

3. If LHO has made a 1/1 response you can hope for some of those missing values to be in partner's hand, but you should still be careful about bidding again.

Neither vul.

W	N	E	S
		1♣	1♢
1♡	pass	1♠	?

♠ K 8
♡ A 10 5
♢ A Q 7 5 4 2
♣ 9 4

Be aware that LHO's 1♡ bid, while not promising a lot, does not deny a good hand. 2♢ is not a safe bid, especially given your partner chose not to raise earlier. It is best to pass.

4. Only when there has been a limited sequence where both opponents have expressed the extent of their values should you be optimistic.

Neither vul.

W	N	E	S
		1♡	1♠
2♡	pass	pass	?

♠ Q J 9 7 6 5
♡ 4 3
◇ A K 7
♣ A 10

Here, for a change, you can rely on partner for a tidbit or two. I would expect partner to have something on the order of 6 points and a couple of spades. Here is a typical layout.

♠ Q J 9 7 6 5	♠ 8 3
♡ 4 3	♡ Q 9 5
◇ A K 7	◇ J 8 6 5 3
♣ A 10	♣ K 9 4

With this boring dummy you can make 1♠ or 2♠ and rate more often than not to push them to 3♡. Note that I even gave partner the ♡Q, which was wasted, rather than the ◇Q. That card would give you a play for 3♠.

Note that all examples of rebidding your suit were at the two-level. It's a rare hand that can overcall one of a suit and then find sufficient justification to be bidding at the three-level opposite a passing partner. One reason for this is that there aren't many 'weak' auctions by the opponents that would force you to the three-level. Most of their limited sequences leave you room for a simple rebid. The times you find yourself contemplating a three-level rebid are when the opponents have good hands, and this should warn you off.

Today you may overcall at the one-level and hear LHO raise opener to the three-level, which is treated by them as weak. I will look at an example of this in one of the following hands.

Neither vul.

W	N	E	S
		1♣	1♡
1♠	pass	2♠	?

♠ J 7 2
♡ A K 10 9 7 5
◇ A Q 2
♣ 3

3♡, with tempered enthusiasm. This is not a true 'weak' auction where you might overcall at the one-level and subsequently try again at the three-level. Note that LHO is still unlimited. This is not an entirely safe action to take. If you were to remove one spade and add a club, then pass would be best. As the hand stands, the ♠J72 suggests a fit. But with the change, there is a quantum rise in risk.

There will be far more occasions for rebidding your suit at the three-level after making a two-level overcall. This is because there is a frequent 'limited' auction that affords you that second chance.

N-S vul.

W	N	E	S
		1♠	2♡
2♠	pass	pass	?

♠ K 8
♡ A Q 10 9 8 6
◇ A Q 4
♣ 3 2

Here is the typical 'limited' auction by the opponents on which you can reasonably rebid your suit at the three-level with a passing partner.

Neither vul.

W	N	E	S
		1♡	2◇
2♡	pass	pass	?

♠ A J 2
♡ 4 2
◇ K Q J 9 8 7
♣ A 8

Again, 3◇. You don't have any reason to expect a fit, but partner can easily have a stray card or two. I would expect to make 3◇ as often as not. Note the following sequence.

LHO	Partner	RHO	You
		1♠	2◇
2♡	pass	2♠	?

Bidding 3◇ would be very unwise. West's 2♡ bid showed good values. You might be safe in 3◇ but you won't be safe higher and if 3◇ is too high, you rate to get doubled. A good time to pass.

Neither vul.

W	N	E	S
		1♣	1♠
2♡	pass	3♡	?

♠ K Q 10 8 7 6
♡ 4 2
◇ K 10 3
♣ A 2

Best to pass. The only reason for bidding 3♠ is that you might find a good save in 4♠. But with relatively balanced shape facing a partner who could not raise to 2♠, you should be content to let this one go. They have almost all of the missing points so you can't hope to find much in dummy. You can imagine dummies that would provide you with eight tricks but it is easier to imagine dummies that have two (or one) spades and which will provide you with only five or six tricks.

Neither vul.

W	N	E	S
		1♡	1♠
3♡¹	pass	pass	?

1. preemptive raise

♠ A Q 10 9 7 6
♡ 4 2
◇ A 10 3
♣ Q 2

Pass. Even though 3♡ is weak, that fact does not make your hand any stronger.

Neither vul.

W	N	E	S
		1♡	1♠
3♡¹	pass	pass	?

1. preemptive raise

♠ A Q 10 8 5 4 2
♡ 4
◇ A Q 3
♣ J 2

It is okay to bid 3♠. You have seven of them. On an auction like this one, if your suit is exceptional you can push a little because your partner usually has a few high-card points.

Neither vul.

W	N	E	S
		1♡	1♠
3♡¹	pass	pass	?

1. preemptive raise

♠ K Q J 10 8 4
♡ A Q
◇ Q 9 3
♣ Q 2

Pass. You have a good suit but you rate to have a lot of losers. Your partner will tend to have 3 or 4 points but that may not be enough on this hand. Judgment counts here.

When should you bid a new suit facing a passed partner?

When partner passes, should you introduce a new suit?
The decision to bid a new suit is similar to deciding whether to rebid your first suit. You need to determine the safety of the auction and consider the values your partner may have.

Neither vul.

W	N	E	S
		1♣	1♠
1NT	pass	pass	?

♠ K J 8 7 5
♡ 3
◇ A Q 6 5
♣ K 4 2

Whereas the auction has strongly warned you off rebidding spades, there is far less objection to bidding a new suit. 2◇ is clear enough to do it just about all the time.

Neither vul.

W	N	E	S
		1♣	1♡
1♠	pass	2♣	?

♠ 6 2
♡ K Q 10 8 7
◇ A Q 6 5
♣ K 2

Bid 2◇, but with the understanding that it is close. Here is a theme that I will dwell on in this set of hands. If you bid 1♡ and then bid 2◇, your partner will suspect you have 5-4 in the red suits. If you had 5-5 you might have bid 2NT, unusual, to show the two lower unbid suits, hearts and diamonds.

Neither vul.

W	N	E	S
		1♣	1♠
1NT	pass	2♣	?

♠ Q J 9 8 7
♡ 3
◇ A Q 6 5 3
♣ K 2

2◇. Read the previous hand again. On that hand I explained why partner would think you might have 5-4 shape. On this auction there is no bid you can make over 1♣ to show spades and diamonds. Barring your playing an unusual convention, you have to bid spades and then diamonds with hands like this one. Given their bidding is not strong, you have plenty to bid 2◇. Be aware that your partner won't have any inference as to your diamond length as he did on the prior hand.

Before getting into what to do after various actions by partner other than a pass, I want to make a few general observations. Some of these have been alluded to extensively already, and some will be mentioned rather frequently as we get more into the ensuing bidding.

First is the state of the auction. Have the opponents shown a fit? Have they shown strength? Have they both shown the limits of their hands? Has either opponent shown the limit of his hand? I'm well aware that I've been carrying on about all of these ideas for some time now and I've stopped to emphasize them on more than one occasion already. Well, it's time to emphasize them again. When you are involved in competitive decisions you have to have a feeling for what your side can do and a conscious recognition of those limitations. In the section just completed, that 'state' of the auction was a major factor in whether or not you bid, as was the presence or lack of a demonstrated fit for the opponents. In the sections about to be covered these factors will be no less important.

I wish there were some way to constantly dwell on these things without sounding like a nag. You get tired of hearing that you didn't shave, or that you smoke too much, or that your breath stinks of onions. After a while you hear these things but they bounce off your consciousness leaving no impression at all. I'd like to be able to make these points so they are heard and understood and used.

What, exactly, is competitive bidding?

One more general observation well worth making. It is this. Competitive bidding at bridge means competitive bidding. If this sounds so obvious that you are wondering why I mentioned it, then compare it with this: competitive bidding is not constructive bidding. What this means is that with some obvious exceptions, your defensive bidding will not be geared to bidding games and slams, but will be geared to competitive actions designed to obstruct the opponents. When you find a fit you may (some of the time) be able to explore for a game. But mostly you will be raising each other in an effort to get the opponents one trick too high, or just one trick higher. This goal dictates that many of your bids will not be forward-going, as they would be in similar circumstances for the side that opened. Instead they will be descriptive bids either looking for a fit or expressing that one has been found.

Remember. The opening side expects the hand belongs to them. The defensive side hopes the hand belongs to them, but generally accepts that it does not and then bids accordingly. Back to cases.

CASE TWO
YOU OVERCALL. PARTNER BIDS A NEW SUIT.

When you overcall you are naturally hoping to initiate a constructive dialogue between yourself and your partner. Very seldom can you compete effectively opposite a passing partner. To this end, there are three contributions he can make. One of these is a raise of your overcall, one is some number of notrump, and the last is a new suit. When partner bids a new suit you should have mixed emotions. On the plus side, you should be happy partner has some values and if you fit his suit, your side will be well placed for further action. On the down side is that partner's bid shows limited values, else he would have made a stronger bid, and he doesn't care for your suit. Further action by you should be in light of the fact that there may be a misfit but that partner is not broke.

Should you introduce the fourth suit? Let's see some examples.

Neither vul.

W	N	E	S
			1♣ 1♠
2♣	2♡	3♣	?

♠ A 10 8 7 5
♡ J 2
♢ K Q 9 6 3
♣ 4

Bid. They have a fit, you should have a fit, and you have an easy method of finding it. Bid 3♢. Note that you are not promising a big hand. Contrary to the principles of the opening side, you can bid your head off on rather weak hands when it is 'safe' to do so.

If you had opened the bidding with 1♠ and partner responded 2♡, a 3♣ or 3♢ rebid by you would show a very good hand. Here, in a competitive framework, you are conducting a similar sequence on a hand not even worth an opening bid.

There is another very important point to be made here. I've discussed it over and over and offer it now in a slightly different light. I've said that the 'state' of the auction is all-important and your bids must always consider the safety or danger of an auction. Keeping this principle in mind leads to another interesting conclusion, which can be treated as one of the basic axioms of competitive bidding.

Very Important Principles:

1. When the opponents have good hands, your partner will always be minimum for whatever actions he takes.
2. When the opponents have minimum and limited hands, your partner may well have a maximum for his actions.

Here are two auctions to emphasize these two points.

LHO	Partner	RHO	You
		1♣	1♠
2♣	2♡		

Partner can have a good hand just short of a strong response. If you have a 10-point overcall, there is room for partner to have as many as 13 points.

LHO	Partner	RHO	You
		1♣	1♠
2◊	2♡		

Partner will always have a good heart suit when he bids after their 2/1 bid, but he will not have a good hand. If you have 10 HCP, your partner will have a maximum of 7 points and could have less.

Neither vul.

W	N	E	S
		1♣	1♠
pass	2♡	3♣	?

♠ A 10 8 7 5
♡ J 2
◊ K Q 9 6 3
♣ 4

Bid 3◊. RHO has shown a good hand but LHO is tentatively weak. Note that LHO may have a good hand with spades, hoping to be able to double, but that fear should only dissuade you from rebidding spades. Other things being equal, you should feel quite comfortable bidding diamonds. This assumes that the opponents are using the negative double. If they are not using it, then LHO does not have a spade stack with a good hand besides or he would have made a penalty double. Regardless of whether they are or are not using negative doubles, this is a 3◊ bid. I have been making note of the times where you might have made a two-suited bid such as Michaels or the unusual notrump. Now and then you will have a two-suited hand that does not have an applicable cuebid. This hand, for instance, has to bid both suits as there is no bid that shows both of these suits at the same time.

3◇, but unenthusiastically. LHO's 1NT bid is not a weak action at all. It shows definite high-card strength. RHO is showing signs of extras too, although they may be in the form of distribution. Or perhaps it's just his turn to bid. In favor of your bidding 3◇ is that you have two hearts (partner's suit) and one club, as opposed to one heart and two clubs. Your spade suit is also well constructed to play in diamonds or, for that matter, hearts. You have the ♠A, not the ♠K or ♠QJ or ♠KJ. Partner, with no apparent interest in spades, may well have a singleton, and if so, he will be pleased to find you have the ace instead of various other combinations.

This hand is the complete opposite of the previous hand. Look at the minuses this hand has. It is hard to know where to start.

1. Partner doesn't care for spades, so your spade values may not be useful.
2. You have a stiff heart, which is poor.
3. Your ♣Q is likely worthless.

Pass is clear.

In the following two layouts, I chose a typical hand for partner to hold. Note how it plays opposite either of the two hands shown above.

Partner's hand	Hand one
♠ 3	♠ A 10 8 7 5
♡ K Q 10 9 6 5	♡ J 2
◇ 10 7 4	◇ K Q 9 6 3
♣ 9 6 3	♣ 4

Partner's hand	Hand two
♠ 3	♠ K Q J 7 5
♡ K Q 10 9 6 5	♡ 3
◇ 10 7 4	◇ K J 8 6 5
♣ 9 6 3	♣ Q 10

In the first layout your side may take eight tricks in hearts or diamonds, but might take nine against soft defense. In the second layout you are in serious trouble. Down three tricks in a red suit is normal and down five is possible.

A useful point from all this is that when partner does not care for your first suit, you should seriously devaluate holdings not headed by the ace. Other combinations are worth much less when not facing a fit.

Should you bid notrump when you overcall and partner bids a new suit?
Sometimes partner will bid a suit after your overcall and your options will include bidding some number of notrump. At the one-level the bid is reasonably commonplace and needs only to be defined. I would guess it to show 11-15 points and no liking for partner's suit. It is not a sign-off in that you can't stand what partner has bid. It does require certain values.

Neither vul.

W	N	E	S
		1♣	1♥
pass	1♠	pass	?

♠ 8 2
♡ A Q 10 7 6
◇ Q 8 2
♣ K J 4

Bid 1NT. Pretty routine. You have more than a minimum and you have notrump values in the 11-15 range.

Neither vul.

W	N	E	S
		1♣	1◇
pass	1♥	1♠	?

♠ Q 10 7
♡ 9 7
◇ K Q J 8 7
♣ A J 7

1NT. When RHO rebids, your 1NT bid shows a better hand than when RHO passed. A good 13-15 is about right.

Neither vul.

W	N	E	S
		1♣	1♥
pass	1♠	pass	?

♠ 3
♡ K Q 10 8 7
◇ J 6 3
♣ A 9 4 2

Pass. No need to continue. Rebidding 2♡ would imply a better suit, and 1NT a better hand. When you overcall you are always hoping for something good to happen, but when it doesn't you should be prepared and willing to give up.

Both vul.

W	N	E	S
	1♣	1♡	
pass	1♠	pass	?

♠ 8
♡ KQJ7
◇ K65
♣ A10875

1NT. Clear-cut. Your bid does not promise any kind of spade support and partner should hesitate to rebid questionable suits. Your stiff spade is not the reason you bid 1NT. The reason is that you have good values.

Notrump calls at the two-level are somewhat rarer. You're a trick higher and that requires extra values to compensate. To start with, there are two auctions where you should forget about it immediately. When LHO bids 1NT after your overcall, or when LHO bids a new suit at the two-level, don't bother.

Neither vul.

W	N	E	S
	1♣	1♠	
1NT	2♡	pass	?

♠ AQ1087
♡ Q2
◇ K65
♣ K95

Pass. Partner has a good heart suit and nothing else. It's right to pass this hand by definition. Note that his expected holding is something like ♡KJ9843 and another little something that he likes. Note too that LHO is more likely than not to have the ♠K, which means your hand is worth a little less than it was a moment ago.

Neither vul.

W	N	E	S
	1♣	1♠	
2◇	2♡	pass	?

It doesn't matter what you have. 2NT is wrong about 99% of the time. It might be wrong even more than that. They have at least 22 HCP and more is likely. The one case where this is not true is when they play negative free bids where the 2♡ bid is not forcing. It can be based on 3-10 points. If you learn they are doing this, you can bid 2NT with some caution.

Neither vul.

W	N	E	S
	1♣	1♠	
pass	2◇	pass	?

♠ Q10876
♡ K3
◇ K9
♣ AQ87

Bid 2NT. The times you do bid 2NT will be when the opponents show weak hands. LHO will usually have passed. The situation will be one where you can hope to find partner with a maximum for his bid. Usually, for you to have any idea where the tricks are coming from, you will have a semi-fit or better for partner's suit. If you don't like his suit and he doesn't like yours, it's going to be tough going to get it all together in time to make 2NT or 3NT on what may be a misfit hand. Therefore, if you don't like his suit you need a much better hand to bid 2NT. Note that 2NT is a forward-going bid. There is no such thing as running from partner's suit to notrump just because you don't like his suit.

Neither vul.

W	N	E	S
		1♣	1♡
2♣	2♢	pass	?

♠ Q 10 8
♡ K Q J 8 7
♢ K Q 9
♣ A 2

This is an incredibly good hand from a high-card point of view. But from a trick-taking point of view, it's a trap. You could bid 2NT or 3NT, but where the tricks are coming from is a mystery. They are going to lead a club, knocking out your stopper, and as soon as they get in they will be placed to run enough tricks to set you. To succeed, you will need nine fast ones. Now if partner has two red aces, fine. But what are the chances of that? You have 17 points, and they have bid and raised. What is left for partner? I doubt he has two aces. But even if he has one of the following hands, 3NT will go down.

♠ A x x   ♡ x x   ♢ A 10 x x x x   ♣ x x

Note partner even has a sixth diamond. And game here requires a spade finesse, which is into the opening bidder. On the other hand, 5♢ is nearly cold. Partner can set up the hearts for needed discards.

♠ K x   ♡ x x   ♢ A x x x x x x   ♣ x x

3NT is down, even though partner has seven diamonds. 5♢ also rates to go down, but not always. Partner might have a singleton club. Perhaps this hand should be considered as an exercise in judgment.

I would suggest bidding 3♣, hoping that partner can make a useful bid for you such as 3♡, which would let you choose 4♡ as your contract. If he does not do that, bid 5♢ and hope it comes home.

Neither vul.

W	N	E	S
		1♣	1♠
2♣	2♢	pass	?

♠ 8 7 6 5 4 2
♡ A Q
♢ K 10 3
♣ K 8

This hand, with far fewer high-card points than the previous hand, may produce 3NT because it has fast tricks. With luck, you can grab your nine tricks without letting the opponents in. This hand and the previous hand clearly show the problems you face when considering notrump against an auction where they have opened and raised. You can anticipate the lead and can judge quite accurately whether your tricks are there at all, and whether you will be able to get at them in time.

When partner bids a new suit, should you rebid your own suit?

There are certainly times where you will want to rebid your suit, but the considerations are somewhat different from other rebids. Firstly, you should expect partner does not like your suit, so there is no future in rebidding anything less than a decent six-bagger. When you rebid your suit, you do so because you have something positive to say. You don't rebid it simply because you don't care for partner's suit. Secondly, you must be aware of the possibility that LHO has your suit and is waiting to double you. This happens frequently against people playing negative doubles. This alone should discourage you from rebidding five-card suits.

When should you rebid your suit and what does it mean?

There are two cases where you can rebid your suit after a new suit bid from your partner.

    1. RHO passes

    2. RHO bids

1. When opener passes

Neither vul.

W	N	E	S
		1♣	1♠
pass	2♢	pass	?

♠ K Q 10 8 7 6
♡ K 4 2
♢ 7
♣ A 6 3

2♠. A very important concept here is that your 2♠ bid shows a good suit. The bid is not made just because you don't like diamonds. If you had a stiff diamond and an average spade suit, you would pass. You are bidding 2♠ because you have something to show. It is not an escape bid.

Neither vul.

W	N	E	S
		1♣	1♡
1♠	2♢	pass	?

♠ J 8
♡ K Q J 10 7 6
♢ K 4 2
♣ Q 2

2♡. 2♢ would obviously be a fine contract, so you need a very good suit of your own to rebid it. Here you are not intending 2♡ as an escape. You are merely showing a good suit. As your support for partner gets better, the quality of the suit you rebid must also get better. The one-loser heart suit here is typical.

Neither vul.

W	N	E	S
		1♣	1♡
pass	2◇	pass	?

♠ A 7 6
♡ Q 10 8 6 5
◇ 2
♣ K 7 5 4

Pass. Your suit is poor and your hand is minimum besides. Add a sixth heart and you should still pass.

Both vul.

W	N	E	S
		1♣	1♠
2♣	2♡	pass	?

♠ K Q J 10 7 6
♡ Q 5
◇ A 10 8 6
♣ 3

This spade suit clearly is worth rebidding and the only question is how many. I'd try 4♠ but would hardly quarrel with three. What has happened that makes this hand worth a jump when it was worth only an overcall in the first place is:
1.   Your ♡Q has become a significant value.
2.   Partner has shown some high cards.
3.   Partner probably has little wasted in clubs, so whatever he has will be useful.

Neither vul.

W	N	E	S
		1♣	1♠
2♣	2♡	pass	?

♠ K Q J 10 8 7
♡ 3
◇ A 10 5 4
♣ Q 2

Only 2♠. The difference between the doubleton ♣Q here and the doubleton ♡Q on the previous hand is enormous. It could easily work out to a difference of three or four tricks.

Neither vul.

W	N	E	S
		1◇	1♠
2◇	3♣	pass	?

♠ Q J 10 7 4 2
♡ A K 2
◇ 7 2
♣ 9 2

Pass. You should be less inclined to remove partner's three-level suit. His suits will be a bit better in general than some of those bid at the two-level. You know you have a couple of clubs for partner. You do not know if he has any spades for you. Assuming your partner is bidding properly, this is a very sane pass. Note that if you also had the ♣K the hand would be worth a 3♠ bid.

Both vul.			
W	**N**	**E**	**S**
		1♡	1♠
2♡	3♣	pass	?

♠ KQJ762
♡ Q2
◇ A42
♣ 32

Still best to pass. With the auction at the three-level, it is more dangerous to continue. There is less space to explore for your best fit. Add the ♠10 and you could rebid them. But without it, caution is best.

2. When opener rebids

When opener rebids you should not feel compelled to persist, so further action by you requires a little extra something. Rebidding your suit is a bit dangerous, remember, because LHO may be waiting (negative double) and partner doesn't like your suit. So you do require a good six-card suit as a minimum. Strangely, you do not need much extra in the way of high cards. Most sound minimums are worth rebidding if the suit quality is adequate. This advice, by the way, is for rebids at the two-level only. Three-level actions require extra.

Neither vul.			
W	**N**	**E**	**S**
		1♣	1♡
pass	1♠	2♣	?

♠ 87
♡ KQ10765
◇ K54
♣ Q3

Pass. The suit is good enough but the hand is minimum with poor high cards. Note that if 2♣ is passed to your partner, he can bid 2♡ if he has two hearts and a decent hand. ♠AJ643 ♡J8 ◇A73 ♣984 is a possible hand for this bid.

Neither vul.			
W	**N**	**E**	**S**
		1♣	1♡
pass	1♠	2♣	?

♠ Q3
♡ AQJ10086
◇ Q102
♣ 96

2♡. Good suit and useful minimum values. The ♠Q is now quite valuable and there is nothing wasted.

Both vul.

W	N	E	S
		1♣	1◇
1♡	1♠	2♣	?

♠ 9 6 2
♡ A 2
◇ K Q J 10 8 3
♣ 4 2

I would bid 2◇, intending to continue with 2♠ if they bid 2♡. This hand is most strongly oriented toward diamonds and game is unlikely. When your maximum is a partscore, you may as well stick to the best suit. If RHO had rebid 2♡, you could have chosen to bid 2♠.

N-S vul.

W	N	E	S
		1♣	1♠
2♣	2◇	3♣	?

♠ K Q J 10 8 2
♡ K 3
◇ A 10 4
♣ J 2

You can bid 3◇, raising partner, or you can rebid 3♠. Or you can bid 4♠, a sane but aggressive choice. I would choose 3♠, showing a good suit and extra values. A 3◇ raise would be competitive, showing a fit while understating both the spades and the values. If RHO had passed, a jump to 3♠ would be best.

Should you raise when partner bids a new suit after your overcall?
Whenever a defender bids a new suit in response to partner's overcall, the most wonderful thing that can happen is to hear partner raise. That raise, more than any other bid, is the catalyst for successful defensive sequences. When your hands fit you can put serious pressure on the opponents, and when your hands fit really well you can create all kinds of chaos. Anything from highway robbery, where you steal the opponents blind, to hands where you can actually make more than the opponents in spite of no high cards. Should you raise partner? Yes. Yes. Yes! For hundreds of pages now, we've been looking at ways to get into the auction. Some of the bids I suggested were dangerous but they were made in the hope of finding a fit. Now that a fit has been found, the dangers are all past and it is again safe to bid. Exploit it.

Neither vul.

W	N	E	S
		1♣	1◇
pass	1♠	pass	?

♠ Q 8 7
♡ 10 2
◇ A K 10 7 5
♣ K J 4

A good minimum raise to 2♠. Partner has five or more spades with a range of 7-12 points. Game is possible and your raise will find it if it exists. Passing would be a serious error.

Neither vul.			
W	N	E	S
		1♣	1♢
pass	1♡	pass	?

♠ 8 5 2
♡ A 9 6
♢ K Q 8 7 4
♣ J 2

Marginal whether you raise or pass. The silence of the opponents suggests partner will probably bid again. Best you should pass. Note that partner can't really have enough for game or he would have made a stronger bid. If opener had bid 2♣, for instance, you would bid 2♡. (See next hand for more on this bid.)

Neither vul.			
W	N	E	S
		1♣	1♢
pass	1♠	2♣	?

♠ K 8 7
♡ 10 6 4
♢ A Q 10 8 3
♣ 4 2

2♠. In competitive auctions you must raise partner when you have a fit. Had opener passed, you would also have passed. But he didn't. When you are raising partner the concept of free bids has almost no meaning at all. In fact, the reverse is true. You raise to show a fit. You don't raise to show a good hand. Points don't count for nearly as much as whether you like or don't like partner's suit. He would far, far rather know if you fit his suit than know if your overcall was minimum or maximum.

Neither vul.			
W	N	E	S
		1♣	1♡
pass	1♠	pass	?

♠ K 8 7
♡ A Q 6 5 4
♢ A 6 4 2
♣ 3

3♠. A straightforward game try. If anything, this is an underbid. This is a rare case where you might make a jump raise with three cards. Partner should have five of them, if not more. If he has four (rare), he will have four good ones.

Neither vul.			
W	N	E	S
		1♣	1♢
1♡	1♠	1NT	?

♠ Q 8 7
♡ A 4 2
♢ A J 8 7 2
♣ 4 2

2♠. While it's possible that you can beat 1NT, you should have little trouble making 2♠. This has the additional effect of keeping LHO from bidding 2♣. Note that when RHO rebids 1NT, he shows a stopper in your trump suit. This isn't all that serious, but it means that games that require a successful trump finesse won't be making.

Neither vul.

W	N	E	S
		1♣	1◊
1♡	1♠	1NT?	

♠ A 10 2
♡ 4 2
◊ A J 9 6 5
♣ 9 6 2

2♠ again. When you have a fit, you should almost always raise unless there is clear reason not to. Had RHO passed instead of rebidding 1NT, you might have considered passing for fear that partner might expect more. But after opener's 1NT rebid the raise to 2♠ is clear-cut. Note that on this hand partner will be able to play the trump suit to best advantage. Whatever spade cards are missing will be in the opener's hand. If RHO has the ♠Kxx, he will be disappointed to find it of no use.

Both vul.

W	N	E	S
		1♣	1♠
2♣	2◊	3♣?	

♠ A Q 9 8 6
♡ 4 2
◊ K J 3
♣ 7 6 3

3◊. This hand is so minimal that some players wouldn't overcall in the first place. Yet when partner volunteers 2◊, it becomes so good that game is not out of the question. Passing 3♣ is terribly conservative. True, you have a minimum, but everything is working overtime.

Both vul.

W	N	E	S
		1♣	1♠
2♣	2◊	3♣?	

♠ K Q 8 6 2
♡ Q J 3
◊ K Q 4
♣ Q 8

3◊, but with none of the enthusiasm of the previous hand. This hand, with no aces, the wasted ♣Q, exactly two clubs, soft hearts, etc, is actually less valuable than the previous hand. I would certainly raise to 3◊, but I wouldn't love it. For the most part, your raise will buy the contract. Rarely, they may compete to the next level. Occasionally your partner will have enough to bid again. It is important on these sequences to judge correctly when to take the push.

Neither vul.

W	N	E	S
		1♣	1♠
2♣	2♡	3♣?	

♠ K 10 8 7 6
♡ K 4 2
◊ A Q 10 7
♣ 3

Bid 4♡. The only reason this hand is included here is that I've seen people actually pass!

What differences exist when you overcall, LHO bids a new suit at the two-level, and partner bids a new suit at the two-level?

So far, the auctions have been safe in that the opponents have limited their hands or at least have not shown much strength. When this is the case you can feel that your side may have a game, and to some degree you bid with this in mind. On other sequences your side will have no game, short of miracle fits, and when this happens your bidding will be purely competitive with no hint of game offered by either defender's bids.

Neither vul.

W	N	E	S
		1♣	1♠
2♦	2♥	3♦	?

♠ A K 10 7 2
♡ J 10 5
♢ 4
♣ 8 6 5 2

3♡. Not because you expect to make it, and not because you hope to get to a game. On this auction, partner won't have many high cards. If he bids 4♡ he will be doing it as a save, rather than expecting to make. The key is for both you and your partner to recognize that their side has the majority of the values. On auctions like this one, your side won't be serious about bidding games. But you may be serious about competing and pushing them around a bit. If you had a doubleton diamond and one less club it would be best to leave them alone.

Neither vul.

W	N	E	S
		1♣	1♠
2♦	2♥	3♦	?

♠ K Q 8 7 6
♡ Q 4 2
♢ K 3
♣ Q 7 4

Pass. You have only defensive values and should not want partner to take any saves. Both your ♢K and your ♣Q may be worthless on offense.

E-W vul.

W	N	E	S
		1♣	1♠
2♦	2♥	3♣	?

♠ A Q J 8
♡ K J 5
♢ 4 3
♣ 9 4 3 2

3♡. Partner has a good suit and you have nothing wasted. Partner should not be disappointed with this dummy. If you wouldn't have overcalled in the first place, that's fine. But if you did make a matchpoint decision to overcall you shouldn't back out now. In a heart contract, you have around 12 or 13 support points. If you look back at the previous hand with its 12 HCP, you should evaluate it at about 8 support points. Some points are worth more than others. Practice evaluating which points go up in value and which go down in value.

N-S vul.

W	N	E	S
		1◇	1♠
2♣	2♡	3◇	?

♠ A Q 8 6 5 4
♡ 10 7 5 4
◇ K 4
♣ 2

4♡. Remember that this is a very dangerous sequence for partner to be introducing a new suit. It must be a good one. This is the sort of hand you need to be bidding a game when the opponents have shown most of the high cards. You have shape. You have good trump. And you have no wasted high cards. Every one of them is working. This is because your side will seldom have more than 15 or so HCP when an opponent makes a 2/1, and if any of your high cards are not working, it will be hard for the rest of them to compensate. In practice, you will usually play in 4♡, doubled, or they will bid on to five of a minor or even six of a minor. Your 4♡ bid will take away some of their useful bidding room and will force them to make a guess much of the time.

N-S vul.

W	N	E	S
		1◇	1♠
2♣	2♡	3◇	?

♠ K J 8 7 2
♡ Q J 4
◇ Q 3
♣ K 10 5

Pass. Your spades are suspect, your clubs and diamonds are worthless, and your distribution is vile. When the state of the auction says it's dangerous for you, do not make questionable bids. On this vulnerability it would be suicidal to keep bidding.

Neither vul.

W	N	E	S
		1◇	1♠
2◇	2♡	3◇	?

♠ K J 8 7 2
♡ Q J 4
◇ Q 3
♣ K 10 5

Here is the same hand again, but with a different auction and with different vulnerability. On this sequence, 3♡ would be acceptable. Note the differences between the evaluation on the two sequences.

On the second auction the opponents are limited. On the first auction they are not.

On the second auction, your partner may have extra values. On the first he does not.

On the second auction your ♣K is worth full value. On the first it is of no value.

On the second auction, your worst result is down one, doubled. On the first it is down four, doubled.

On the second auction, you aren't vulnerable. On the first auction, you are.

On the second auction, no one will be inclined to double you. On the first, either opponent will be inclined to double you. I could go on.

Once again, the state of the auction continues to influence the bidding and what you can and can't do. On the last two example auctions you should have felt strongly against bidding when it was wrong and you should have known why you felt that way, and conversely for the case where it was right to bid.

Neither vul.

W	N	E	S
		1♡	1♠
2♣	2♢	2♡	?

♠ QJ654
♡ Q2
♢ KQ6
♣ K42

You could bid 3♢, but nothing much will come of it. The opponents are going to continue on, likely to 4♡, and you don't really want to hear partner saving in 5♢. As usual, when the opponents are having a strong sequence your decision whether to raise should be influenced by the number of questionable cards you hold. Here the only sure values you have are the ♢KQ. And even the queen may be overvalued. It is possible that of your 13 HCP, only the ♢K will carry full weight.

When is it best to pass when partner bids a new suit after your overcall?
The only important point to make here is that you can indeed pass if you feel it best. A bid by you is forward-going in that you are looking for something. You should not be running from partner's suit just because you don't like it.

Neither vul.

W	N	E	S
		1♠	2♣
pass	2♡	pass	?

♠ K62
♡ 3
♢ K54
♣ AQ9654

Pass. You want better clubs to rebid them and you want a better hand to try notrump. Your stiff heart will be a bigger liability at notrump than at hearts. Your partner's 2♡ bid was not what you wanted at all. Having gotten bad news, passing is often the best way to keep the bad news from getting worse.

Both vul.

W	N	E	S
		1♡	1♠
pass	2♢	pass	?

♠ KJ876
♡ K2
♢ 7
♣ K9654

Pass again. Some of the time you have to be content with showing part of your hand. You can pass. 2♢ is not forcing. Give it up. Imagine that you bid 3♣ and your partner gave you a preference to 3♠. Would you like it? Would you like it if LHO doubled 3♠? This hand is typical of those where you might make a Michaels cuebid. A 2♡ bid would show spades and a minor, but your hand is not good enough to force to the three-level, vulnerable. Better, when you can't do everything, is to do *something* if it is reasonable.

Neither vul.

W	N	E	S
		1♡	1♠
2♡	3♣	pass	?

♠ Q 10 8 7 6 5
♡ A J 2
◇ 4 2
♣ K 3

Pass. This should be a fine spot if you are allowed to play it. Rebidding spades or notrump would be poor. You have some decent cards for partner's 3♣ contract, but overall this hand is nothing special.

Neither vul.

W	N	E	S
		1♡	2◇
2♡	3♣	pass	?

♠ A 8 7
♡ K 5 4
◇ K Q 10 6 5 2
♣ 3

Pass. No reason to expect diamonds is a better contract than clubs. You have a decent overcall which didn't improve when partner bid clubs. You can pass. Do so.

N-S vul.

W	N	E	S
		1♡	2◇
2♠	3♣	3♠	?

♠ A 3
♡ J 5 4
◇ K Q J 10 5
♣ Q 8 7

Pass. The bidding tells you the opponents have extra high cards so your partner is not bidding with strength, he is bidding with a good club suit. I'm not sure this was a 2◇ bid in the first place, but even with partner bidding clubs I don't care for this hand much. If I bid 4♣, my partner would be justified in bidding 5♣ as a save against 4♡ or 4♠ by the opponents. My hand has too many losers to invite partner to do that.

CASE THREE
YOU OVERCALL. PARTNER MAKES A JUMP SHIFT

This one is pretty easy. Partner's jump is either invitational in some way, or it is weak and preemptive. The important point is to understand which type exists.

Type one - The invitational jump shift in response to your overcall

When you overcall and LHO passes, raises, bids a new suit at the one-level, or makes a negative double, partner's jump shifts are invitational and show a good hand (12-15 HCP) and a good six- or seven-card suit. You are allowed to pass, but that would require both a minimum and a misfit as well.

LHO	Partner	RHO	You
		1♣	1♡
pass	2♠		

Invitational jump shift. Opener's partner passed.

LHO	Partner	RHO	You
		1♣	1♡
2♣	3◇		

Invitational jump shift. Opener's partner raised opener's suit.

LHO	Partner	RHO	You
		1♣	1◇
1♡	2♠		

Invitational jump shift. Opener's partner bid a new suit at the one-level.

LHO	Partner	RHO	You
		1♣	1♡
dbl	2♠		

Invitational jump shift. Opener's partner made a negative double.

In all four of these cases, opener's partner made a bid that promised no more than 6 points. Following are some example problems.

Neither vul.

W	N	E	S
		1♣	1♡
pass	2♡	pass	?

♠ 8 2
♡ A Q 10 7 6
◇ Q J 7
♣ K 10 5

2NT, but just barely. You would like the ♣J too. Here are a couple of typical hands partner may have.

♠ A Q J 7 5 4   ♡ 5 4   ◇ A 9 4   ♣ Q 7
♠ K Q 10 9 4 3   ♡ K J   ◇ 9 4   ♣ A 7 4

The clear point of these two examples is that you see partner has real values. He might have a point more. On both of these hands, he will raise to 3NT. If he had a seventh spade or if he had a better suit with serious distribution he would rebid 3♠, or perhaps 4♠.

Both vul.

W	N	E	S
		1♣	1♠
2♣	3♡	pass	?

♠ Q J 9 7 6 5
♡ 4
◇ Q 2
♣ A 6 5 4

Pass. Even though you have a club stopper, you have a poor minimum. As long as it is understood that you can pass, those hands where it is correct are fairly clear-cut.

Neither vul.

W	N	E	S
		1♣	1◇
2♣	3♠	pass	?

♠ Q 2
♡ 8 6 5
◇ A K Q 8 3
♣ 9 6 4

Bid 4♠. You have a fine hand for partner, which includes a fit and a convenient source of tricks. If your partner can get in before they take four tricks he should be able to make this.

Neither vul.

W	N	E	S
		1♡	2♣
2♡	3♠	pass	?

♠ 10 2
♡ 3
◇ A 8 6 5
♣ A Q 10 8 6 5

Bid 4♠. Partner's bid shows six or a super five cards in spades so ♠102 is adequate support. The rest of your hand is minimum, but it will be useful. You have a singleton heart and you have aces and you have a likely source of tricks in clubs. Compare it with the next hand.

Neither vul.

W N E S
    1♡ 2♣
2♡ 3♠ pass ?

♠ 10 7
♡ Q 3
◇ K J 7
♣ K Q J 10 8 7

Pass. This hand includes far more losers than the previous hand. The heart holding is the worst possible and you have no aces. Best to go quietly. But note that you are not passing just because you have only two spades. You are passing because you have a stinky hand that got worse when hearts were raised.

Both vul.

W N E S
    1♡ 2♣
2♡ 3♠ pass ?

♠ 10 6 2
♡ 3
◇ Q 3 2
♣ A K J 10 7 2

You might not make a vulnerable 2♣ bid with this hand, but if somehow the auction had gone as indicated you would raise to 4♠ and be concerned that you could (rarely) be missing a slam. The trick is not to think you overcalled with a weak hand but to evaluate how good your hand is now.

Both vul.

W N E S
    1♣ 1♡
pass 2♠ pass ?

♠ 3 2
♡ A K Q 8 7
◇ A J 4
♣ 9 4 2

Bid 3♣. This is a situation where game is almost sure, but which one is unclear. You hope partner can bid 3NT. Failing that, 4♡ or 4♠ will be worth trying.

Neither vul.

W N E S
    1♣ 1♠
2♣ 3♡ pass ?

♠ A Q 10 8 7 6
♡ 3
◇ A J 7 6
♣ Q 2

Bid 3♠. The question here is whether or not a rebid of your suit is forcing when partner makes a jump shift. There are probably good reasons for playing it non-forcing, but my impression is that it should be treated as forcing. This hand is shown only to let you consider the possibilities.

Neither vul.

W	N	E	S
		1♣	1♠
2♣	3♡	pass	?

Pass is probably best. If you play that 3♠ is non-forcing you could bid that, but that is not the recommended treatment. (See above hand.)

♠ KJ8764
♡ —
◇ KJ75
♣ Q82

Neither vul.

W	N	E	S
		1♣	1♠
pass	3♡	pass	?

Pass. The question here is whether a new suit after partner's jump shift is forcing. Again, without getting into an involved discussion, I suggest it should be forcing. Here you have a minimum hand. 3♡ is likely to be a good enough contract. Leave it alone.

♠ KJ872
♡ 3
◇ A10974
♣ Q3

Type two - The preemptive jump shift in response to your overcall

When you overcall and the next player makes a strong bid such as 1NT or 2NT, a new suit at the two-level, or a cuebid of your overcall, a jump in a new suit by your partner is preemptive.

Most of the time your side will be poorly placed to find a contract that will make because the opponents have the majority of the high cards. Usually your best strategy will be to pass and hope that partner's preempt has upset the opponents' exchange of information. On occasion, though, you may be able to continue the auction, but this will be the case only when you have a fit. Remember your side will have fewer than half the high cards, so fit alone will give you cause to bid. Here are some example auctions when you overcall and your LHO shows some values.

LHO	Partner	RHO	You
		1♣	1♡
1NT	3◇	pass	?

Partner's 3◇ bid is not invitational. The 1NT bid showed 8-10 points, which means your side won't have any games. 3◇ shows a respectable suit and some expectation of not getting killed. This is an easy sequence for them to double so partner will be showing a little caution.

LHO	Partner	RHO	You
		1♣	1♠
2◇	3♡	pass	?

They have shown game values or close to it with their 2◇ bid so your partner's 3♡ jump is preemptive.

LHO	Partner	RHO	You
		1♣	1♡
2♡	3♠	pass	?

The 2♡ cuebid showed a limit raise or more (one of my least favorite conventions) and that means your partner's 3♠ jump is weak.

Here are some examples of hands where your LHO shows values over your overcall. Your partner's jump shifts on these auctions are weak. Generally, you should be cautious except when you have an unexpectedly good fit for partner's suit. Remember that you won't be bidding any games to make, barring miracle fits. Mostly, if you bid you will be trying to cause problems for them.

Neither vul.

W	N	E	S
		1♣	1♠
1NT	3◇	pass	?

♠ K 10 8 7 6
♡ A 9 3
◇ 8
♣ A J 5 4

Pass. No other choice. Once you realize what the opponents have shown it is clear partner is weak. There is no possible future for his hand other than 3◇. What does partner have? Here is one possible hand:

♠ 3   ♡ J 10 4 2   ◇ Q J 10 7 6 5 2   ♣ 7

Neither vul.

W	N	E	S
		1♣	1♠
2◇	3♡	4♣	?

♠ A Q 8 7 6 5
♡ 3
◇ K 7 5
♣ A 4 2

Pass again. This decision is easy to make if you accept that partner is weak. Partner's 3♡ bid may have kept them out of a cold 3NT. Why bid something now and ruin partner's good work?

W	N	E	S
		1♣	1♠
2◇	3♡	pass	?

♠ K Q 9 8 7
♡ 2
◇ K 9 7
♣ K Q 7 3

Still pass. Under no circumstance should you try 3NT. There's a good chance that LHO is about to bid 3NT. And he has a much better chance of making it than you do. In fact, if LHO does bid 3NT I wouldn't double with this hand, which shows how unsound it would be to bid 3NT.

Neither vul.

W	N	E	S
		1♣	1♠
2◇	3♡	pass	?

♠ Q J 10 8 7 6 5
♡ —
◇ K 8 7
♣ A 5 4

Even with this hand, pass might be best. If you do decide to bid 3♠, however, it should be treated as non-forcing given the opponents have promised values. As far as bidding another suit, you probably shouldn't bother. Much of the time there won't be a fourth suit to bid, as in this auction. But if it should ever happen that there is an unbid suit and you feel the need to bid it, it should be non-forcing.

So far all the hands in this section have been misfits and the proper action after partner's jump shift was a pass. On some hands, however, you will have a fit and it will be correct to bid. You must be aware that you are not bidding with intention to make something. True, you may get to a successful contract, but it will be the exception. Instead, most of your actions will be save-oriented and both you and partner should realize this.

Neither vul.

W	N	E	S
		1♣	1♠
2◇	3♡	pass	?

♠ A Q 8 7 6
♡ K 6 4
◇ 7 6 5 4
♣ 9

Bid 4♡. A case could be made for 5♡. The point of this hand is that you have a fit, you have an offensive hand, you have no reason to expect to be able to defeat any game contract (or for that matter a slam) and you can make a useful bid that takes up more bidding room from the opponents' progress. Have no doubt about it, this hand belongs to the opponents.

E-W vul.

W	N	E	S
		1♡	1♠
2♣	3◇	3♡	?

♠ A Q 6 5 4
♡ 9 2
◇ K 10 8
♣ 10 8 7

Bid 5◇. The opponents surely have a game and maybe a slam. As with most preemptive actions, by bidding the maximum immediately you force the opponents to guess. If you pass or bid 4◇ now and then bid 5◇ later, the opponents will have exchanged more information and can better judge the situation. Bidding 5◇ directly creates problems and among other things takes away their cuebids and their Blackwood. An important aside is the vulnerability. They are vulnerable, you are not. If you bid 5◇ and get doubled you can afford to be down three, meaning your partner only has to take eight tricks to make it a worthwhile save against a game.

CASE FOUR
YOU OVERCALL, PARTNER RAISES

Of all the things that can happen when you overcall, this is about the best. When you make any defensive bid at all you are always hoping for a fit, and when partner raises your overcall you will have found one. Now it remains to exploit this fit to its fullest. When you have a fit the problems you face are far different from the many cases where you haven't got a fit. But they are nice problems with relatively safe solutions.

After a simple raise by partner
When this happens, you have to decide:

1. Do you have a sure game?
2. Do you have a potential game?
3. Should you compete?
4. Should you double?
5. Should you quit?
6. Should you save?

By now, you know that the answers to these questions will be largely predicated on the state of the auction. On some sequences, game will be unlikely or impossible and your activities will be competitive or save-oriented. Other sequences will leave open the possibility of game and you will have genuine cause for optimism. Here is a reminder that will save you a lot of grief.

When partner raises, always consider what he shows and do not forget about the bids that he did not make.

The various ways your partner can raise you

In an earlier section, I discussed a number of possible bids partner can make to show you support. He has these bids available when there has been competition.

He can make a simple raise. Usually this is a boring 7-9 point hand, usually with only three trumps.

He can make a preemptive jump raise.

He has the cuebid, usually showing a balanced raise with 11+ points.

He has the jump cuebid, showing a shapely limit raise or better with four trumps.

In an upcoming section I will introduce two more possible bids for partner to make. Read through the next few pages and then be ready to look at something new.

When can you be optimistic?

On sequences where LHO has passed, raised opener, made a negative double, or bid a new suit at the one-level and your partner raises, you can feel that your side may own the hand. This doesn't mean that the hand belongs to you, but it means that the possibility exists. What is happening is that LHO's bids do not promise good hands. This means there are more points unaccounted for, which may be in the form of a good overcall in your hand or a maximum raise in partner's hand.

1. Do you have a sure game?

Neither vul.			
W	**N**	**E**	**S**
		1♣	1♠
2♣	2♠	pass	?

♠ A Q 8 7 6
♡ A Q 5
◇ K J 7 2
♣ 3

Bid 4♠. Quite routine. This hand will make game easily. If the opponents save you may have to decide what to do, but that is a later problem. If you play it in 4♠ you will have the benefit of having heard descriptive bids from both opponents, particularly from LHO. This should make it easy for you to decide which high cards are where.

W	N	E	S
		1♣	1♠
pass	2♠	3♣	?

N-S vul.

♠ A J 8 7 6 5
♡ K 8
◇ K 10 8 7
♣ 7

The auction by definition is one where game for you is possible. Here, you have the additional knowledge that your finesses will work. I would just bid 4♠ and not even bother with a game try. Curiously, if I had opened 1♠ and partner raised to 2♠ I would probably pass. But on the example auction you know the cards are well placed for you. It's almost as if you had another ace. Note also that the auction has suggested that partner's values will be outside of clubs. Most of the time his high cards will be working.

W	N	E	S
		1♣	1◇
1♡	2◇	pass	?

Neither vul.

♠ 4 2
♡ A K 3
◇ A Q 6 5 4 2
♣ K 3

3NT. When your major-suit overcall is raised, you usually do not look for notrump. But when your overcall is in a minor suit you may well make the switch. This hand looks like it should produce at least nine notrump tricks while offering no such assurances about 5◇. Note that the spade suit is not a threat. Neither opponent has five spades. Partner therefore has three and probably more. If LHO hadn't bid 1♡, but had passed instead, then he might indeed have five spades but without the values to bid them. The spades are a bigger danger to 3NT with LHO passing throughout than with him bidding 1♡.

2. Do you have a potential game?

When the auction is safe there is a real chance your side has a game. If you think this is the case, you make a game try.

W	N	E	S
		1♣	1♠
2♣	2♠	pass	?

Neither vul.

♠ Q 10 8 7 2
♡ K 2
◇ A Q J 3
♣ K 2

Any finesse you need rates to work and that is a good sign. This hand is worth a game try of 3◇. This hand brings up an old question. How do you play a 3♣ bid at this point? It can be played as invitational and as preemptive. Your choice. Be sure you and partner are in agreement.

Both vul.

W	N	E	S
		1♣	1◇
1♡	2◇	pass	?

♠ K 2
♡ K 9
◇ K Q J 10 8 3
♣ Q 10 5

2NT. Partner will remember that you overcalled 1◇, not 1NT.

E-W vul.

W	N	E	S
		1♡	2◇
3♣	3◇	pass	?

♠ K J 7 3
♡ 4 2
◇ A Q 8 7 6 5
♣ 4

I would try 5◇. This is not a hand to make a game try. It is a hand where you need to realize you are outgunned. LHO's 3♣ bid showed a good hand. I expect them to have a game somewhere and if so, all our side needs is eight tricks to make a save worthwhile. That should be easy. By bidding 5◇ now, you put pressure on LHO to make a good guess at the five-level. He won't always get it right.

Both vul.

W	N	E	S
		1♣	1♠
2♣	2♠	pass	?

♠ Q 9 7 6 5
♡ 3
◇ A Q 10 9
♣ A Q 2

3♠ if invitational. It's useful to play that when RHO passes, the 3♠ bid asks for good trumps. Had RHO bid 3♣, the 3♠ bid would have been competitive. This is an issue your side needs to discuss.

Neither vul.

W	N	E	S
		1◇	1♠
2◇	2♠	3◇	?

♠ A Q 9 7 6
♡ Q 3
◇ 4 2
♣ A K 10 5

This hand presents a problem in that you would like to make a game try but there is no clear-cut game try available. You would like to be able to bid 3♠ to show a forward-going hand, but as you will see in the next section, that bid is best reserved as a competitive effort. This leaves 3♡ as the only legal bid left that can be construed as a game try. Scientific? Yes. But not unreasonable. If you don't like to get involved in this you have to use 3♠ as invitational, but that means you won't be able to compete on many other hands.

Both vul.

W	N	E	S
		1♡	1♠
2♡	2♠	3♡	?

♠ K 10 7 6 5
♡ 4 2
♢ A Q
♣ A Q 8 7

More problems. Again, you would like to make a game try but the only bid you have is 3♠. And that is competitive. Or is it? Here are some possible solutions.

1. Play that when there is no game try available, a bid by you is constructive. 3♠ now would be invitational and not competitive.

2. Play that double is an artificial game try and 3♠ remains competitive. This loses the penalty double and runs the risk of someone forgetting a convention.

3. Perhaps you should play double as a game try only when they have established a fit.

Anything will work okay as long as you remember what's happening.

Neither vul.

W	N	E	S
		1♢	1♡
1♠	3♡	pass	?

♠ A Q 9
♡ K J 8 7 4
♢ 4 2
♣ A 8 4

Your partner's 3♡ bid is preemptive. Even though you have a sound overcall, your chances of making game are close to zero. There is a good chance LHO has spade values and your shape leaves you with a lot of losers. I doubt you can make 3♡. Why bid more? Partner's hand is:

♠ 10 7 4 3 ♡ A 9 6 3 ♢ J 8 5 ♣ J 7

Neither vul.

W	N	E	S
		1♢	1♠
2♢	2♠	3♢	pass
pass	3♠	4♢	?

♠ Q J 8 7 4
♡ 8 4 3 2
♢ 4
♣ A Q 10

What kind of hand does partner have to raise to 2♠ and then compete to 3♠? He must have four trumps, for starters. This is a rule you do not want to break (without excellent reasons). And he ought to have a little useful shape. His typical hand is something like ♠K932 ♡KJ76 ♢975 ♣98. This is a maximum normal raise. Note that while it does not have a lot of points, it plays a lot better than normal raises such as this one with only three-card support: ♠A62 ♡QJ95 ♢105 ♣J642. Dummy's fourth trump is a big asset that helps you a lot. In a later section I will introduce a way to show this hand right away. Were you wondering what to bid with this hand? I am not giving you a bid. Rather, I am giving you an opportunity to consider what your partner has.

Both vul.

W	N	E	S
		1◇	1♠
2◇	Dbl	pass	2♡
pass	2♠	pass	?

What is partner doing? His double was responsive, tentatively showing hearts and clubs. You chose hearts and partner went back to spades. What does he have? He should not have a limit raise. A possible holding is a good hand with a doubleton spade honor. This auction is fairly rare.

♠ A Q 9 7 6
♡ Q 3 2
◇ K 2
♣ J 8 4

Neither vul.

W	N	E	S
		1◇	1♠
2◇	3◇	4◇	?

Partner shows a limit spade raise or better. Because their bidding did not leave room for partner to bid 2◇, his 3◇ bid doesn't give you an accurate description of his hand. He has at least limit raise values but you can't tell if he has three-card support or four-card support. If you knew, you would be better placed than you are without that knowledge. You have to use some judgment. My guess is to bid 4♠ on the theory that my hand could be weaker. It has nice honor cards, good shape, and even the ♠108 may be useful.

♠ K 10 8 5 3
♡ A 10 7 3
◇ 4
♣ A 10 8

3. Should you compete?

On auctions where it is 'safe' to continue, you should feel quite free to do so. Only when it is clearly wrong to continue should you give up.

Neither vul.

W	N	E	S
		1♣	1♡
1♠	2♡	2♠	?

3♡. This is a typical competitive action. Note that RHO rebid, so your 3♡ bid is defined as competitive. You have only a normal overcall but it is offensive in nature without excess defensive values. The opponents have found what rates to be a good two-level contract, so it behooves you to get them out of it. If you had one less diamond and one more club, bidding again would be too much. Note that partner will have three trumps much of the time. Do not make the automatic wish that he will turn up with four. In the next section I will show you how a new bidding trick will help you on some (not all) hands in this family.

♠ 8 2
♡ A Q 9 6 5
◇ K Q 9 3
♣ 4 2

Neither vul.

W	N	E	S
		1♣	1♠
2♣	2♠	3♣	?

♠ Q 9 8 7 3
♡ A 9 2
◇ K J 5 4
♣ 3

Pass. You should be aware of many things.

1. You have a poor trump suit.
2. It is possible that they will get a bad trump break.
3. They are at the three-level. When the opponents are at the three-level you should give more consideration to defending than when they are at the two-level. This is because you have a better chance of defeating a three-level contract than a two-level contract. Here are some additional things to worry about.
4. Your partner may have only three trumps.
5. While you have nice values, overall, this is a minimum overcall.
6. You still have a partner. He may be able to bid something if 3♣ gets back to him. He might bid 3◇ or 3♡. This may be a bit of a dream but both of these bids are in the realm of possible choices.

N-S vul.

W	N	E	S
		1◇	1♡
1♠	2♡	3♣	?

♠ 5 3
♡ A J 8 7 5 3
◇ K 10 8 5
♣ 3

3♡. This is a competitive bid only and partner is not expected to do any further bidding. This hand offers many points of interest.

1. You are vulnerable, so you need additional safety to continue.
2. A good six-card suit which has been raised is a good basis for competing.
3. The opponents are at the three-level so the need to compete is less urgent.
4. The opponents have no fit yet, which suggests slight caution.
5. Your shape is sensational.

N-S vul.

W	N	E	S
		1◇	1♡
1♠	2♡	3♣	?

♠ Q 3
♡ K 10 9 5 4
◇ K J 3
♣ K 4 2

Good time to pass. You have a defensively-oriented hand. Your shape is minimal. The opponents don't have a known fit. Your suit is poor. Your ♠Q is of marginal value. You are vulnerable. This sequence and vulnerability are the same as the preceding hand, but that's as far as it goes. I would rather bid 4♡ on the previous hand than 3♡ on this hand.

Neither vul.

W	N	E	S
		1♡	1♠
2♡	2♠	3♡	?

♠ J10 8 7 6 5
♡ 3
◇ A8 6
♣ A4 2

The answer to this depends on your competitive agreements. If you play 3♠ is forward-going, you have to pass. If you play it as competitive, you can bid. The reason so much time has been devoted to this is that partscores have far more importance than might first be appreciated. At matchpoints, +100 instead of +110 or +140 can be a zero. And at IMPs, if you allow the opponents to steal a partscore you lose 5-7 IMPs. Two such losses is more than a game swing of 11 IMPs.

With partscores being so important, your bidding should recognize their value. Many bids will be made solely to win in the partscore battle. Nonetheless, games are worth more than partscores, and for this reason competitive bidding situations should not conflict with the ability to bid games intelligently.

Neither vul.

W	N	E	S
		1♠	2♣
2♠	3♣	3♠	?

♠ 3
♡ QJ2
◇ K87
♣ AQ8765

It looks reasonable to bid 4♣, but it is not automatic. The opponents have been pushed to the three-level, which is one of the goals of competitive auctions. Your stiff spade is good for a club contract but the odds are good that your partner has four spades, and that will make life difficult for RHO. Having pushed them to the three-level is a nice achievement. You should go to the four-level with extra caution.

4. Should you double?

The main point of this section is that when you have established a fit, you should not rush to double your opponents. If they have a fit you should be very cautious about doubling. If they have not found a fit, you can double more frequently.

Neither vul.

W	N	E	S
		1◇	1♠
2◇	2♠	3◇	?

♠ KJ876
♡ A82
◇ A972
♣ 3

They have a fit. Doubling is less safe than if they do not have a fit. I would pass. If partner has four spades and any kind of hand at all, he will bid 3♠.

An aside. Do not lead a club. You don't want ruffs. Lead a spade and hope that you can force declarer to ruff, which may achieve trump control for your side.

In comparison, if LHO had not raised to 2◇, you could double them. Declarer has a good diamond suit but your four trumps won't be easy for him to get around.

N-S vul.

W	N	E	S
		1◇	1♠
2◇	2♠	3◇	?

♠ K J 4 3 2
♡ K J 3
◇ J 2
♣ A J 3

You have a good enough hand to consider bidding 3♠, but it's nothing special. You are balanced and you have defense. Passing could easily be best. What I would not do is make a penalty double. 3◇ might go down but there isn't enough of a guarantee to risk it. Note that if you pass your partner may be able to bid 3♠, which would promise four spades and some shape. You would rather be in 3♠ because your partner chose to bid it than because you guessed to bid it.

Neither vul.

W	N	E	S
		1♠	2♣
pass	3♣	3♠	?

♠ Q 10 8 3
♡ A 2
◇ 3
♣ A Q 8 7 6 5

This one you can take to the bank. When one hand is doing all the bidding for the other side you can be aggressive with your penalty doubles. Had LHO raised to 2♠ instead of passing, it would not be nearly as clear to double. On the given auction your partner can have anything from one to three spades. But if LHO raised spades, your partner will have zero or one spade. This reflects enormously upon the defensive and offensive potential of this hand, given either sequence.

After a jump raise

When partner gives you a jump raise you have to decide whether to pass or to continue to game, and your definition of partner's values will help you decide. My suggestion is to play all jump raises of your overcalls as weak.

Neither vul.

W	N	E	S
		1♣	1♠
dbl	3♠	pass	?

♠ K 10 7 6 5
♡ 3
◇ A 10 4 2
♣ K 10 3

Pass. Partner's bid is weak, showing about 5 or 6 points, some shape and four or more trumps. His hand will be something in this family: ♠Q843 ♡Q874 ◇Q73 ♣82. It has the required four trumps, some shape, and a few values.

Both vul.

W	N	E	S
		1♡	1♠
pass	3♠	pass?	

♠ A Q J 3
♡ A Q 6 2
◇ K J 5 2
♣ 5

An automatic 4♠ bid. The only minus you have is the lack of a fifth trump. But as long as partner has four or more, you have plenty to make up for the trump suit. One item of note. There are players who make preemptive raises on zero points and four trumps. I recommend that you produce at least a few high card values for the simple reason that if you bid with nothing and your partner continues, it may lead to assorted disasters, plus your partner won't know what to expect.

Neither vul.

W	N	E	S
		1♣	1♠
pass	3♠	pass?	

♠ K Q 7 6 5
♡ K 2
◇ K Q 5
♣ Q 8 7

Pass. Partner's raise is weak. If he has the ♠A, you probably have four losers elsewhere. If he does not have the ♠A you rate to have a different selection of four losers. You may even have five losers if LHO has a high heart or a high club.

Both vul.

W	N	E	S
		1◇	1♠
pass	2◇	pass	2NT
pass	3♠	pass	4♠
pass	pass	pass	

♠ K 8 7 6 5
♡ 4 2
◇ A Q 8
♣ A J 5

The main bid here is declarer's 2NT bid. He shows extra values for this bid. Partner then shows that his cuebid was based on a nice raise and game is reached. If you err by rebidding 2♠ after the 2◇ cuebid, partner will usually pass and game will be missed. Do not forget that partner can't jump to 3♠ to show a limit raise. His jump raises are weak, not invitational.

Both vul.

W	N	E	S
		1◇	2♣
dbl	4♣	4♡?	

♠ A J 4
♡ 4 3
◇ K 8 7
♣ K Q J 8 3

Pass. The raise to 4♣ is weak, just as if he had made a jump raise after a major-suit overcall by you. Partner will show up with something like this: ♠10732 ♡Q102 ◇6 ♣A10954. If you go to 5♣ you will get doubled and will go down three tricks most of the time. In 4♡, you have chances of setting them one or two tricks. Always consider your defensive values before taking a further bid after a preemptive raise.

CHAPTER SIXTEEN
CONTINUING THE AUCTION WHEN PARTNER RAISES YOUR OVERCALL

Deciding whether to continue bidding after partner raises your suit often depends on which of the many ways he chose to make that raise.

WHEN PARTNER MAKES A SIMPLE RAISE AFTER THEY SHOW STRENGTH

When you overcall and LHO bids any number of notrump or a new suit at the two-level or higher, and your partner raises, you should feel that your side has no game. Either your trump suit will be offside or you will be seriously outgunned point-wise. In either case, a successful game contract by you would be exceptional. In such circumstances, when you can't really expect to have a game, it is reasonable to give up all your invitational sequences and play instead that your bids are all competitive. It's easy to recognize when this applies and it is only necessary to make the definition. Obviously, it won't be good if one person makes a weak, competitive bid and gets it raised to game.

Both vul.

W	N	E	S
		1♣	1♠
1NT	2♠	3♣	?

♠ A J 8 7 6 5
♡ K 10 5 4
◇ 3
♣ K 2

Bid 3♠. On an auction where LHO is known to have a spade trick plus some additional high cards as well, you have to be cautious. Had LHO raised to 2♣ instead of bidding 1NT, you would have bid 4♠. But under the circumstances, a non-invitational 3♠ is best. If you can't stand it, you could try 3♡ as a game try.

Neither vul.

W	N	E	S
		1♡	1♠
1NT	2♠	3♣	?

♠ K J 7 6 5
♡ 7 6 5
◇ A Q 7
♣ K 2

This hand, as good as it is, has too many minus features to go on. Your suit is full of holes and your heart holding is just awful. I would rate 3♠ as barely acceptable at matchpoints, but with the understanding that you expect to go down. At IMPs this would be too dangerous. One thing you have going for you if you do decide to bid is that partner needs a good hand to raise after the 1NT bid. From his point of view, you might have overcalled on a four-card suit so he won't be bidding on three small with questionable values. Finally, you can fall back on the wish that your partner may be able to bid 3♠ himself. Don't count on it.

Neither vul.

W	N	E	S
		1♡	1♠
1NT	2♣	3♣	?

♠ K Q 9 7
♡ A 10 6 5
♢ 3
♣ Q 10 9 7

Double. This is the sort of good result that can occur when you make a well-judged overcall on a four-card suit. If your partner pulls this double, he must have four spades. If he pulls it with three spades I can virtually guarantee that he made a bad bid.

Neither vul.

W	N	E	S
		1♠	2♡
2NT	3♡	pass	?

♠ 4 2
♡ A Q 10 6 5 4
♢ —
♣ A 8 6 5 3

Pass. Looks like game is possible, but you should be warned by that 2NT bid. You rate to have two spade losers and a heart loser, so you have to lose no clubs. With a spade lead and trump return, 3♡ will be the probable limit. Who knows. You might yet get doubled in 3♡.

An aside: The reason you did not bid 2♠, Michaels, over 1♠ is that you have six hearts and five clubs. A general rule is that when you use one of these bids, the higher-ranking suit is never longer than the lower suit.

Neither vul.

W	N	E	S
		1♡	1♠
2♣	2♠	pass	?

♠ A 10 7 6 5
♡ K Q 7
♢ A 10 5
♣ 3 2

Given the 2♣ bid, game is out of the question. You might feel willing to go as high as 3♠, but no higher. I suggest passing. If you pass, LHO will bid something. He may bid 2NT, he may bid 3♣, he may raise opener's hearts. If he bids 3♣ and it is passed to you, you can consider bidding 3♠. Here is a hand your partner might have. Look at it very carefully and remember it.

♠ Q J 8 3   ♡ 8 4 3   ♢ J 3   ♣ 10 7 6 4

He doesn't have very much. But given the bidding, you can't expect much more. RHO has an opening bid. You have 13 points. LHO may have 10 but can have more. Add it all up and your partner has up to 6 points but usually less. He made an aggressive raise, *typical of this bidding situation,* expecting that you would not take him seriously. He has something good but darn little of it. Be aware that a 2/1 response by your LHO is a big warning. Do not ignore it.

	Neither vul.		
W	**N**	**E**	**S**
		1♡	1♠
2♣	2♠	pass	?

♠ QJ8765
♡ A642
◇ 42
♣ 7

This is a good example of a competitive 3♠ bid. If you can bid 3♠ with the security that partner will pass, you can make it difficult for LHO to continue. If they were vulnerable you could even bid 4♠. Remember, partner should not raise on this sequence unless he has either good trump or good shape. A random 7- or 8-count with bad trump is not worth a raise.

	Neither vul.		
W	**N**	**E**	**S**
		1♣	1♠
2♡	2♠	3♡	?

♠ AK872
♡ KJ3
◇ Q54
♣ Q2

Clear to pass. You have a defensive hand poorly suited to competing. Partner's values are likely to include a singleton heart and that isn't much use to you. It is clear that partner has a very minimum raise, which means you will find precious few high cards in dummy. You won't make much in spades, your good hand notwithstanding.

	E-W vul.		
W	**N**	**E**	**S**
		1◇	1♠
2♡	2♠	3♡	?

♠ AJ8765
♡ 5432
◇ K3
♣ 2

Bid 3♠. Even 4♠ might work. You usually find three trumps in dummy, but you have six and you have good shape. Also, your ◇K should be worth something.

	N-S vul.		
W	**N**	**E**	**S**
		1♣	1♠
2♡	2♠	3♣	?

♠ AJ872
♡ 42
◇ KQ765
♣ 2

With a good offensive hand, a save might be in order. But the opponents have yet to find a fit, and even with game values they may have trouble making a game. Rather than bidding 4♠ you might bid 3◇, which helps your partner's judgment.

When Partner Makes a Preemptive Jump Raise

Neither vul.

W	N	E	S
			1♣ 1♠
2♡	3♠	pass	?

♠ K Q 8 7 5
♡ K Q 4
◇ K J 7
♣ 4 2

Pass. The problem here is not whether or not you have a good overcall. The question is what your partner's 3♠ bid shows. If you play it as preemptive, something I have suggested, your decision is clear. You should pass.

Years ago, it was common to play the jump raise as strong or invitational. That was fine then. Today, players are bidding better than ever and you need tools to combat this. Using the jump raise as preemptive is more valuable today than it was in the past. The sequence here is such that if you count the missing high-card points, you will conclude that partner has a weak hand. There are only a few high-card points available for partner to have.

Both vul.

W	N	E	S
			1♣ 1♡
2◇	3♡	4♣	?

♠ K 10 7 6
♡ K 9 8 4 3 2
◇ 3
♣ K 2

Bid 4♡. This is the sort of hand where you might continue after a weak jump raise by partner. Very seldom will you continue as a result of high cards alone. If you bid again, it will be because you have distribution such as you have here. All you need from partner to make 4♡ is a doubleton spade and four hearts to the ace and a little luck. You may not make 4♡ but the possibility exists. Note that your knowing of four trumps or more in partner's hand is a huge plus for you.

When Partner Uses a Cuebid Raise

If you overcall and your partner makes a cuebid at the two-level, he usually shows a balanced limit raise of your suit. You should bid on that assumption.

Neither vul.

W	N	E	S
			1♡ 1♠
pass	2♡	pass	?

♠ K 10 7 6 4
♡ K 9 8
◇ A Q 4
♣ 10 2

Bid 2♠, suggesting a minimum hand. You expect partner to have around 11 support points, probably with three trumps. If he has this hand, he will pass 2♠. If he has much more, he will bid again. If he has a big hand with a suit of his own, he will show his suit. For now, your hand is worth a minimum bid only. This is not a bad hand, though, and you will continue to game if partner raises to 3♠.

Neither vul.

W	N	E	S
		1◊	1♠
pass	2◊	pass	?

♠ A 10 7 6 4
♡ 9 8
◊ 8 7
♣ A K Q 7

Bid 3♣. When you go beyond two of your suit you promise more than a minimum. Bidding 2♠ would show less and might be passed. It is possible that you might bid a three-card suit just as a waiting bid. The big deal is that you do not make the weak bid of 2♠.

WHEN PARTNER DOUBLES THEIR RAISE

Neither vul.

W	N	E	S
		1◊	1♠
2◊	dbl	pass	?

♠ Q 10 7 6 4
♡ 9 8
◊ 8 7
♣ A Q J 4

When you overcall and they raise, a double by partner is takeout for the other two suits. Your correct bid is 3♣. As minimum as this hand is, it has a huge value in the four good clubs.

WHEN PARTNER MAKES A JUMP CUEBID RAISE

Neither vul.

W	N	E	S
		1◊	1♠
dbl	3◊	pass	?

♠ Q 10 7 6 4
♡ A 9
◊ 8 7
♣ K J 7 4

Bid 3♠. Partner has a distributional limit raise with four trumps but you have a minimum with only modest shape. If you bid 3♠ partner is not obliged to pass. If he has 11 or 12 support points, he will pass. If he has more, he will consider bidding game.

Neither vul.

W	N	E	S
		1♣	1♡
1♠	3♣	pass	?

♠ Q 8 3
♡ A J 8 7 3
◊ K Q 8 3
♣ 4

You have two reasonable choices. You can bid 3◊, which is a game try of sorts. Or you can just take your chances and bid game. This is not a huge hand but your shape is good, you know you are going to find four trumps in dummy, and your values are all likely to be working. You have nothing wasted in clubs, which is a good thing. Hopefully your ♠Q will be useful. LHO's bid of 1♠ is not a scary thing since he rates to have a weak hand. He does not have to have good spades.

N-S vul.

W	N	E	S
		1♡	1♠
dbl	3♡	4♡	?

♠ K Q J 5 4
♡ 7 3
◇ 8 3
♣ A Q 8 4

Bid 4♠. You have a hand worth around 15 points and your partner is promising around a dozen. Game should be on. Do not spend time looking for reasons not to bid game. Just take the view that partner thinks enough of his hand to invite game and you have more than you might.

WHEN PARTNER MAKES A CUEBID RAISE IN COMPETITION

Reminder. When you overcall and LHO raises opener, a singularly annoying situation arises.

LHO	Partner	RHO	You
		1♡	1♠
2♡	?		

Partner no longer has room to make a simple cuebid of 2♡ or a jump cuebid of 3♡. That little raise takes away some of your valuable tools. Partner no longer has room to do everything he wishes. A 3♡ bid by partner says he has a limit raise or better but he is not able to tell you whether he has a balanced hand or a shapely hand.

Look for the later section on modern methods. It brings you some new tools to help in moments like this one.

Both vul.

W	N	E	S
		1◇	1♡
2◇	3◇	4◇	?

♠ K 4 2
♡ A 8 6 5 3
◇ K 10 7
♣ J 10

First, you must remember that partner has a limit raise or better with three *or* four trumps. With a balanced hand and barely more than a minimum, you shouldn't bid 4♡. If anyone is going to bid 4♡ on this hand it will have to be partner. One bid that you might like to try is double. You have a heart winner, a diamond winner, and you might even have two diamond winners. You have an excellent defensive card in the ♠K and so far you have not credited partner with anything. Another issue here is that if you double, you should lead the ♣J, not the ♡A. Leading aces belongs in another book (my book *Opening Leads*, for one), but it is worth a mention here.

Summary of Standard Methods

I don't claim at all to have done a complete job of discussing overcalls and the ensuing auctions. High-level decisions, slam methods, saves, penalty doubles, and many other specific situations have been barely touched upon. And the problem of what to do with really big hands when RHO opens has been totally ignored. I promised earlier to discuss some of these topics, but for the time being they will have to wait for another book. What I have done instead has been to dwell on the early decisions made by both the overcaller and his partner. A foundation has been created which will help make later decisions easier. Bids have been defined and common problem situations identified and some suggestions offered.

Update to 2009

In fact, there are two such books now that tidy up some of the odds and ends. I wrote *The Complete Book on Takeout Doubles* and later, *Double! New Meanings for an Old Bid*. There are many excellent authors writing about topics which never saw print until recently.

CHAPTER SEVENTEEN
MODERN METHODS

Throughout this book I have been hinting at some new bidding tricks that have come about in recent years. I wish they had been available a long time ago. The new methods are aimed at helping you bid when your partner overcalls at the one-level in a major. The opponents may or may not do something.

In this section I will discuss bidding when your partner overcalls 1♡ or 1♠ and your RHO does something that is not a jump bid.

THE NEW TOOLS AND SOME OLD TOOLS

In brief:

New tool #1 – The 2NT bid
New tool #2 – The mixed raise
New tool #3 – Doubles are not for penalty. See later discussion for more.
New tool #4 – Two- and three-level cuebids. See discussion for more details.
Old tool #5 – Responsive doubles
Old tool #6 – Snapdragon doubles. Some new situations for this one.

NEW TOOL #1 — THE 2NT BID

Let's face it. When was the last time your partner overcalled with 1♡ or 1♠ and you jumped to 2NT showing 12-13 balanced HCP? It is one of those albatrosses that sit in the back of your convention card and never make an appearance. Given that this bid is so rare, some players decided to find a meaning that made sense and which also had a good frequency of coming up. A typical example:

Neither vul.

W	N	E	S
1♣	1♠	dbl	?

♠ K J 5 4
♡ Q 3
◇ A J 8 4
♣ 8 7 4

Bid 2NT. This shows a limit raise with four trumps and shape. In the old style of responding this hand would bid 3♣, a jump cuebid, to show a limit raise with four trumps. The 3♣ bid now has a different meaning which I will show you shortly.

Neither vul.

W	N	E	S
1♣	1♠	dbl	?

♠ Q 2
♡ A J 7 3
◊ J 10 8
♣ K Q 10 6

This is the hand that you used to bid 2NT with. Now that 2NT is used as a raise, you need another approach. The way to show this hand now is to redouble, ostensibly showing 11 or 12 points with a doubleton spade, and then follow with 2NT. Fortunately, this is unlikely to come up.

NEW TOOL #2 — THE MIXED RAISE

The mixed raise is an elegant name for a hand that has four trumps, some shape, and values to raise to the two-level but with enough stuff that if given a second chance, you might compete to the three-level. When you have such a hand, you show it by cuebidding their suit at the three-level. If they have bid two suits, you cuebid the lower-ranking suit. One small caveat. Keep the vulnerability in mind when you make this bid. Here are some examples.

Neither vul.

W	N	E	S
1◊	1♡	pass	?

♠ A 8 7 3
♡ K 10 4 3
◊ 5 4
♣ J 10 4

This hand is worth a raise to 2♡ and if they bid again, you would consider continuing to 3♡. Using this mixed raise convention, you would jump to 3◊ and get this hand off your chest immediately, thus describing your values to your partner and making life a little harder on your opponents.

Neither vul.

W	N	E	S
1◊	1♡	2◊	?

♠ Q J 4
♡ A J 8 7
◊ 5 4
♣ 9 7 6 3

Bid 3◊, the mixed raise showing a good raise to 2♡ with at least four trumps. Admit it. If you bid 2♡ and opener continued to 3◊, would you not feel like bidding 3♡? This hand is not good enough to consider it as a limit raise and it is too good for a weak raise of 3♡. Getting to the three-level first and forcing them to guess is better than letting them have an extra round of bidding to discuss things.

Neither vul.

W	N	E	S
1◊	1♡	2♣	?

♠ J 9 8 7 3
♡ Q J 7 4
◊ 5 4
♣ K 9

Bid 3♣, the mixed raise. The rule when responder goes to the two-level in a new suit is that a three-level cuebid in their *lower* suit shows the mixed raise. Note that when they show good hands you should be careful in making this bid. Be sure to have the four trumps, good values, and decent shape. 3◊ is the higher cuebid and it shows something else. It is a preemptive raise that will be discussed shortly.

Neither vul.

W	N	E	S
1◇	1♡	1♠	?

♠ A J 10 8 7 5
♡ K 4
◇ 8 7 5 4
♣ 3

Bid 2♠. When RHO bids 1♠, a new suit at the one-level, a cuebid by you is natural. The mixed raise cuebids apply only to opener's suit or to responder's suit that he bid at the two-level. Remember that if they have bid two suits, the three-level cuebid of their lower suit is a mixed raise. For the record, if you bid 3♠ here, that would be a splinter bid in support of hearts.

NEW TOOL #3 — DOUBLES AND REDOUBLES

Your partner overcalls 1♡ or 1♠ and your RHO does anything that is not a jump bid. If you double his bid, you show a raise of some sort. Here is a discussion of what RHO might bid and what a double by you shows.

Let's dispense with the odd case first.

LHO	Partner	RHO	You
1♣	1♡	dbl	rdbl

If RHO makes a negative double and you redouble, you show 10 or more points and a doubleton in partner's suit. This bid is intended to show your values and it allows your partner to bid again on some hands where your message is appropriate to his hand. He may decide to double them if they run to a suit he likes. He knows you have 10 points and he knows you have two cards exactly in his suit.

Neither vul.

W	N	E	S
1♣	1♡	dbl	rdbl

♠ Q J 8 4
♡ Q 7
◇ A J 10 5
♣ J 8 4

You have the needed 10 or more points, you have two cards in partner's heart suit, and you have no other bid that screams for you to make it. Whatever partner does now will be informed.

LHO	Partner	RHO	You
1♣	1♡	1♠	dbl

Snapdragon double. This double shows the unbid suit (diamonds) and a heart tolerance. A tolerance is defined roughly as a doubleton jack or better, or perhaps three small cards. If your hand is suitable to raise partner, do that instead. You need around 8-10 points for this, but can have a lot more. Two example hands:

♠ A 5 4	♠ 8 4 3
♡ J 3	♡ 10 8
◇ K J 9 8 4	◇ A K J 8 7
♣ 9 8 4	♣ A J 7

LHO	Partner	RHO	You
1♣	1♡	1NT	dbl

Responsive double. When there are two unbid suits, a double shows the two suits. You need a decent hand since there might not be a fit, so you need a good 8-10 points again. Be aware that doubling 1NT for penalty is not a good idea. A theme I have expressed often is that if they bid to 1NT, they tend to have their values. If you have a good hand your partner has a minimum overcall. It's best to use double to show a hand that you are likely to have; that is, two suits. One example hand:

♠ A J 8 5 4
♡ 3
◇ Q J 9 7 4
♣ 9 4

LHO	Partner	RHO	You
1♣	1♡	2♣	dbl

When RHO raises opener, your double is also responsive. There are two unbid suits, which is a requirement for a responsive double to be in effect.

Neither vul.

W	N	E	S
1♣	1♡	2♣	dbl

♠ K Q J 4
♡ 3
◇ Q J 10 9 3
♣ 9 4 2

You usually have five cards in each suit but these suits are good ones. For the record, your three little clubs suggest your partner has short clubs, which increases the chance that he likes one of your suits. If he rebids 2♡, just pass.

LHO	Partner	RHO	You
1◇	1♡	2♣	dbl

On this auction, your RHO is bidding a new suit at the two-level that is *lower* than his partner's suit. A double by you is snapdragon, showing a tolerance for hearts and the unbid suit, spades. Because RHO is showing a good hand, you better have useful values. You do not need a big hand but you need a likely home. (Note that on this sequence you can bid 2◇. That bid shows a nice raise for partner's hearts. More on this shortly.)

Two example hands:

Neither vul.

W	N	E	S
1◇	1♡	2♣	?

♠ A Q J 9 8
♡ J 3
◇ 9 3
♣ 9 5 4 3

You can double 2♣ with care and some hopes. The best part of this is that if LHO declares the hand, your partner will have strong reason to lead a spade. It is true that if partner has no spade fit and has a minimum heart suit you could be in trouble. Bidding when they show values is always a nervous affair.

Neither vul.

W	N	E	S
1◇	1♡	2♣	?

♠ Q 9 8 4 2
♡ K 3
◇ J 3
♣ Q 5 4 3

Pass this one. Your ♡K is nice, and that is the last of the good news. You have a poor spade suit and you have cards in the minors that may bother them but won't help your partner.

LHO	Partner	RHO	You
1♣	1♡	2♢	dbl

On this auction the opponents have shown two suits and RHO is bidding a suit that is *higher* than opener's suit. When this happens, you have less bidding room. This leads to your using double as a nice heart raise, in the 7-9 point range. You would raise to 2♡ with a good but lesser hand. Two examples:

Neither vul.

W	N	E	S
1♣	1♡	2♢	?

♠ K J 3
♡ Q J 8
♢ 4 3
♣ J 8 7 6 4

Double. Since you have two ways to raise hearts here, your partner will know from your double that you have a good raise, not one that you dragged up for the heck of it.

Neither vul.

W	N	E	S
1♣	1♡	2♢	?

♠ 10 7 5 4
♡ A 9 4
♢ 8 7
♣ 9 8 3 2

Bid 2♡. You can raise with minimum values if your hand is good in that context. This hand has an important heart honor and it has a ruffing value. Keep these two hands in mind when you are considering raising after the bidding shown in this example where RHO makes a 2/1 in a suit higher than his partner's.

NEW TOOL #4 — TWO- AND THREE-LEVEL CUEBIDS

Your partner overcalls 1♡ or 1♠ and they bid a new suit at the two-level. On some sequences you can cuebid one of their suits at the two-level. Sometimes when they bid two suits you have to go to the three-level to make a cuebid. All of these cuebids have meanings, which I have touched on already. The discussions below will fill in the details.

LHO	Partner	RHO	You
1♣	1♠	2♡	?

Here, you can cuebid 3♣ or 3♡.

  3♣ Cuebidding their lower suit at the three-level shows a mixed raise.
  3♡ Cuebidding their higher suit at the three-level shows a good preemptive raise.
  3♠ A jump raise to the three-level shows a lousy preemptive hand.

Here are a couple of examples of 3♡ and 3♠ bids for comparison.

Neither vul.

W   N   E   S
1♣ 1♠ 2♡ ?

♠ K 10 7 5
♡ 4
◇ Q 9 8 7 4
♣ 9 4 3

3♡. This hand has a little something of value.

Neither vul.

W   N   E   S
1♣ 1♠ 2♡ ?

♠ J 7 6 4 3
♡ 8 7 2
◇ 8 7 4
♣ Q 7

3♠. This hand, with five trumps, is still lousy. 3♠ is enough with this. Mind you, when you make your choice of bids, you should always consider the vulnerability.

LHO	Partner	RHO	You
1♡	1♠	2♣	?

Here, you can cuebid 2♡ or 3♣ or 3♡. Here is what these bids would mean.

2♡   This one was discussed earlier. If they go to the two-level and you can make a two-level cuebid, you show a good 7-9 point raise, assuming you do not have a better bid.

Neither vul.

W   N   E   S
1♡ 1♠ 2♣ ?

♠ K 9 8 4
♡ 9 8 3
◇ K J 3
♣ 10 5 2

You have your points but you do not have shape. Best to bid 2♡, showing a decent spade raise. You won't often have four-card support for this bid.

Your points are pretty good so this is worth a 2♡ bid. If you didn't have the ◇K you would be welcome to bid 2♠.

♠ K 9 4
♡ J 8 3
◇ K J 3
♣ 10 5 4 2

3♣   Mixed raise. The cheapest cuebid at the three-level shows the shapely 7-9 point raise with four trump.

Ballpark for a mixed raise.

♠ A J 7 3
♡ 8 3
◇ Q 7 6 5 4
♣ J 10

3♡   When they make a strong bid, you do not use splinter bids anymore. Your side just can't have the values to do this constructively. The 3♡ bid says you have a good preemptive raise. 3♠ would show the lousy preemptive raise.

Bid 3♡.

♠ 10 7 6 4
♡ 9 8 4 3
◇ A 8 7 3
♣ 8

The following were shown in the previous discussion on doubles and redoubles.

OLD TOOL #5 - RESPONSIVE DOUBLES

A reminder. If partner overcalls 1♡ or 1♠ and RHO bids 1NT or raises opener, a double by you is always responsive, showing the unbid suits. There are a few additional situations for responsive doubles, which will be shown in the following discussions.

OLD TOOL #6 - SNAPDRAGON DOUBLES

Some new situations for this one.
A reminder. When your partner overcalls 1♡ or 1♠ and RHO makes a 2/1 bid, a double by you can be either snapdragon or support. See discussion following for full details.

Here is a compilation of modern-method bids you can make when your partner overcalls 1♡ or 1♠. You will note that there are various situations depending on what your RHO bids over your partner's overcall.

WHEN PARTNER OVERCALLS A MAJOR AT THE ONE-LEVEL AND RHO PASSES

LHO	Partner	RHO	You
1♣	1♡	pass	?

Note that RHO passed. When RHO bids something, things can change. For now, stick with this auction where your partner overcalled and RHO passed. Here are the tools you will use.

Pass   Nothing to say.
1♠   New suit at the one-level. Five-card suit. Modest values. Not forcing.
1NT   8-10 points (maybe a boring 11) with a stopper or near stopper.
2♣   Cuebid, normally showing a limit raise with three-card support.
2◇   New suit at the two-level. Five-card suit. Decent values. Not forcing.
2♡   Raise, usually showing three trumps. Normal values.
2♠   A jump shift. Natural. Shows invitational values. On auctions where RHO does bid something, the meaning for 2♠ may be weak.
2NT   A new bid. Shows a limit raise or better with four or more trumps.
3♣   A new bid. Jump cue shows a nice four-card raise.
3♡   The jump raise remains preemptive.

WHEN PARTNER OVERCALLS A MAJOR AT THE ONE-LEVEL AND RHO BIDS SOMETHING

LHO	Partner	RHO	You
1◊	1♡	1♠	?

When your partner bids a major at the one-level and your RHO bids something at the one-level or makes a negative double, you can use all of the tools in your arsenal. You can use the 2NT raise and you can use the mixed raise, and all of your other tools remain unchanged.

Here is a list of your possible bids.

Pass	Nothing to say. Might have a good hand that intends to double something later.
1NT	8-11 points with suitable stoppers.
2♣	Natural and not forcing.
2◊	Cuebid, most likely with a balanced limit heart raise.
2♡	Normal raise. Three trumps usually, four rarely.
2♠	Natural!
2NT	Limit raise with four trumps and shape.
3♣	Natural. Invitational values.
3◊	Jump cuebid is the mixed raise.
3♡	Preemptive.
Dbl	Snapdragon. You have the unbid suit (clubs in this case) and two cards in hearts. Note that snapdragon doubles are used only when your partner can bid the unbid suit at the one- or two-level.

LHO	Partner	RHO	You
1◊	1♡	1NT	?

When RHO bids 1NT, things are slightly different. You have to be aware that your RHO has something in your partner's suit so you can't be entirely cavalier about bidding.

Pass	Nothing to say.
2♣	Natural and not forcing.
2◊	Cuebid, most likely with a balanced limit heart raise. Just remember that you rate to have a trump loser or two.
2♡	Normal raise. Three trumps usually, four rarely.
2♠	Natural.
2NT	Limit raise with four trumps and shape.

3♣	Natural. Preemptive but with a decent suit.
3◇	Jump cuebid is the mixed raise. Use judgment here since RHO says he has something in hearts.
3♡	Preemptive.
3♠	Good preemptive spade hand.
Dbl	Responsive, showing the two unbid suits. Do not bother doubling 1NT for penalty. They always have their values. If you have a good hand you will find that it is your partner who is bidding a lot, not the opponents.

When Partner Bids a Major at the One-level and RHO Raises His Partner

LHO	Partner	RHO	You
1◇	1♠	2◇	?

Pass	Nothing to say.
2♡	Natural with normal (6-10 point) values.
2♠	Normal raise. Three trumps usually, four rarely.
2NT	Limit raise with three or four trumps; the only time where a 2NT bid is ambiguous about the number of trumps.
3♣	Natural. Mildly invitational values.
3◇	Three-level cuebid is a mixed raise.
3♡	Preemptive.
3♠	Preemptive raise.
Dbl	Responsive, showing the two unbid suits. After a raise, just as after a 1NT bid from RHO, a double is responsive, showing the two unbid suits.

When RHO Bids a Suit at the Two-level and the Suit He Bids is Lower Than Opener's Suit

LHO	Partner	RHO	You
1♡	1♠	2♣	?

Oddly, this 2/1 bid is easier to bid against than when RHO raises his partner. On the sequence shown here, you have room to cuebid opener's suit so you have all of your tools.

Special note: When RHO's 2/1 suit is lower than opener's suit, a cuebid of opener's suit shows a good three-, perhaps four-card raise.

Pass	A likely bid. They have values so you won't often have anything to say.
2◇	Natural. A pretty good suit and not that many points.
2♡	The simple cuebid of opener's suit shows a 7-9 point raise.
2♠	A minimum raise. You may be extra aggressive in competition when RHO has made a strong bid such as a 2/1.
2NT	A shapely limit raise with four or more trump. In fact, you will seldom have a full limit raise. The 2NT bid shows as good a raise as you rate to have.
3♣	A mixed raise. When there are two suits to cuebid at the three-level, the lower cuebid shows the mixed raise.
3◇	Preemptive.
3♡	The three-level cuebid of their higher-ranking suit shows a good preemptive raise.
3♠	Preemptive.
Dbl	Snapdragon, showing five or more cards in the unbid suit and a tolerance for partner's suit, spades. After a 2/1 from RHO, the snapdragon double only applies when RHO's suit is lower than opener's suit.

RHO Bids a Suit Higher Than Opener's Suit

LHO	Partner	RHO	You
1◇	1♠	2♡	?

RHO's 2♡ bid took away your 2◇ cuebid. Fortunately, you still have many tools remaining.

Special note: When RHO's 2/1 suit is higher than opener's suit, a double by you shows a good three-, perhaps four-card raise.

Pass	A likely bid. They have values so you won't often have anything to say.
2♠	An aggressive raise in the range of 3 useful points up to a 6- or 7-point hand.
Dbl	A good, balanced raise in the area of 7-9 points, usually with three trump.
2NT	A shapely limit raise with four or more trump. You won't have the usual values associated with this bid. Note that you will never have the balanced limit raise after RHO's strong bid.
3♣	Natural and competitive only.
3◇	A mixed raise. When there are two suits to cuebid at the three-level, the lower cuebid shows the mixed raise.
3♡	The higher cuebid shows a good preemptive raise.
3♠	The jump raise shows a weak preemptive raise.

THE ODD CASE

Inevitably, there will be a time when the bidding goes this way.

LHO	Partner	RHO	You
1◇	1♡	2♠¹	?

1. Weak, 3-5 HCP with six spades (or similar)

Against this sequence, I suggest the following. *Note* that 2NT is no longer artificial because it is the only bid you have to show a good balanced hand.

Pass Nothing to say. You may have a hand that wishes to double 2♠ and are hoping your partner can reopen with a double.

Dbl A limit raise or better. Usually you will have a balanced hand or a minimum shapely limit raise.

2NT Natural. 11 or 12 HCP.

3♣ Natural with mildly invitational values.

3◇ Mixed raise.

3♡ Decent 7-10 point raise, probably with three trumps.

3♠ Cuebid for hearts. Some kind of hand that thinks there is a possible slam. Don't expect to see this bid.

4♡ A decent hand. This is not preemptive. When RHO preempts, you do not use preemptive bids too. You might bid 4♡ with a hand that normally would make a shapely limit raise.

QUIZ PART ONE

Your partner overcalls. What do you bid?

This quiz will show a variety of hands using the new structure. Assume LHO is the dealer on all of these hands and assume that neither side is vulnerable. I will leave it to you to make appropriate adjustments for different vulnerabilities. Note that in the previous discussion, I gave a basic message and in some cases suggested alternatives. In the hands that follow I am using only the basic new materials. I am ignoring the more complex methods. If you wish to use them, you will have to experiment to see if you like or do not like them.

LHO	Partner	RHO	You
1♣	1♡	pass	?

♠ Q873
♡ Q74
◇ QJ
♣ 9874

Raise to 2♡. Nothing new here.

♠ Q10732
♡ 74
◇ AQJ
♣ 974

Bid 1♠. A modest hand with five spades. Not forcing but not hopeless either.

♠ 73
♡ Q742
◇ K8743
♣ 94

Raise to 3♡. This is preemptive but does promise a few values along with four trumps and some shape.

♠ J74
♡ 10874
◇ 74
♣ Q743

Pass. Some would bid 3♡, a preemptive bid. My view is that this is too much. Many have different views on this and would bid 3♡. Not my style. But I won't tell you not to do it. Just be aware that your partner may hope for a bit more.

♠ K8754
♡ Q74
◇ KQJ
♣ 84

Bid 2♣, a cuebid, normally promising a balanced limit raise. Your partner will expect three trumps but if you are 4-3-3-3 it is okay to make this bid with four trumps.

♠ K 4 3
♡ Q 8 4 3
◇ Q 7 4
♣ 8 4 3

Just raise to 2♡. You normally have three trumps but hands like this one don't really relish being at the three-level.

♠ A K 5 4 3
♡ J 5 3 2
◇ K 3
♣ 10 5

Bid 2NT. This is a shapely limit raise or better. Until recently you would have bid 3♣, a jump cuebid, to show this hand. Now the jump cuebid shows a mixed raise and the 2NT bid is the limit raise.

♠ A 4 3
♡ J 10 3 2
◇ Q J 8 4
♣ 10 6

Bid 3♣, the mixed raise. If you had 3-4-3-3 shape you would just raise to 2♡.

LHO	Partner	RHO	You
1♣	1♡	dbl[1]	?

1. Negative

♠ K 5 4 3
♡ A 7 4
◇ 9 7 5 3
♣ 9 6

Raise to 2♡. Don't forget to raise when you have similar values. Normally you have three trumps for this bid.

♠ A 8 4
♡ 8 4
◇ K Q 7 4
♣ Q 10 7 4

Redouble. When you redouble over their negative double, you tell your partner that you have 10 or more good points and exactly a doubleton in his suit. You are helping partner know when or if he should compete. Also, if he wishes to double something, he knows you have values.

♠ 5 4
♡ J 8 5 4
◇ A K 3
♣ 10 5 4 2

Bid 3♣. You show a hand that is worth a raise and which might consider bidding again. This hand feels too good for a raise to 2♡, a bid that can be made with a boring 7-count, and it is not strong enough to invite game. Sort of half and half. The mixed raise jump cuebid lets you have the best of all worlds without misleading partner.

♠ 10
♡ J 10 7 4
◇ Q J 7 5 4
♣ J 8 4

Raise to 3♡. Preemptive with a little something.

♠ A Q 7 3
♡ K J 7 4
♢ A 8
♣ 7 5 4

Bid 2NT, showing a limit raise or better with four-card support. You will continue to game, which will tell partner you have extras. Bidding 4♡ immediately would not help partner if the bidding continued. For instance, if opener bid 5♣, your partner would have to guess if you had a preemptive hand or a real hand.

♠ J 10 7 5 3
♡ K 7 5 4 3
♢ 10 3
♣ 4

Raise to 4♡. This raise shows a weak hand, just like the situation where you raise partner's opening 1♡ bid to game. When your partner overcalls, you must be careful to choose the right way to raise.

♠ 8 4
♡ A J 3
♢ Q 8 7 5
♣ A 7 5 4

Bid 2♣. The simple cuebid always (99%) shows a balanced limit raise or more. This is one of the most important bidding tools you have. When your RHO bids something to get in the way of this cuebid, you lose an important bid. Note that on rare occasions, the cuebid will actually turn out to be a big hand with a suit of your own. Given that RHO made a negative double, the chances of your having a big hand are slight.

LHO	Partner	RHO	You
1♣	1♡	1♠	?

When RHO bids a suit at the one-level you have all of your tools. You can do just about anything you like.

♠ K J 9 8 7
♡ 4
♢ A 8 7 4
♣ J 10 7

Pass. Do not double. A double for penalty is silly since their bidding has just started. If you pass, you may get a chance to double something later when they are higher. In any event, a double should show something else, according to your agreements. You can use double to show some kind of heart raise and you can use double to show you have the unbid suit, diamonds, and something in hearts. Anything is better than doubling for penalty.

♠ 8
♡ 8 3
♢ K Q 10 8 4 3 2
♣ A Q 3

Bid 3♢. I suggest this be played as natural with invitational values.

♠ A Q	Bid 3♣, the mixed raise showing a good four-card raise with
♡ Q 7 5 4	decent points. It is a hand that is happy to raise and is willing
◇ 9 7 6 5	to be at the three-level.
♣ 9 5 4	

♠ K 8 4	Bid 2NT. This special raise shows a limit raise with four
♡ Q 7 4 2	trumps. You might have game points and if so, will show
◇ A Q 4 3	them on the next round if necessary.
♣ J 10	

♠ K 3	Bid 3♡. No need to bid 4♡ because you have five of them.
♡ J 8 7 5 4	Why offer the opponents 800 when you have a balanced
◇ J 10 4	hand?
♣ 9 8 4	

LHO	Partner	RHO	You
1♣	1♡	1NT	?

Be a little careful with your excesses here. RHO has hearts stopped, something that you fortunately are now aware of. Because you have all the bidding room you need, there is little restriction on your bidding as long as you heed the warnings of that 1NT bid.

♠ J 8 4 3 2	Double. This is responsive, not penalty. You show the unbid
♡ 9 3	suits with this kind of shape.
◇ A K J 3 2	
♣ 10	

♠ Q J 10 7	Pass. The important thing is to realize that double is responsive,
♡ J	not penalty. You can count on their side to have half of the
◇ K J 3	deck. It looks like your partner has bid on a good heart suit
♣ A J 10 7 4	and a prayer. If you set 1NT it will probably turn out that it
	was not easy. They might make it, too. Best to save double
	for the more common situation where you have the unbid
	suits and wish to show them, as in the previous hand.

♠ K J 3	Without RHO's 1NT bid you would have bid 3♣, the mixed
♡ 9 7 5 4	raise. Here you are warned that RHO has something in hearts.
◇ A 9 8 4	Bidding just 2♡ is best.
♣ 10 4	

♠ K J 3
♡ K J 4 3
◇ 4 3
♣ 9 7 5 4

I mentioned in the introduction that when RHO bids 1NT you need to show some judgment. This hand is worth a 3♣ raise since it has a little extra and it has good enough hearts that you may be able to negate RHO's heart holding.

♠ Q J 8 7 4
♡ A 10 8 4
◇ K J 4
♣ 8

2NT. Your shapely limit raise. If you had the same hand with one more club and one less spade you would bid 2♣, cuebidding opener's suit to show a good balanced raise.

LHO	Partner	RHO	You
1♣	1♡	2♣	?

This is the innocent raise that brings unexpected irritations to your bidding. Losing the ability to cuebid 2♣ is not trivial. I discussed this issue earlier. Here are a few reminder thoughts.

The raise to 2♡ is the same as always.
The raise to 3♡ is the same as always, preemptive.
The 3♣ cuebid is the same as always, a mixed raise.
A new suit bid, jump or otherwise, is the same as always.
2NT is a limit raise but it does not distinguish between three- and four-card support.
A double is takeout for the two unbid suits. When they bid and raise, a double by you always shows the two unbid suits.

Regrettably, if you have a game-forcing bid in another suit or a natural 2NT hand you have to start with double and then show your real hand. In practice, this has not come up in my experience.

♠ A K 10 8 7 4
♡ K 3
◇ K J 8 5
♣ 3

This is a double followed by a strong spade bid. If you think about it, there is close to zero chance that you will have this hand. LHO has about 12-14 points, your partner has 9 or 10, and responder has 5-9. Your share after this is 14 at most, but it's usually in the 7-11 point range.

LHO	Partner	RHO	You
1◇	1♠	2♡	?

When you hear a sequence like this you should confirm if 2♡ shows a good hand, as it does in most systems. If your RHO shows 11 or so points, your bidding is no longer as constructive as before. Here are some of the changes you have to make.

♠ K 8 5
♡ 8 6 5 4
◇ 4 3
♣ J 9 7 4

Raise to 2♠. When they make a strong bid (2♡) your bidding is aimed at obstruction, not construction. Your side can't make anything but you can be a pain to their bidding if you use caution. A raise by you now should say you have something good for spades but not necessarily a good hand. If partner bids again you want to be able to put something down in dummy that you know he will like. See the next hand for a comparison.

♠ J 8 7 4
♡ Q 8 3
◇ 9 8 3
♣ Q J 3

Why bid 2♠? The bidding is going to continue and, importantly, you do not want partner to keep bidding. Your shape is lousy and your high cards, with the possible exception of your club holding, are bad. Worse, on defense you have some stuff that may mean they cannot make a game. Here's a leading question. If they bid 4♡, would you rather save in 4♠ or defend against 4♡?

♠ Q 8 4 2
♡ 8 3
◇ 9 8 4
♣ K Q 7 5

Bid 3◇. This is the mixed raise and, in context, says you have a decent raise with four trumps and values your partner rates to appreciate.

♠ K J 4 3
♡ 4 3
◇ 8 3
♣ A J 7 6 3

Given that you can't have a good hand, you can bid 2NT with this. Partner will play you for this kind of hand. Good spades, better than normal shape, and useful cards. Partner will not play you for a balanced limit raise.

♠ Q J 8 5
♡ 8 4 3 2
◇ 5 4
♣ J 10 7

Bid 3♠. A preemptive raise. You would be happier if they were vulnerable but they aren't. At least you have excellent spades, shape, and a pusher in clubs. In addition, you do not have defense. I have said that a preemptive raise should promise a few points. When RHO makes a strong bid you are welcome to make a weak jump raise with less than usual since their chance of having a game or slam has increased. You can more easily afford to go down 300 or 500 when they have games or better their way.

♠ A Q 5
♡ 8 7 3 2
◇ 9 4
♣ J 8 7 4

Double. When RHO bids a new suit at the two-level that is higher ranking than opener's suit, a double by you shows a good raise of 7-9 points. The good spades put this hand in this category.

♠ Q 10 8 5 3
♡ 8 4 3
◇ 5 4
♣ K 4 3

Bid 3♡. Bidding their higher suit at the three-level shows a preemptive raise but one that has a few cards.

LHO	Partner	RHO	You
1♡	1♠	2◇	?

Note that this sequence gives you more room to bid. Responder's suit is lower than opener's, leaving you more choices and hence more room to bid.

♠ K 9 4
♡ 7 4
◇ 9 8 5 4
♣ Q 9 7 4

With RHO showing a good hand, you can afford to bid 2♠ without worrying that your partner will take you seriously. Do not overlook raises like this one.

♠ A J 2
♡ 8 7 4 3
◇ 9 3
♣ K 10 7 4

Their auction has left you room to cuebid at the two-level. Bid 2♡, showing a good balanced raise. Given that RHO made a strong bid, you won't have much more than this and your partner should make allowances for the way the bidding has gone.

♠ J 4
♡ J 9 8 4
◇ 9
♣ K Q J 8 6 4

This is what a snapdragon double would look like. You have a good holding in the unbid suit and you have a tolerance for partner's suit, spades. You will note that given their strong bidding, you can't have much more than this. Worse, if partner has a fair spade suit and no club fit, you might be down a lot in whichever suit you play. I do not like snapdragon doubles after a 2/1 bid by RHO. They work best when RHO's bidding is weak (he bids a new suit at the one-level), in which case your side may have the values to compete.

♠ K J 8 5
♡ 8 7 4
◇ 9 3
♣ A J 7 4

This is about as good a hand as you will have after partner's overcall and RHO's 2/1 bid. You can bid 2NT to tell partner that you have four trumps, some shape, and something like a minimum limit raise.

QUIZ PART TWO

You overcall 1♡ or 1♠ and partner bids. What do his bids mean?

Using modern methods, you (South) overcall 1♡ or 1♠ and the auction continues. Following are a number of auctions where partner bids something. All that is asked of you in this quiz is what you think partner is doing. Keep in mind that some of partner's bids change according to what your LHO has done. Assume neither side is vulnerable for now.

West	North	East	South
		1♣	1♠
pass	2♠		

North's raise usually shows three trumps or a balanced and boring hand with four. He has normal values for a raise. Nothing special about this bid.

West	North	East	South
		1◇	1♡
pass	2◇		

North's cuebid usually shows a balanced limit raise or better. He may have a big notrump hand and he may have a huge hand with a suit of his own. He will have the balanced raise over 95% of the time.

West	North	East	South
		1◇	1♡
pass	3◇		

The three-level cuebid in opener's suit is a special bid known as the mixed raise. Partner shows a hand that he normally would raise to 2♡ but which is good enough that he might consider bidding 3♡ in competition. His 3◇ bid does the job immediately, anticipating more bidding. He hopes to distract their auction with this bid. Remember that this mixed raise promises four or more trump.

West	North	East	South
		1◇	1♡
2♣	3♣		

Here, they bid two suits and partner cuebid the lower of them at the three-level. The rule that applies is this. If partner cuebids the lower of their suits at the three-level, it shows a mixed raise. Because they have shown values, the mixed raise can be bid a little more freely than normal. It will still include some distribution.

West	North	East	South
		1◇	1♡
2◇	3◇		

The mixed raise again. The cuebid shows something like the following:

♠ Q 7 6 4 3   ♡ K J 5 4   ◇ 2   ♣ 9 4 3

West	North	East	South
		1♣	1♠
pass	2NT		

When you overcall 1♡ or 1♠, all 2NT bids by partner show a limit raise or better. Most of the time, with one exception, partner's hand has four trump with some shape.

West	North	East	South
		1♣	1♠
2♣	2NT		

Partner's 2NT bid shows a limit raise or better. This is the one time you cannot tell what kind of limit raise he has. He may have a balanced hand with three or four trump and he may have a shapely hand with four or more trump. This happens only when you overcall and LHO raises opener to the two-level.

West	North	East	South
		1◊	1♡
1♠	dbl		

When they bid two suits at the one-level, a double is snapdragon. North has a tolerance for hearts and he has a club suit.

West	North	East	South
		1◊	1♡
2◊	dbl		

If they bid and raise and partner doubles, it is responsive, showing the unbid suits. He rates to have 5-5 but may have 5-4 if he has good suits with suitable values.

West	North	East	South
		1◊	1♡
1♠	3♡		

A jump raise is always preemptive. If LHO has not shown a big hand, North's raise promises a little something. He won't have a Yarborough.

West	North	East	South
		1◊	1♡
2♣	3♡		

On this sequence, West showed a good hand. North's 3♡ is preemptive and may be bid with a lesser hand than when West passes or makes a weak bid such as a raise.

West	North	East	South
		1◊	1♡
1NT	dbl		

Double is takeout. We have no penalty doubles when you overcall and LHO bids something that is not a jump bid. The double shows the unbid suits, probably 5-5, and enough values to be safe. Judgment rules here.

West	North	East	South
		1◇	1♡
2♣	dbl		

Note that West's suit is lower ranking than opener's. A double in this instance is snapdragon, showing a heart tolerance and the unbid suit, spades.

West	North	East	South
		1◇	1♡
2♣	2◇		

They made a 2/1 bid and it left room for partner to cuebid opener's suit. This shows the 6-9 point raise. If North had bid 2♡ instead, that would show a weak raise with some reason to bid.

West	North	East	South
		1◇	1♠
2♡	dbl		

Do not forget that when you overcall and they bid a new suit, there are no penalty doubles unless they are making some kind of jump. When they make a 2/1 bid and you do not have a two-level cuebid to make, the double shows your nice 6-9 point raise that was not suited to one of the other raises you have. Here, West bid 2♡, a higher-ranking suit than opener's. You can not cuebid at the two-level now. Had West bid 2♣, you would have room for a two-level cuebid of 2◇.

West	North	East	South
		1◇	1♡
2♣	2♡		

When they make a 2/1 response, it is clear that your side is outgunned. In this situation, your partner is allowed to make really aggressive raises. His hand falls into the range of 4-6 points. The most important thing is that his values will be useful to you. He should not raise with six lousy points. Here is one example of a 6-point hand that should not raise to 2♡:

♠Q874 ♡J64 ◇94 ♣QJ63

You have nothing that you know your partner will like. This hand is a wishy-washy pile of junk.

West	North	East	South
		1◇	1♡
2♣	3◇		

If North had bid 3♣, that would have shown an aggressive mixed raise. When they make a 2/1 bid, a cuebid in their higher-ranking suit shows a fair preemptive raise.

West	North	East	South
		1◇	1♡
2♣	3♡		

North's 3♡ bid is weak — with a vengeance. When they have proven values, your preemptive jumps are really preemptive.

♠9 8 4   ♡Q 8 7 6 5   ◇9 8 4   ♣10 4

West	North	East	South
		1◇	1♡
pass	4♡		

Jumps to game are preemptive. Do not jump to game when you have a good hand. There is some chance the opponents will continue bidding and partner needs to know what you are likely to have. Mind you, jumping to game with some good hands may be wise if you are terribly afraid of giving the opponents a second chance. But remember that your partner will expect you to have a weak hand.

West	North	East	South
		1◇	1♡
pass	2♠		

Partner's jump shift when LHO shows a weak hand shows an invitational hand with a six-card suit or rarely, a good five-card suit.

West	North	East	South
		1◇	1♡
pass	3♣		

New suit jumps to the three-level also show invitational hands. At the three-level, your partner promises six cards in his suit, and may even have seven.

West	North	East	South
		1◇	1♡
2◇	3♠		

If their auction is not strong, as occurs here, the jump is invitational. North has six spades plus a fair hand.

West	North	East	South
		1◇	1♡
1NT	3♣		

If they make a strong bid (1NT is counted as strong for this purpose) a jump in a new suit is preemptive. Since a penalty double is possible, North will have a good suit.

West	North	East	South
		1◇	1♡
2♣	3♠		

If they show strength, as here, the jump to 3♠ is preemptive. Given that they have shown a lot of strength, the 3♠ bid can be more aggressive than normal.

West	North	East	South
		1◇	1♡
2♠¹	?		

1. Weak, 3-5 points, six cards.

Do you remember what each of partner's possible bids means in this singular situation?

Pass   Nothing to say. Partner may have a stack in spades and be hoping you can reopen with a double.

Dbl   A limit raise or better. Can be shapely or balanced. This is the most important bid. Remember that doubles are not for penalty.

2NT   Natural, 11 or 12 HCP.

3♣   Natural with mildly invitational values.

3◇   Mixed raise.

3♡   Decent 7-10 point raise.

3♠   Cuebid. Either a good hand for hearts or perhaps willing to look for 3NT.

4♡   A decent hand. This is not preemptive. When an opponent preempts, you do not use preemptive bids too. Partner has something over there. He might even have a fair hand that does not want to leave the opponents bidding room.

Bidding When RHO Opens 1NT

This section reflects hundreds of requests that I include this topic when *Overcalls* was updated. I will do that here but suspect that some will be disappointed in that there are no examples. What you will find in this section is a selection of hands where you are asked if you would bid. I do not ask what you would bid, however. That is left to you.

Why?
The reason I am not offering any advice is that there are dozens of conventions in use when RHO opens 1NT, and there is always the tried-and-true method of just bidding suits naturally.

Do you need a convention?
This question is easy to answer. You need a convention. Let's say that RHO opens 1NT showing 15-17 points. You have this hand.

♠ A J 8 7 4 ♡ 4 ◇ Q J 8 7 4 ♣ K 4

This hand has a lot to offer and your wish is to let partner know what you have so he can bid a lot if his hand is suitable, and can stop the bidding if his hand is not suitable. If you are not playing a convention you have to guess whether to bid 2♠, 2◇ or pass. Do you know what the best bid is? Neither do I. Do you agree that bidding is a good idea? Me too. The key to many of your decisions is to have a convention to use and the wisdom and experience to use it appropriately and properly.

Here is a short list of conventions you might play after an opening 1NT.
  Hamilton/Cappelletti (These two conventions are actually the same, each being invented at approximately the same time.)
  DONT
  Landy
  Hello
  Astro
  Aspro
  Mohan
  Woolsey
  Scum
  Submarine
  Transfer bids
  Rabbit
  And a lot more that do not come to mind right now.

Don't bother looking up these names. Some of them were in use a long time ago and have fallen out of favor. The first two, Hamilton/Cappelletti and DONT, are widely used.

My advice? Pick a popular convention, get your partner to agree to it, and play it. The reason for playing a popular convention is that if you play with many partners you will be playing a convention that they are likely to know. You won't waste time getting a lot of zeros while you teach it to your partner.

Here are some hands that you might have after hearing RHO open a strong notrump. My comments will not include what to bid, but rather what your approach should be.

Neither vul.

W	N	E	S
		1NT	?

♠ Q J 9 8 7
♡ K 9 7 6 5
♢ 5 4
♣ 9

Bid something. Most conventions include ways to show two-suited hands. Some of them show the suits immediately, and that is always good since your partner knows what to expect. On this hand you do not seriously expect to make anything significant, but with these values you suspect they have a game or a slam. Sitting back quietly will give them room to use their system.

Here is a possible auction you might hear if your opponents are allowed to bid by themselves.

LHO	Partner	RHO	You
		1NT	pass
2♠	pass	3♢	pass
3♠	pass	4♣	pass
4♡	pass	4NT	pass
5♡	pass	6♢	all pass

Here is what their bids mean. 2♠ asks for the minors and 3♢ shows four. 3♠ shows a singleton spade. 4♣ is a cuebid looking for a slam. 4♡ is another cuebid and 4NT asks for aces. West shows two keycards and East bids a slam. This was easy and their side is probably pleased to have had their bidding tools come up.

Now let's say you poke your nose into the bidding with 2♡. For the sake of discussion, the 2♡ bid shows hearts and spades as in the DONT convention. Do you think that your opponents will know how to bid their hand to slam now? They may, but they may not. Your 2♡ bid forces them to work a lot harder.

What I am suggesting is that with shape you should bid and without shape you should pass, or perhaps make a penalty double should that be one of your alternatives.

E-W vul.

W	N	E	S
		1NT	?

♠ 7
♡ K J 9 8 7 6
◇ Q 8 7 4
♣ 10 9

Worried that you have only 6 points? That is valid. What you do have is a fair six-card suit and distribution which, if you find partner with an acceptable 6-count, will take five tricks, which will add up to a 500-point penalty. That is less than the value of their expected game.

What bid should you make to do this? Here are some choices.

You can bid 2♡, natural. This is part of many conventional treatments.

You can bid 2◇, a transfer to hearts, if you play transfer bids.

You can bid 2♣, showing a one-suited hand, if this is the convention of your choice.

You can bid 2◇, showing either spades or hearts, again, depending on the convention you are using.

E-W vul.

W	N	E	S
		1NT	?

♠ K J 8 4
♡ 4
◇ A 10 7 6 4
♣ 8 7 3

It is nice to have 5-5 shape when you enter the bidding with two suits, but experience has shown that getting into the bidding with 5-4 shape is a winning deal in the long run as long as you have decent suits. This hand has two semi-decent suits, and what you have going for you, as usual, is that you are making them work for their result as opposed to letting them bid unmolested. They may miss a chance to double you and set you a lot. But the upside is that your partner will fit one of your suits and you can either outbid them or push them too high.

E-W vul.

W	N	E	S
		1NT	?

♠ Q 8 7 5
♡ K
◇ Q 8 7 6 5
♣ Q 9 4

Pass. This hand has the same shape as the one above and it even has one more point. But the suits are crummy and the values are poor. You don't have a single card that you can count on. Your ♡K has the potential to be worthless.

Neither vul.

W	N	E	S
			1NT ?

♠ K J 4
♡ K J 8 7 4
◇ A Q
♣ Q 9 4

Here is a hand that, if given to a hundred players, would induce a huge number of bad decisions. I would hazard that the bids would fall along these lines.

Pass – twenty votes
Double (intended as penalty) – twenty votes
2♡ (or the artificial equivalent) – sixty votes

Double would get more votes than twenty except for the fact that many players use a convention that uses double as some kind of artificial bid.

What is my opinion of bidding on these cards? Keep in mind that I am answering this question: "It is right to bid something or is it right to pass?" I am not touting a specific bid.

I would pass. Doubling with a broken hand is unwise. There are about 8 points unaccounted for and these will often be divided evenly. You may end up defending 1NT with half of the deck and you will find that defense is not so easy. Declarer will know about your points and he will play the hand way better than you want to see.

Bidding 2♡ by whatever method you have is also not a good idea. If your partner fails to put down a few trumps, you will find that 2♡ is not a winning contract. You need entries to dummy to take finesses, and they won't be there. You will spend much of the time leading out of your hand.

Here is a truth you can appreciate. If your partner has the few high-card points you need to make eight tricks in hearts, you will find that those points will usually allow you to set 1NT. If he does not have them, you will often go down quite a few. Points are nice but they do not take tricks.

FINAL QUIZ

The following section includes hands that will reflect on the important points made throughout this book. These are not presented in any particular order so you won't always know the theme of any given hand. The answers will be based on the original methods and if modern methods would have been applicable, that will be mentioned in the discussion.

To get the most out of these hands, I suggest you get a card or some similar device and cover up the bids attributed to your hand. Look at the auction and decide on your choice of calls. Do this for each round of the auction to its completion.

One additional idea. As you bid these hands keep in mind how your hand is changing in value according to the auction, and keep in mind the state of the auction. Recognizing a dangerous auction as opposed to a safe auction will be a strong beginning to effective defensive bidding.

Note that on some sequences there are quite a few bids. I only discuss the ones that need discussion. Usually these bids will involve judgment or system.

HANDS WHERE YOU OVERCALL. YOU ARE SOUTH.

W	N	E	S
		1♣	1♠
1NT	2♡	pass	3♡
all pass			

Neither vul.

♠ 8 7 6 4 2   ♡ A 10 7   ◇ 3   ♣ A Q 9 3

A classic bad-suit overcall. North's 2♡ bid is not forcing but South likes hearts a lot. 3♡ gets the nod but 4♡ is possible too. I would award 100 to 3♡ and 70 to 4♡.

W	N	E	S
		1♣	1♠
2◇	2♠	3♣	pass
3◇	all pass		

E-W vul.

♠ K 8 6 5 3   ♡ 3 2   ◇ K J 3   ♣ A 5 4

South is barely able to find a 1♠ bid. In fact, I prefer bidding 1♠ on the previous hand. West's bidding shows real values so South is not tempted to bid again with this hand. Note that North should not raise to 2♠ after West's strong 2◇ bid unless he has good values for spades, not just three spades and some random points.

W	N	E	S
		1♡	1♠
2♡	2♠	pass	pass
3♡	pass	pass	3♠
all pass			

N-S vul.

♠ Q 10 8 6 5 4   ♡ A 9 3   ◇ 4   ♣ K 10 6

South is entitled to compete to 3♠ based on his six-card suit, his expectation of short hearts in the North hand, and his nice shape. An easy bid.

W	N	E	S
		1♡	1♠
2♡	dbl	pass	4♣
all pass			

Neither vul.

♠ A 10 8 6 5   ♡ 3   ◇ K 4 2   ♣ K Q 7 6

You know North has the minor suits. You love clubs. Jump to 4♣, or even 5♣. If North has the minors, he will judge what to do. A rare hand that North can have is an 11- or 12-point spade raise with a doubleton spade. If he has this hand he will make as good a guess as he can. If you choose not to include this treatment in your responsive doubles, you won't be giving up much.

W	N	E	S
		1♣	1♠
2♣	dbl	pass	2♡
pass	pass	3♣	3♡
all pass			

Neither vul.

♠ A Q 8 6 4 3   ♡ J 8 4 2   ◇ Q 3   ♣ 7

Bid 2♡ and be willing to compete to 3♡ as shown.

W	N	E	S
		1◇	1♠
2◇	dbl	pass	2♡
3♣	pass	3◇	all pass

N-S vul.

♠ K 7 5 4 3 2   ♡ A 9 6   ◇ K 5 3   ♣ 7

Bid 2♡. As hands go, this one is pretty good for hearts. You expect (hope) partner has five so this hand will be adequate for a heart contract.

W	N	E	S
		1◇	1♠
2◇	dbl	pass	2♡
3♣	pass	3◇	all pass

N-S vul.

♠ J 5 4 3 2   ♡ A 9   ◇ A 7 3 2   ♣ K 8

2♡. Same auction as the previous hand. But this time you do not have a three-card suit to bid. I suggest bidding 2♡, which is inelegant at best. The reason I show this hand is that this kind of situation does happen now and then. You do not have enough to bid notrump and rebidding this spade suit is a bad choice. You could, if you like living on the edge, pass 2◇ doubled. Beating it is possible.

W	N	E	S
		1♣	1♠
2♣	dbl	pass	2♠
pass	pass	3♣	all pass

E-W vul.

♠ K Q J 10 6 3   ♡ 9 5 4   ◇ K 2   ♣ 7 3

Just rebid spades. At the end of the auction, you might bid 3♠ instead of passing it out. A close decision.

W	N	E	S
		1♣	1♠
2♣	dbl	pass	2♡
pass	3♡	all pass	

Both vul.

♠ A J 8 7 5   ♡ Q 5 4   ◇ K 2   ♣ 8 5 3

Bid 2♡. North usually has five of them so 2♡ will be a fine spot. If North bids 2♠, very unlikely, you will pass that too.

W	N	E	S
		1♣	1♠
2♣	dbl	pass	2♠
pass	pass	3♣	3◇
all pass			

E-W vul.

♠A Q J 10 8 7 ♡Q 2 ◇K 7 3 ♣9 5

Bid 2♠. You are close to bidding 3♠. Your red-suit honors are good since North is promising something in both of these suits. At the end, you can compete and the issue is whether to bid 3♠ or 3◇. Your partner will know you have six good spades and probably three diamonds. You would have bid diamonds earlier if your spades were not excellent.

W	N	E	S
		1♣	1♠
1NT	all pass		

Neither vul.

♠K 9 7 6 4 3 ♡K 3 ◇A Q 2 ♣Q 5

West's 1NT bid and North's silence should warn you. If you had the ♠J10 too, bidding 2♠ would be okay. You would be happy to trade the ♣Q for the ◇J.

W	N	E	S
		1◇	1♠
2◇	pass	pass	2♠
pass	pass	3◇	pass
pass	3♠	all pass	

N-S vul.

♠J 10 8 7 6 4 ♡A K ◇A 2 ♣K 4 3

You are entitled to hope for partner to have a few points and a couple of spades. Their bidding is not scary at all. Pass if partner later competes to 3♠. His first pass denies values for game.

W	N	E	S
		1♡	1♠
2♣	pass	2♡	pass
3♣	all pass		

Both vul.

♠A Q J 4 2 ♡4 3 ◇Q 7 6 5 3 ♣A

This auction is dangerous. Letting them play in 3♣ is okay. You might have a partscore but you won't have a game. South had another decision of note. He might have used Michaels and didn't because his spades were so good and his diamonds so flimsy.

W	N	E	S
		1♡	1♠
pass	2♡	pass	2♠
pass	3♠	pass	4♠
all pass			

Neither vul.

♠Q J 10 9 2 ♡8 7 ◇A Q 5 ♣K 9 5

You have a sound overcall. After signing off in 2♠, you were asked if you have a dog overcall or a little something. As minimum hands go, this one is good. You can bid 4♠ now.

W	N	E	S
			1♣ 1♡
pass	2♣	pass	2♠
pass	3♢	pass	3♡
pass	4♡	all pass	

Both vul.

♠ A Q 2 ♡ A K 8 6 5 ♢ 4 2 ♣ 8 5 3

The important bid is South's 2♠ call. He has too much to rebid 2♡, which would be weak. The rest of the auction includes a forcing 3♢ bid from North and a neutral 3♡ bid from South. North's hand? ♠K43 ♡Q9 ♢AKQ1095 ♣94. North looked for game in diamonds or notrump, and settled on game in hearts.

W	N	E	S
			1♣ 1♠
2♣	3♣	pass	?

Both vul.

♠ A Q 9 7 5 ♡ K J 7 ♢ Q 5 4 2 ♣ 8

Bid 4♠. North's cuebid shows a limit raise in spades or better. You have a sound overcall and are entitled to bid a game. If you are using the modern methods, 3♠ shows a good spade raise in the 7-9 point range with four trumps and some shape. Bid only 3♠ if partner's 3♣ bid is the newer version of the cuebid. Here is an example of a modern 3♠ bid: ♠KJ103 ♡10862 ♢K6 ♣1073.

W	N	E	S
			1♣ 1♠
2♣	2NT	pass	?

Both vul.

♠ A Q 9 7 5 ♡ K J 7 4 ♢ Q 4 2 ♣ 8

This sequence shows how bidding has changed over the years. Normally, the 2NT bid shows a notrump hand with invitational values and a club stopper. This is a rare occurrence. If 2NT is used this way, South has real choices. I think I would bid 3♡.

If using the new methods, the 2NT bid shows a limit raise or better for spades. If West hadn't raised clubs, 2NT would promise a limit raise with shape. Partner would cuebid 2♣ with a good, balanced limit raise. With West bidding 2♣, and with your partner's 3♣ bid being used to show a good competitive raise, the 2NT bid now shows a limit raise but with unknown shape. He can be balanced or unbalanced. You do have a good overcall in either case and should bid 4♠.

W	N	E	S
		1♣	1◇
pass	2♣	dbl	rdbl
pass	2◇	pass	3♣
pass	3◇	pass	3NT
all pass			

E-W vul.

♠ Q 2　♡ A 4 2　◇ K Q 8 7 5　♣ A 8 4

Your redouble shows a good hand with at least half a club stopper. North signs off and South rebids 3♣. He intends to reach 3NT but wants it played by North if North has something in clubs. If North denies a club stopper, South will bid 3NT himself. Given South's values and North's promised values, 3NT should be okay if North is willing to play it there.

W	N	E	S
		1♣	1♡
pass	2♣	pass	2♡
pass	2♠	pass	3♣
pass	4♣	all pass	

Neither vul.

♠ Q 8　♡ A K J 6 4　◇ J 1 0 3　♣ 8 7 3

The mechanics of this auction are the key. North cuebids and South shows a minimum. North's 2♠ bid is natural and forcing. South chooses 3♣, which is not perfect but probably best.

W	N	E	S
		1◇	1♡
pass	2◇	pass	2♡
pass	3♣	pass	3◇
pass	3NT	all pass	

Neither vul.

♠ 4 2　♡ A Q 1 0 8 4　◇ J 8 7　♣ K 1 0 5

South overcalls and then shows a minimum. North's 3♣ bid shows a big hand, so now South is interested in game. His 3◇ bid looks for 3NT, which North bids. Note how useful a card the ♣K has become after partner showed a strong hand with clubs.

W	N	E	S
		1♡	1♠
2♣	2◇	2♡	5◇
pass	pass	dbl	all pass

E-W vul.

♠ Q 1 0 9 8 6 4　♡ 3　◇ A Q 8 2　♣ 8 5

The early auction suggests they have a game, and your partner's bidding shows he has good diamonds and not much else. I like 5◇, can understand 4◇, but don't like a wimpy 3◇, or worse, a pass. You won't make 5◇ but this bid will make life difficult for them. West likely wanted to show heart support, but his exploration room was gone.

W	N	E	S
		1♣	1◇
1♡	1♠	2♡	3♠
pass	4♠	all pass	

Both vul.

♠ A J 8　♡ 4　◇ A 1 0 9 7 3　♣ K 9 7 5

South overcalls 1◇ and gets a 1♠ bid from North. North tends to have a good five-card suit with at least 8 points. The best bid is 3♠, with 2♠ being a lazy choice.

W	N	E	S
		1♡	1♠
2◇	pass	2♡	pass
3♡	all pass		

Neither vul.

♠K 10 8 6 5 4   ♡Q 3   ◇K 9 5   ♣A Q

South recognizes that West has a good hand and North has a lousy hand. South correctly bids 1♠ and then quits when North is silent. Remember this important guideline. Don't rebid on marginal hands when the opponents have shown strength, such as West's two-level response of 2◇. Be aware of the exception – when an opponent uses a 'negative free bid' in which a bid of a new suit in competition is no longer forcing.

W	N	E	S
	pass	1♡	1♠
2♡	3◇	3♡	4◇
4♡	pass	pass	?

Neither vul.

♠K Q 10 8 4   ♡3   ◇A Q 4   ♣J 8 5 2

If you are thinking of bidding 5◇, consider that their bidding is not confident. There is nothing about this sequence that suggests they will make 4♡. You should pass.

W	N	E	S
	pass	1♡	1♠
2♡	3♡	4♡	4♠
all pass			

N-S vul.

♠K 7 5 4 3 2   ♡4   ◇8 3   ♣A Q 7 5

Your partner, a passed hand, still felt he had enough to invite game. You have as much as you can possibly have. Bid 4♠ for sure. Note that if you are using the new methods, North's 3♡ bid shows a good, normal raise with four trumps. South would tend to bid 4♠ over that, too.

W	N	E	S
	pass	1♡	1♠
2♡	dbl	pass	3♣
3♡	all pass		

Neither vul.

♠K Q 7 5 3   ♡A J 4   ◇7 4   ♣J 7 3

The double is responsive. South bids 3♣ and then quits, happy to have pushed them to the three-level.

W	N	E	S
	pass	1♡	1♠
2♡	dbl	pass	3♣
3♡	pass	pass	4♣
all pass			

Neither vul.

♠Q 10 8 5 3   ♡4   ◇Q 10 2   ♣A Q 9 5

Your partner promises the unbid suits. You should show your clubs. When 3♡ is passed to you, you have enough to compete. Your fourth club is a very big deal.

W	N	E	S
		1♡	1♠
pass	3◇	pass	3♡
pass	4◇	all pass	

Neither vul.

♠A K 8 7 4   ♡8 5   ◇K J   ♣Q 10 5 2

North's 3◇ bid was just invitational. South saw a lot of potential tricks and invited 3NT by asking for a heart stopper. North said no and South gave up.

W	N	E	S
		1♣	1♠
pass	2♣	pass	2◇
pass	2♠	all pass	

Neither vul.

♠A Q 10 6 ♡3 ◇10 7 5 3 ♣A J 9 5

North's cuebid and return to 2♠ suggests a good raise with three trump. South has extras but only a four-card suit. He passes 2♠.

W	N	E	S
		1♣	1♠
pass	2♠	3♣	all pass

Neither vul.

♠A Q 10 5 3 ♡Q 8 3 ◇Q 9 3 ♣Q 9

North's raise usually shows only three spades. If he does have four, he will have a poor raise. South has 12 points, bad shape, and a wasted ♣Q. South should definitely pass over 3♣.

If you are using the new methods, your partner can either jump to 3♠, weak, or to 3♣ to show a nice raise with four trumps and shape. When he just raises to 2♠ he won't have a flavorful four-card raise, which you need to go further with this hand.

W	N	E	S
		1◇	1♠
1NT	pass	2◇	3♣
3◇	4♣	4◇	pass
pass	dbl	pass	?

N-S vul.

♠A J 10 5 2 ♡10 3 ◇8 ♣K Q 10 9 3

This hand shows a common decision. South bid 1♠ and then bid 3♣. North raised to 4♣ and then doubled 4◇. Should South sit? The answer is that South ought to pass. The reason is that South has not shown much of a hand so far. What he has is about par. In other words, South has what North will expect. Further, South does have some defense. It is likely that North has 1-4-4-4 shape, in which case East will have problems in the play.

W	N	E	S
		1♣	1♠
pass	2♣	pass	3♣
pass	3◇	pass	3NT
all pass			

E-W vul.

♠A Q 5 3 2 ♡A Q 5 ◇5 3 ♣K 9 7

South is not sure that North has spades on this sequence, but he is sure North has a good hand. South tried to get North to bid notrump and now has to do it himself.

W	N	E	S
		1♣	1♡
pass	2◇	all pass	

E-W vul.

♠K Q 8 ♡J 10 8 7 6 ◇4 ♣A Q 6 2

South's 1♡ bid is fine but it didn't get the response he was hoping for. North's 2◇ bid is not forcing. With a misfit, South correctly passes.

W	N	E	S
		1♣	1◇
1♡	1♠	2♣	2♠
pass	3♣	pass	4♠
all pass			

Neither vul.

♠ J 8 7 ♡ 8 3 ◇ A K 10 8 4 ♣ A 10 3

An easy valuation problem. South overcalls 1◇ and North bids 1♠, not forcing. South raises and North invites. South has solid values given the bidding and accepts the invitation.

W	N	E	S
			1♡ 1♠
pass	2◇	pass	2NT
pass	3◇	all pass	

E-W vul.

♠ A Q 9 8 ♡ K 9 8 6 3 ◇ J 3 ♣ A 4

North's 2◇ bid is not forcing but it does show something. Since South has a mild fit he is right to bid 2NT, invitational. If South had a weaker hand he would pass 2◇. North rejects the invitation, rebidding his diamonds, and South accepts his decision.

Note South's 1♠ overcall. This is the kind of hand where you either bid now or likely get shut out of the bidding. I approve.

W	N	E	S
		1♣	1♠
pass	1NT	pass	3NT
all pass			

Both vul.

♠ A J 10 8 4 ♡ A Q 2 ◇ K J 4 ♣ J 5

A 1NT response to a one-level overcall promises at least a fine 8-count and normally has 9-11. South has a comfortable raise to game.

W	N	E	S
1♣	pass	1♡	1♠
2♣	2♠	3♣	pass
pass	3♠	all pass	

E-W vul.

♠ K Q J 5 ♡ A J 8 7 4 ◇ 3 ♣ 10 6 3

With a four-card overcall, South does well to bid just once and quit over 3♣. One note of extreme importance is that North should have four spades in order to justify raising spades a second time. This is a standard consideration. If you raise a one-level overcall with three trump, it is almost always wrong to rebid your raise later.

W	N	E	S
		1♣	1♠
1NT	all pass		

N-S vul.

♠ A K J 9 7 ♡ K Q 4 ◇ Q 4 ♣ Q 10 7

South is very wise to pass 1NT. East-West rate to have at least 21 HCP and West is likely to have four spades. This is a well-judged pass by South.

W	N	E	S
	pass	1♡	2♣
2♡	2♠	all pass	

Neither vul.

♠A 8 7 ♡Q 6 4 ◇8 3 ♣A K 10 7 4

Believe it or not, this isn't a safe 2♣ bid. You have a ton of losers in a balanced hand. South was lucky in that North made a bid South liked. South should pass 2♠ in spite of his fit. North is a passed hand and the South hand is just too balanced to continue. You will probably make 2♠. South should be aware that he got lucky.

W	N	E	S
	pass	1♡	2♣
2♡	pass	pass	2♠
pass	3♣	all pass	

Both vul.

♠K J 8 4 ♡4 3 ◇3 ♣A Q J 8 6 3

When the opponents show weakness, as they did here, you can continue bidding with such hands. 2♠ is routine, as is passing 3♣.

W	N	E	S
		1♡	2♡
3◇	3♠	4◇	4♠
5♡	all pass		

Neither vul.

♠Q J 10 8 3 ♡4 ◇3 ♣K Q J 8 7 5

This sequence shows an example of a two-suited cuebid. South's 2♡ bid shows spades and a minor. When North can show a spade fit, South continues even though he has a weak hand. The importance of this example is to show how you might continue the auction with the South hand. How would you approach this hand if not using the Michaels cuebid?

W	N	E	S
1♣	pass	1♡	pass
2♣	all pass		

Neither vul.

♠K 10 7 5 3 ♡Q 4 2 ◇8 5 ♣K J 3

South properly refrains from bidding 1♠ and when they fail to find a fit, South does well again by not balancing.

W	N	E	S
		1♠	2♡
2♠	pass	pass	3◇
all pass			

E-W vul.

♠8 2 ♡A Q 10 8 3 ◇K Q J 8 ♣4 3

South trades on the weak-sounding auction to compete with 3◇. This is not guaranteed but is an excellent choice at matchpoints. Remember, when the opponents have a fit and have limited their hands, it is relatively safe to compete. If partner doesn't seem to like your first suit, try again.

An aside: You should not forget that if you are using the modern methods, a 2NT bid by North would have shown a limit raise or better for hearts. Either balanced or with shape.

W	N	E	S
pass	1♠	2♣	
2♠	dbl	3◇	4♡
4♠	pass	pass	5♡
all pass			

Both vul.

♠ 4   ♡ K J 8 5   ◇ 8 5   ♣ A Q J 9 7 6

Partner makes a responsive double, showing the unbid suits. South has a super hand for hearts and bids game. If they bid 4♠ as shown, South has a new decision. Bidding or passing are both acceptable guesses. South might choose to bid 5♣ at his last turn, which lets partner know of his extra shape in case North is willing to play in clubs.

W	N	E	S
pass	1◇	2♣	
2◇	2♠	pass	3♣
all pass			

Both vul.

♠ 4   ♡ A J 8 5   ◇ 9 4   ♣ K Q J 8 5 3

South overcalls and hates his partner's 2♠ bid. Passing is an option, but with super clubs it is best to rebid them. There is no way to get hearts into the auction.

W	N	E	S
		1♠	2♣
pass	2♠	pass	3♣
pass	3♡	pass	3NT
all pass			

E-W vul.

♠ K 3   ♡ 8 6   ◇ 9 7 5   ♣ A Q J 10 8 5

South overcalls and North cuebids, showing a big hand. With a minimum and with good clubs, South rebids them. When North bids 3♡, showing a forcing hand with good hearts, South can now bid notrump without overbidding his hand. Since South has no diamond stopper at all, a 4♡ bid might work best. Hard to say.

W	N	E	S
		1♠	2♣
2♡	3◇	3♡	5◇
dbl	all pass		

E-W vul.

♠ 8   ♡ 8 5 3   ◇ Q J 8   ♣ A K 10 9 6 3

This hand shows a bidding tactic known as the premature save. South overcalls 2♣ and North bids 3◇, not forcing. South assumes the opponents can make game so he bids 5◇ right away, putting pressure on West. 5◇ does not rate to make but it shouldn't be down many. Assuming 4♡ will make, 5◇ doubled will be a good save.

W	N	E	S
		1♠	2♣
2♠	3◇	3♠	4◇
4♠	all pass		

E-W vul.

♠ 8   ♡ 8 5 3   ◇ Q J 8   ♣ A K 10 9 6 3

This is the same hand as above but the bidding is different. East-West aren't bidding with the same confidence so letting them play in 4♠ is not a bad idea. North can bid 5◇ if he wishes, and in this case he didn't. His pass is an opinion that defending 4♠ suits him just fine.

W	N	E	S
		1◇	1♡
2◇	3◇	dbl	?

E-W vul.

♠ 8 3   ♡ K Q J 8 3   ◇ 8 7 3   ♣ K J 2

In standard bidding, North's 3◇ bid shows a limit raise of unspecified quality. If you are using the new methods, the 3◇ bid shows a nice heart raise in the 7-9 point range with four trumps and a bit of shape. It is a hand that would like to bid 2♡ but which is willing to compete to 3♡ if necessary. There is a useful agreement you can have over East's double.

Read this distinction carefully. If 3◇ is the old-fashioned limit raise or better, then when East doubles 3◇, South passes with a dog and bids 3♡ with a useful minimum hand. If 3◇ is the new raise, showing a nice 6-8 point raise with four trump, then South just bids 3♡ on all minimum hands. If South wishes to make a game try, he redoubles and leaves it up to partner.

W	N	E	S
		1♠	2♡
2♠	3♣	dbl	all pass

E-W vul.

♠ 8 3   ♡ Q J 9 7 5 3   ◇ A Q 7 5   ♣ J

This nice hand has turned to garbage. You actually have three choices and none of them are good. You can bid 3◇, 3♡, and pass. I would tend to pass, thinking that partner could have shown both minors and he does know that I have a good heart suit. No guarantees with this one.

W	N	E	S
		1♠	2♡
2♠	pass	pass	dbl
pass	3◇	3♠	pass
pass	4♣	all pass	

Neither vul.

♠ 3   ♡ A Q J 8 6   ◇ A Q 4   ♣ J 10 8 4

This hand shows a bidding sequence that is worth knowing. South overcalls 2♡ and when 2♠ is passed to him he doubles, showing good hearts and support for both minors. You do not promise four cards in either or both minors but you do have at least three-card support and a solid overcall. Your partner bids diamonds and later competes in clubs. You should note that if he had a really decent hand with both minors he would have doubled 2♠. You know he did not have enough to bid earlier, hence you should pass 4♣. A possible hand for North: ♠1074 ♡– ♢K10753 ♣Q7632.

W	N	E	S
		1♡	2♣
2♡	2♠	3♡	3♠
all pass			

Neither vul.

♠Q74 ♡84 ♢K4 ♣AQ10972

A normal sequence. You overcalled and partner bid a new suit. You should raise. Do not overlook this bid. Here, a raise to 3♠ is fine. If East passes 2♠, it is close whether you should raise to 3♠ or pass. Partner can have 6-11 points (typically) with five or six spades. Game will have chances facing some of partner's maximum hands.

W	N	E	S
		1♠	2♡
2♠	dbl	3♠	4♣
all pass			

E-W vul.

♠843 ♡AKQ85 ♢10 ♣K1073

Partner ostensibly has shown the minors. You have a good hand for clubs and are worth a 4♣ bid. If partner has a singleton spade you might have a game.

W	N	E	S
		1♠	2♢
2♡	pass	2♠	pass
2NT	all pass		

E-W vul.

♠853 ♡KQ ♢KQ9864 ♣AJ

South has his overcall but there are too many danger signs to continue. West has a strong hand and South has a terrible spade holding. With West bidding notrump, South has been warned that his diamond suit is not as good as he might have hoped. It is clear to bid 2♢ and it is clear to quit after that.

W	N	E	S
		1♠	2♣
2♡	3♣	3♡	5♣
5♡	all pass		

E-W vul.

♠1054 ♡3 ♢K106 ♣AQ10863

South knows he has a good club fit and the bidding hints strongly that they have a game. South bids 5♣ now instead of passing and doing it later.

W	N	E	S
		1♡	2♣
2♠	4♣	4NT	6♣
pass	pass	dbl	all pass

Neither vul.

♠8 ♡74 ◇K 10 8 5 ♣A Q 9 7 5 3

Once again, South overcalls and the opponents conduct a strong auction. North's 4♣ bid is weak so South can imagine East-West have a game or a slam. With East bidding 4NT, slam looks likely. South should bid 5♣ or 6♣ over 4NT to impede their bidding. I do not like a pass by South, which lets the opponents use all of their science unimpeded.

W	N	E	S
		1♠	2♣
pass	2♠	dbl	rdbl
pass	2NT	pass	3NT
all pass			

Both vul.

♠Q 4 ♡A 7 4 ◇8 5 ♣A Q J 10 7 3

South bids 2♣ and North bids 2♠, usually showing a good club raise. East doubles. South redoubles to show a good overcall with something in spades (a half stopper or more). North bids 2NT, showing spades are stopped, and South goes on to game. Won't always make but it should have a play. Your six-card club suit suggests that this could be a hand where 3NT makes with only 22 points in the combined hands.

W	N	E	S
		1◇	2♣
2◇	dbl	pass	2♠
pass	3♠	all pass	

E-W vul.

♠K 8 7 ♡J 2 ◇8 5 ♣A Q 10 8 7 5

South overcalls and North makes a responsive double. North usually has the unbid suits so South shows his three cards in spades. North raises and South, with a minimum, gives up.

W	N	E	S
		1♡	2♣
2♡	dbl	3♡	3♠
all pass			

Both vul.

♠K Q 7 ♡9 7 ◇7 2 ♣A Q J 8 6 4

South overcalls and North makes another responsive double. When East competes with 3♡, South has plenty to bid 3♠. He has only three of them but usually North will have five.

W	N	E	S
1♣	pass	2♣	2♠
3♣	3♠	all pass	

Both vul.

♠K 10 8 5 3 ♡K 2 ◇A J 4 ♣10 6 5

Just a routine auction. South bids 2♠ on a 'safe' auction and North raises. South has no reason to continue.

W	N	E	S
1♡	pass	2♡	3♣
pass	pass	3♡	all pass

Both vul.

♠ A 3   ♡ 8 5 3   ◇ 8 4   ♣ A Q J 9 7 4

South bids 3♣ and gives up. Not all of your overcalls will strike gold. There is still some good news. North will lead a club, which is likely best for your side.

W	N	E	S
1◇	pass	2♣	pass
2◇	pass	2NT	pass
3NT	all pass		

E-W vul.

♠ K Q 8 6 5   ♡ A Q 7   ◇ K J 2   ♣ 10 5

South correctly stays out of this very dangerous auction. Beware of sequences that begin with a 2/1 response. Partner's hand? He has about what you would expect, which is not much. ♠942 ♡9853 ◇83 ♣J873. Given your diamonds are likely worthless, your chances of setting 3NT are slim. Had you bid 2♠, you would have been in jeopardy of going down 800.

W	N	E	S
1♠	pass	2♡	pass
3♡	pass	4♡	all pass

Neither vul.

♠ K 3   ♡ 8 3   ◇ A K 4   ♣ K J 9 7 5 3

Even this South hand is best kept out of the bidding. Note that South would have to bid at the three-level, even more dangerous than on the previous hand.

W	N	E	S
1♠	pass	2♣	2♡
2♠	3♡	3♠	4♡
4♠	pass	pass	5♡
dbl	all pass		

E-W vul.

♠ 8 5 3   ♡ A Q J 10 8 6   ◇ Q 5 2   ♣ 9

South's overcall after a 2/1 shows a good suit and not much of a hand. 4♡ is an acceptable bid. North's raise should show a willingness to save, not just some high cards. He rates to have a few useful values. Hence, the save in 5♡. You will surely be doubled but getting eight tricks ought to be doable. Also, there is a decent chance they will continue bidding.

W	N	E	S
1♠	pass	2◇	3♡
3♠	4♡	4♠	all pass

E-W vul.

♠ 8 5   ♡ Q J 10 9 7 5 3   ◇ K 3   ♣ 6 4

The main bid here is South's 3♡ bid. It shows a preempt, which is precisely what he has.

W	N	E	S
1♣	pass	2♣	3♠
pass	4♠	all pass	

Neither vul.

♠K Q J 8 7 5 4 ♡A J 4 ◇Q 2 ♣7

South makes another bid that is exactly defined. A jump overcall when they bid and raise shows an invitational hand with an excellent suit. North knows he can raise with 7 or 8 useful points and a doubleton or more in your suit. There is no need to preempt when they bid and raise because opener has learned most of what responder has to offer.

W	N	E	S
		1♣	1♠
2♣	dbl	pass	2♡
3♣	all pass		

Neither vul.

♠K Q 10 7 5 ♡K 5 4 ◇Q 2 ♣J 7 5

North's double is responsive. South duly shows his hearts.

W	N	E	S
1◇	pass	1♡	dbl
2◇	2♠	3◇	pass
pass	3♠	all pass	

Both vul.

♠A J 10 8 ♡J 4 2 ◇3 ♣A Q 8 5 4

South doubles instead of overcalling. This is best given you have two suits that can be shown via a takeout double. North is just competing when he bids 3♠.

W	N	E	S
1♣	pass	1♠	pass
2♣	all pass		

E-W vul.

♠8 6 3 ♡K J 9 7 5 ◇A 3 ♣K 5 4

There is no really safe moment in the bidding for South to bid. His hand is not good enough to overcall and there are worries in spades and clubs that warn against balancing in 2♡. I imagine that many would bid here, but there are good reasons not to.

W	N	E	S
1♡	pass	1♠	2◇
2♡	dbl	all pass	

Neither vul.

♠K 10 8 6 4 ♡3 ◇A K 10 9 6 ♣J 3

Not everyone would bid 2◇ with this. I like the bid. East's spade bid hints there may be a fit and if there is, your hand will be valuable. When North doubles, it is easy to pass. You have better defense than you might. North can easily have five hearts and good values.

W	N	E	S
1♣	pass	1♠	2♠
all pass			

Neither vul.

♠ K Q 10 9 4 2 ♡ A J 3 ◇ Q J 3 ♣ 3

This is an example of an unusual bid. When your RHO responds at the one-level, he often has a ratty four-card suit. You can bid his suit naturally on hands like this one. You have a good six- (usually) card suit and you have approximately an opening bid. I promise you that if you do not abuse this bid, it will work. Note that you cannot make this kind of bid in the suit that LHO opened. On this auction, for instance, you cannot bid 2♣ to show a club suit. More on this in one of the upcoming hands.

W	N	E	S
1♡	pass	1♠	pass
2♡	all pass		

E-W vul.

♠ Q 5 ♡ K J 7 ◇ K J 9 8 7 ♣ A 4 2

Another example of a good hand with lousy points and poor shape. Passing this one out is clear.

W	N	E	S
1♣	pass	1♡	1♠
pass	2♠	all pass	

Both vul.

♠ 8 6 5 4 2 ♡ A Q 10 8 ◇ A Q ♣ A 4

Having bid 1♠, a reasonable choice, you now have to decide whether to continue. I wouldn't mind a game try with these values but passing is acceptable too.

W	N	E	S
1♡	pass	1NT	all pass

E-W vul.

♠ K 3 ♡ Q 7 5 ◇ K Q 9 6 4 ♣ K 10 7

South should pass. East's bid could easily include some diamonds. Further, much of South's hand is made up of soft cards. Passing is wise. Note that this is true regardless of whether 1NT is forcing or not forcing. A forcing 1NT response tends to show a 6-9 point hand. Only a few of the forcing 1NT responses turn out to include something extra.

W	N	E	S
1◇	pass	1NT	2♠
all pass			

N-S vul.

♠ 9 8 6 5 4 2 ♡ A J 10 ◇ A K ♣ 8 4

With a six-card suit and decent values, you can risk 2♠. You know East doesn't have four spades. You must still hope that West doesn't have a lot of them. At matchpoints, bidding is a long-term winner.

W	N	E	S
1♡	pass	2♡	2♠
3♡	3♠	all pass	

Neither vul.

♠Q J 8 7 5   ♡A 8 3   ◇8 6   ♣A 10 3

When they bid and raise you can be aggressive if you can overcall at the two-level.

W	N	E	S
1◇	pass	2◇	2♡
3◇	3♡	pass	4♡
all pass			

E-W vul.

♠A J 3   ♡K 10 8 6 4 3   ◇A 9 7   ♣3

The bidding tells you that North is short in diamonds. This is good news that you can use.

W	N	E	S
1♣	pass	2♣	2♡
3♣	3♡	all pass	

Neither vul.

♠A J 3   ♡K 10 8 7 5 4   ◇A 9 6   ♣4

This auction does not inform you of useful distribution in your partner's hand. It is reasonable to pass 3♡ here.

W	N	E	S
1◇	pass	2◇	2♠
pass	3♠	pass	4♠
all pass			

N-S vul.

♠10 8 6 5 4   ♡4   ◇A Q 4   ♣A K Q 8

You have some minuses but you have so many pluses that going on is acceptable. Consider that you may get a nice diamond lead.

W	N	E	S
1♣	pass	1♡	2♡
3♣	all pass		

E-W vul.

♠K 2   ♡K J 10 8 7 5   ◇A J 5 3   ♣3

Here is another overcall in responder's suit. Note that your bid gets in the way of opener's ability to bid 1♠. Note that South has good heart spots. Do not make this bid with suits like KJ6543.

W	N	E	S
1♣	pass	1♠	2♣
2♠	3◇	all pass	

E-W vul.

♠K 2   ♡A 10 7 4   ◇K Q 9 7 6 5   ♣4

On this sequence, South cuebids opener's suit. There are many ways to play this bid. The way demonstrated here shows four cards in the unbid major and six in the unbid minor. Another possible meaning is to play that the cuebid shows 5-5 in the unbid suits. And finally, it is possible to play it as natural. I am not fond of this last treatment because if opener has good clubs, he is over you and can double effectively. Your choice of meanings is probably fine but be sure you discuss it.

W	N	E	S
pass	pass	1♣	1♠
2♣	2NT	pass	3◇
pass	4♠	all pass	

E-W vul.

♠ A J 8 7 4 ♡ 4 ◇ A Q 10 3 ♣ J 10 8

On this hand North is using the new methods. His 2NT bid shows a limit raise that can be balanced with three or four trump, or with shape and four trump. West's 2♣ bid took away the ability for North to clarify the kind of good raise he has. South might bid 4♠ here, but making a game try of 3◇ is fine. North, a passed hand, will evaluate his cards in light of your bid and whatever he chooses will be okay with you.

W	N	E	S
1◇	pass	1♡	pass
2♡	pass	pass	2♠
pass	pass	3♡	all pass

Neither vul.

♠ K J 8 4 ♡ 4 ◇ A Q 10 9 7 4 ♣ 8 4

Who knows what is correct? South cannot bid 2◇ because natural cuebids apply only to a suit RHO bid. A 2◇ bid would show something else. One possibility would be four spades and five or more clubs. You do not need 2◇ as Michaels because you also have a takeout double and you have the unusual 2NT. At the end, you can try 2♠ if you like to gamble. Winning bridge is not always good bridge.

W	N	E	S
	pass	1◇	1♠
3◇	dbl	pass	4♡
all pass			

Both vul.

♠ A Q J 8 4 ♡ K 10 7 4 ◇ 8 4 3 ♣ 5

Partner's double shows hearts and clubs. In support of hearts you have a great hand. Bid game.

W	N	E	S
		1♣	1♠
2♣	2♠	pass	pass
3♣	3♡	all pass	

E-W vul.

♠ A K J 8 ♡ 9 2 ◇ A 4 3 2 ♣ 10 6 5

South correctly bids 1♠ and then gives it up. When you overcall with a four-card suit you usually leave the running to your partner.

W	N	E	S
		1◇	1♠
2◇	dbl	pass	3♣
3◇	dbl	pass	3♡
all pass			

E-W vul.

♠ 10 8 7 6 5 ♡ K J 4 ◇ 2 ♣ A Q 7 5

You need to know what partner is up to. His double says he has the unbid suits or a huge hand with one suit. You bid 3♣. North's second double is not for penalty but says he has a maximum hand. Your 3♡ bid shows a willingness to play there. Your partner knows you have a hand like this one and he will choose the best contract.

W	N	E	S
1♡	pass	2♣	3♠
4♣	pass	5♣	all pass

Both vul.

♠K Q 10 9 8 6 5 ♡5 3 ◇Q J 9 ♣7

South made his obstructive 3♠ bid and got no interest from partner. Pass it out. Note that when vulnerable you need a decent hand for your 3♠ bid.

HANDS WHERE YOUR PARTNER OVERCALLS. YOU ARE SOUTH

W	N	E	S
1♣	1♠	dbl	2♠
3♡	all pass		

E-W vul.

♠K 8 4 ♡4 3 ◇K 10 8 5 4 ♣J 7 4

North overcalls and East makes a negative double. You should raise in this situation if you can. A raise shows three trump, usually, and about 6-9 support points.

W	N	E	S
			pass
1♡	2♣	2♡	2♠
pass	3♠	all pass	

Neither vul.

♠K J 10 8 4 ♡J 5 4 ◇8 4 2 ♣K 9

South makes a pushy 2♠ bid based on his nice ♣K, his decent spade suit, the weakness of their bidding, and the expectation that North has short hearts. A sane but aggressive bid.

W	N	E	S
1◇	1♡	2♣	pass
2◇	all pass		

Both vul.

♠K J 9 7 4 ♡J 3 ◇Q 10 7 ♣J 7 3

East's 2/1 bid of 2♣ should warn South against bidding.

W	N	E	S
1♣	1♡	2◇	2♠
3♣	pass	3◇	pass
3NT	all pass		

E-W vul.

♠Q J 10 8 4 3 ♡Q 4 ◇9 7 5 4 ♣7

This is the kind of hand and suit that can bid freely after partner's overcall and RHO's 2/1 bid.

W	N	E	S
1◇	1♡	2♣	3♠
4♣	pass	4◇	pass
5◇	all pass		

Both vul.

♠K Q 9 7 6 5 3 2 ♡J 4 ◇9 4 ♣3

Normally, a jump response to partner's overcall is invitational. This is not the case after RHO's 2/1 bid of 2♣. Jumps are preemptive after a 2/1 by RHO.

W	N	E	S
1♣	1♡	pass	2♠
pass	3♠	pass	4♠
all pass			

N-S vul.

♠K Q 10 9 7 5　♡Q 8　◇A Q 5　♣8 4

A jump response in a new suit usually shows an invitational hand. North raises and South accepts. Compare this with the previous hand where East made a 2/1 response.

W	N	E	S
1♠	2♣	2♡	4◇
4♡	dbl	all pass	

Both vul.

♠8 6 2　♡—　◇K Q 10 8 7 6 4 3　♣J 9

South makes a weak jump shift after East's 2/1 response and North doubles.

Rule

When you have shown all of your hand and partner doubles, pass.

W	N	E	S
1◇	1♡	2♣	4♠
5♣	pass	pass	5♡
dbl	all pass		

E-W vul.

♠K Q J 8 7 5 4　♡10 7 5 3　◇3　♣4

South's 4♠ bid is a practical guess. He has heart support but experience shows that when you have a suit this good, it should be trump. The important thing here is to bid a lot.

W	N	E	S
1♣	1♠	pass	3♣
pass	4♠	all pass	

Neither vul.

♠Q 9 6 4　♡A J 10 7 5　◇K 4　♣8 4

The 3♣ bid shows a limit raise with shape and four trump. This bid describes your hand and lets North make the final decision.

If you were using the new methods, you would bid 2NT with this hand. 3♣ would show a good four-card raise with normal values.

W	N	E	S
1♣	1♠	2♡	3♠
pass	4♠	5♣	pass
pass	dbl	all pass	

Neither vul.

♠J 10 8 4 2　♡8 3 2　◇Q J 9　♣8 2

Your 3♠ bid is weak. You might even bid 4♠ but your shape is poor. Five trumps is not, of itself, reason to jump to the four-level. When North doubles 5♣ you should pass. Partner knows your hand; you don't know his. Respect his educated opinion. Bidding 5♠ would be a terrible choice.

W	N	E	S
1♥	2♠	3◇	5♠
dbl	all pass		

E-W vul.

♠Q8654 ♡854 ◇9 ♣J1072

Partner made a weak jump overcall and East is bidding strongly. The theme here is that if you think you might consider saving in 5♠, you should bid to 5♠ immediately, not later.

W	N	E	S
1♣	1♠	pass	pass
dbl	2◇	2♡	all pass

Neither vul.

♠J2 ♡J975 ◇Q73 ♣K853

You have a weak hand with no particular fit. Passing is okay when you have nothing to say. Do not go looking for bids to make.

W	N	E	S
1♣	1◇	1♡	1♠
2♡	2♠	pass	pass
3♡	pass	pass	3♠
all pass			

Both vul.

♠KQ975 ♡843 ◇K104 ♣J8

It is reasonable to bid 3♠. You have a spade fit and a diamond fit. Nine tricks are likely. Being vulnerable, you should not bid willy-nilly, but this time you have your bid. Note that hands like this one often produce nine tricks for both sides. Make your bid confidently, and that in itself may keep someone from doubling you.

W	N	E	S
1◇	1♠	2◇	2♠
3◇	all pass		

N-S vul.

♠K107 ♡QJ96 ◇K85 ♣J54

You were entitled to raise to 2♠. With a questionable ◇K, bad shape and only three trump, you can pass. Keep in mind the minimum hands your partner can have.

W	N	E	S
1♣	1◇	pass	1♡
2♣	pass	pass	2◇
pass	pass	3♣	all pass

Neither vul.

♠754 ♡AJ984 ◇QJ4 ♣75

South has done it all. He bid his heart suit and then raised diamonds. He has nothing left to say. If partner wants to bid again, he may do so.

W	N	E	S
1♣	1♠	2♣	2♠
3♣	pass	pass	3♠
all pass			

Neither vul.

♠K Q 7 5   ♡8 2   ◇Q J 8 7   ♣10 8 7

Raise to 2♠ and if the auction permits, as it does here, continue to 3♠. If using the new methods South can bid 3♣, showing this exact hand. Four trumps, a good normal raise, and a bit of shape. It is almost predictable that East-West will keep bidding and you will too. Since this is often the case after their raise, you can now show your hand immediately and keep them from having an easy time of continuing.

W	N	E	S
1♣	1♠	2♡	pass
3♣	pass	3◇	pass
3NT	all pass		

Neither vul.

♠8 7 4   ♡K J 6 4   ◇Q 9 8   ♣Q J 3

The idea here is that South has a lousy 9 points with little redeeming value. When partner overcalls and they get into a 2/1 auction, your raises should show good values for partner, not boring hands. Take credit if you saw the reasons for South's pass. At the end, South could consider a double of 3NT if he was in search of something special.

W	N	E	S
1♣	1♠	2♡	3♠
pass	pass	4♡	all pass

Both vul.

♠Q 9 8 7   ♡3   ◇J 10 8 7 5 4   ♣9 7

South makes a preemptive raise and leaves the rest of the bidding to partner.

W	N	E	S
1♡	1♠	1NT	pass
2♣	all pass		

Neither vul.

♠9 5 3   ♡K 8 5 4   ◇K 9 2   ♣Q 10 7

With questionable values and with three small spades, South notes East's 1NT bid and stays out of the auction. Knowing when to pass is an important skill.

W	N	E	S
1♣	1♠	1NT	2♠
pass	pass	3♣	all pass

Neither vul.

♠8 6 5 4   ♡8 7 5   ◇K 10 9 6 4   ♣5

South has been warned that East has something in spades. Still, with four spades and good shape, South is entitled to raise to 2♠.

W	N	E	S
1♣	1♠	1NT	3♠
all pass			

Neither vul.

♠ 8 6 5 3 2   ♡ K J 9 7 5   ◇ 8   ♣ Q 9

South would normally jump to 4♠. The 1NT bid alerts South that East has a trick (or two) in spades, and that causes South to be careful.

W	N	E	S
1◇	1♡	pass	2◇
pass	2♡	all pass	

Neither vul.

♠ 8 2   ♡ K Q 7   ◇ K 9 5 4   ♣ A 9 8 5

South cuebids 2◇ and accepts North's sign-off. This is a wise decision. Keep in mind that partner can bid 1♡ with a 10-count. Also, the ◇K may be bad.

W	N	E	S
1♣	1♠	2♣	3♣
pass	3◇	pass	3♠
pass	4♠	all pass	

E-W vul.

♠ K J 7   ♡ A Q 7 5 3   ◇ Q 7 3   ♣ 5 2

South cuebids to show (probably) a limit raise in spades. This cuebid doesn't say if you are balanced or have shape. This is not the usual case since their raise got in the way of your science. If you were using the new methods, the correct bid with this hand would be 2NT, showing a limit raise of ambiguous quality.

W	N	E	S
1♣	1♠	pass	2♣
pass	2♡	pass	2♠
all pass			

N-S vul.

♠ 9 5 3   ♡ A K 8   ◇ A 10 7 3   ♣ J 7 3

South has lousy spades and lousy shape, but he has super high cards. Note that North's 2♡ bid does not promise extras.

W	N	E	S
1♣	1♠	pass	2♣
pass	2♠	pass	3♡
pass	3♠	pass	4◇
pass	4♡	all pass	

Both vul.

♠ 3   ♡ A K J 8 5   ◇ A K Q 8 4   ♣ 8 5

Here is one of the problem areas of bidding. South has a huge hand and must cuebid first, then show his hearts. When North denies hearts, South shows his diamonds. When you cuebid, any new suit bid subsequently is forcing until game is reached. Note that North rates to have just two hearts. In spite of South's great hand, 4♡ may be an impossible struggle.